Travels with Sophie

The Journal of Louise E. Wegner

Edited with Commentary by
Gene L. LaBerge and Michelle L. Maurer

PRAIRIE OAK PRESS
Madison, Wisconsin

D1208349

First edition, first printing
Copyright © 1999 by Gene L. LaBerge and Michelle L. Maurer

Typeset by Quick Quality Press, Madison, Wisconsin
Printed in the USA by Sheridan Books, Chelsea, Michigan

Library of Congress Cataloging-in-Publication Data

Wegner, Louise E., 1893–1968.
   Travels with Sophie : the journal of Louise E. Wegner / edited with commentary by
Gene L. LaBerge and Michelle L. Maurer.
      p. cm.
   Includes bibliographical references (p.).
   ISBN 1-879483-64-5 (alk. paper)
   1. Wegner, Louise E.--Diaries.   2. Teachers--United States--Biography.   3.
Education--Wisconsin--History--20th century.   I. LaBerge, Gene L.   II. Maurer, Michelle L.   III. Title.

LA2317.W37 W44 1999
370'.92--dc21
[B]   99-050308

To Louise

Contents

Map showing some of the main cities and towns referred to in this book.

Acknowledgments

Many people, mainly descendants and relatives of Louise, have contributed materials that have helped to make this project possible. Their assistance is acknowledged with gratitude. To Phyllis LaBerge Dailey we owe a debt of gratitude for saving Louise's journals and for providing them for this project. We offer our special thanks to Betty LaBerge Silvernale for her endless efforts in locating reference material and photographs pertinent to the story. Without her help this project would have been much more difficult, or incomplete. Special thanks also to Jim Labre of the University Publications office at the University of Wisconsin–Oshkosh for turning the many faded eighty- to ninety-year-old negatives into usable photographs. Without his expertise there would be few photographs to augment the text. The Media Services at the University of Wisconsin–Oshkosh resurrected the 1915 road map of Rusk County from a microfilm copy of an old newspaper and rendered it into a legible document for the book. Mount Senario College generously lent its microfilm copy of the newspapers for research of most of the years covered in the book. The Rusk County Historical Society also lent copies of period newspapers and photographs from its archives, and these materials are acknowledged with thanks. These old newspapers enabled us to document most of the dates, places, and events not covered in Louise's ledger and journals. Larry Easton, archivist of the Soo Line Historical and Technical Society, provided information about trains. Finally, sincere thanks to Sally LaBerge, wife and mother, as well as to the LaBerge siblings for their support in the project.

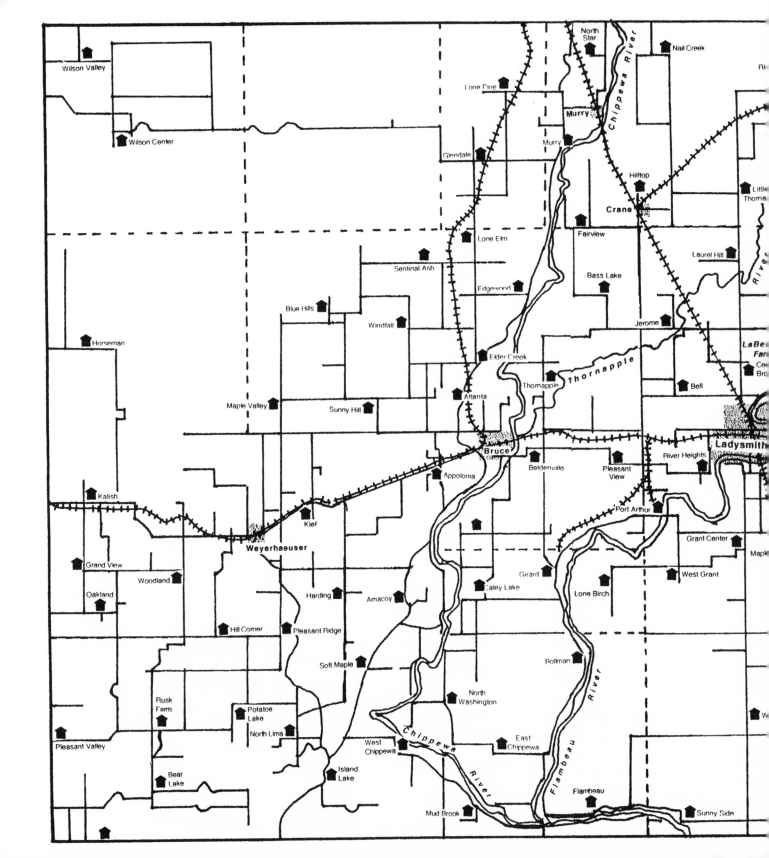

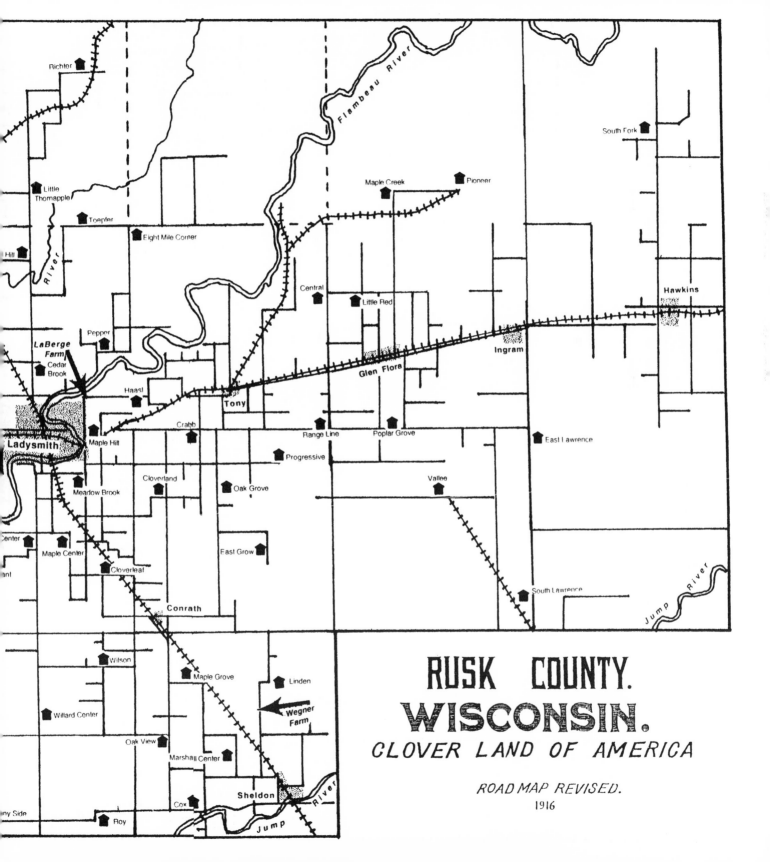

Richter

Little Thornapple

Toepfer

Hill

Eight Mile Corner

River

Flambeau River

South Fork

Maple Creek

Pioneer

Central

Little Red

Hawkins

Pepper

LaBerge Farm

Cedar Brook

Haasl

Ingram

Glen Flora

Ladysmith

Maple Hill

Tony

Crabb

Range Line

Poplar Grove

East Lawrence

Progressive

Meadow Brook

Cloverland

Oak Grove

Vallee

Center

Maple Center

East Grow

Cloverleaf

Conrath

South Lawrence

Jump River

Wilson

Maple Grove

Linden

RUSK COUNTY.

Willard Center

Wegner Farm

WISCONSIN.

Oak View

CLOVER LAND OF AMERICA

Marshall Center

ROAD MAP REVISED.
1916

ny Side

Cox

Sheldon

Jump River

Roy

Jump

Travels with Sophie

Introduction

In 1915 the Wisconsin State Legislature established the position of county supervising teacher in an effort to provide assistance to rural schoolteachers throughout the state and to ensure some degree of uniformity in education. The first county supervising teacher in Rusk County, one of the larger counties in northern Wisconsin, was Louise Wegner, who at twenty-two had already taught for five years in Rusk County's rural schools. The Committee on Common Schools made the selection on October 5, 1915, and Louise

Louise Wegner with her younger brother Victor in 1895.

assumed her duties shortly thereafter at a salary of seventy dollars per month plus necessary expenses for travel and lodging.

In the diaries published here Louise recounts some of the experiences and adventures she had while traveling among the various rural schools, but her stories are also about the period. The first entry in this particular series of writings is dated October 29, 1917. America had entered World War I, the influenza epidemic was decimating the country, and new technologies, such as the moving picture, the automobile, and the telephone, were changing the world. With her own brand of humor and insight, Louise tells how these events affected rural Wisconsin, and therein lies the charm of her stories. No matter how grand the subject—whether world war or epidemic—the stories remain firmly rooted in rural life. In this regard, they are unique and valuable historical timepieces.

In addition, Louise and her three sisters were talented amateur photographers, and in compiling this book, the editors discovered that for almost every diary entry Louise made, someone had snapped a photo of the event. Thus Louise's ecstatic account of the spontaneous armistice celebrations of 1918 in Ladysmith, the county seat, is captured just as vividly on film.

The diaries and photographs, however, drop us into the middle of the story. Louise began her career as county supervisor in 1915 and kept a ledger account of her expenses, the schools she visited, and other travel related to her position. Her ledger record begins in August 1916, but her personal diaries begin in late 1917. Apparently there were other diaries of these early years that unfortunately are lost. This lapse, therefore, requires some introduction to both the period in which Louise lived and her life up to the time she tells about it in her own words.

Before 1915, the education available to a child living in the isolated rural regions of Wisconsin was not standardized. No set curriculum for grades had been established, nor was there any way to monitor the rural educators. In part, the creation of the county supervisor position was a sign of the times. Wisconsin, along with the rest of the country, was on the brink of a great transition, a movement from the pioneer days of its formation as a state into the "modern era." Log cabins, dirt roads, small farms, and horse-drawn carriages were still the norm for most of the state, but road signs, telephone lines, and motor cars were increasingly commonplace. Dramatic improvements in transportation and communication eased but by no means erased the isolation of the more rural regions. The railroad had brought together many of the small towns, and better roads and the Model T made travel easier, though still an adventure. Life in these areas was a unique hybrid of the pioneer past and the brand new twentieth century, and individuals had to be competent in both worlds.

One such area was Rusk County, located in the heavily forested northwestern part of Wisconsin. In the late 1800s, the logging industry was the primary draw for the many immigrants who settled there. Just a few decades earlier, northern Wisconsin was a forested wilderness where the few scattered settlers made their living by trapping and trading with the Indians. The sale of large tracts of land to logging companies who cleared the timber from the seemingly endless forests paved the way for more extensive settlement of the region. The industry attracted many immigrant families, as well as Indians and other woodsmen. French Canadians from Quebec, Norwegian and Swedish, German and Polish, and English lumberjacks, some with experience in the forests of New England or Michigan, arrived to make their living

Cut-over forest area, typical of large parts of Rusk County in the early 1900s. Much of the area was actually more open than it is now. (Photo: State Historical Society of Wisconsin.)

in the lumber camps. Nearly all the camps were in remote areas with few amenities, and working conditions were strenuous and dangerous. For the times, however, the pay was good, and many a young man, sometimes only in his early teens, went off to spend the winter in the woods working at one of the many logging jobs.

As the lumber companies cleared land and built the first roads through this northern wilderness, farms sprang up. Many of the men had worked in the logging industry in their younger years and dreamed of becoming farmers, for the concept of land ownership was very strong in the minds of these European settlers. As more families settled and began homesteading in the region, the need for schools arose. Because many of the immigrants had difficulty learning the language of their new country, they felt strongly that their children should get an education and learn English so that they might have a better life. In fact, some of the settlers felt so strongly

about educating their children that they built the schoolhouses themselves. Even in the early twentieth century, many schools were still primitive; Louise recalled many with no bathroom or plumbing, no insulation, and heat only from a wood-burning stove. Some schools had no well, and drinking water had to be carried in a bucket from a neighboring farm.

The structure was not the only rudimentary element of the rural schools. Initially, there was little or no standardization of the curriculum. Teachers had only a high school education, perhaps not even a diploma. They taught what they felt they could, concentrating on the basics of reading, writing, and arithmetic. Since each area had its own school—because all of the students had to walk to school—the number of rural schools continued to increase as settlement of the area progressed. About 125 rural schools—most consisting of one room and one female teacher—were scattered throughout Rusk County. Where a large number of

A typical rural school in Rusk County in the early 1900s. Most schools were built by the local settlers.

settlers had begun homesteading, a school might have as many as thirty or forty students; schools elsewhere might have fewer than ten students.

However crude and ill equipped the building may have been, the community spirit associated with the schools demonstrated a commitment to learning. Young women played an important role in the developing communities because teaching was one of the few career avenues open to them then. Two-thirds of the 706,000 teachers nationwide were women, and the percentage was increasing—in Rusk County, 114 of the 125 teachers Louise was in contact with were women. Thus, it was primarily the young women who provided the education so essential to a group of largely immigrant pioneers. When school opened in the fall, teachers encountered a wide variety of languages that reflected the wide variety of immigrants in the area. One of the first tasks that teachers faced therefore was

to establish some means of communication. Their duties, however, ranged far beyond this basic need.

Gertrude Moe Endthoff, a long-time teacher in northern Wisconsin, described the rural school:

The elementary rural school day was from 8 a.m. to 4 p.m. There was a one-hour lunch and play period. In the winter the day was shortened by one-half hour by shortening the lunch time. There were usually twenty-three class preparations to meet the needs of eight grades. The curriculum was adjusted for even and odd years. Third and fourth, fifth and sixth, and seventh and eighth grade classes were combined and each two grades were taught together. All grades but the first and second were combined to cut the number of daily classes. Odd year courses of study were taught in odd numbered years. . . .

Attending a rural school provided an education equal to the ability and expertise of the teacher. Rural school teachers were masters of and manipulators

The student body of a large rural school in Rusk County, 1910. (Photo courtesy of the Rusk County Historical Society)

of knowledge, keeper of books and records, disciplinarians, fire builders and tenders, janitors, nurses, supervisors of play, trouble shooter in case of emergency, trimmer and filler of the lamps and librarians. They were the drama coach, producer and director of entertainment—the quality of the Christmas program has been known to determine the renewal or rejection of a teacher's contract for another year. Those of you who have not performed in, rehearsed for, planned or directed a rural school Christmas program have missed one of life's great experiences. There were recitations, acrostics, songs, skits, plays and monologues to locate, learn, rehearse and perform. Sometimes the curtains were strung on a wire stretched from one side of the room to the other. Each pupil had a place in the spot light. The age range in a rural school was from six years to about fourteen. . . .

There were no telephones and there also was no electricity. Kerosene lamps provided light at night or on dark days. Fuel for the furnace was hardwood. Fires were usually built and kept by the teacher. The chalkboards and floors were cleaned daily. Snow was shovelled, water was carried in from the well. The flag was put up and taken down daily. We had a good time.

Rural school students were expected to be good, independent workers while other classes were in session. Generally if clear concise directions with ample challenging assignments were given, students worked and learned well.*

Schools became part of the community almost as soon as families had settled the land. In addition to educating the community's youngsters, the rural schools played the important role of social center. Before the days of good roads and reliable cars, many communities held dances and "socials" almost weekly in the local school. Those with musical talent brought instruments and played for the neighbors. Sing-alongs and dances were customary. For pie socials and basket

socials women brought pies or baskets of food, and the men bid to win the pie or basket and the company of its creator for the evening. Occasionally the high bidder met a stiff challenge if he got the "eating rights" to the pie of the ladyfriend of a suitor. But whatever the outcome, these social events served their purpose of providing a place where neighbors could get acquainted in their newly adopted community. The conclusion of each school year in early June was celebrated with a potluck picnic for all the students and their families, which provided a welcome opportunity for neighbors to visit and learn what others in the community had been doing. While the children were out on the playground, the parents set out the food, and there always was a great plenty to eat. Usually after the meal

Albert Wegner and his sister-in-law, Ella Ketel, in about 1895.

---

* *History of Rural Schools of Rusk County, Wisconsin* (Ladysmith: Rusk County Historical Society, 1985), pp. 24-25.

the younger members of the crowd played softball until it was time to go home. Such events helped establish the ways in which people dealt with one another throughout their lives and served as a small melting pot from which they emerged as Americans.

As for Louise herself, she was the first child born to Albert and Martha Wegner on February 20, 1893, in Neillsville, Wisconsin. As a young man Albert had emigrated with his family from Germany and still spoke German. Martha Ketel Wegner was descended from the Muellers, some of the early settlers in the Milwaukee

Louise Wegner's high school graduation photo, 1910

area. She was a third-generation German American whose parents had moved to the Neillsville area to begin farming and raising a family. As a result of their heritage, the children grew up speaking both German and English. Like most other pioneer families in Wisconsin in the late 1800s, the Wegners were farmers. When Louise was still quite young, the family moved to the larger town of Marshfield where Albert had gotten a job at a factory.

It was in Marshfield that some of Louise's younger siblings came into the world: three brothers, Victor, Robert, and Clarence, and three sisters, Dorothea, Gertrude, and Margaret. All the children were christened with nicknames as well as given names. Predictably, Victor became Vicy, and Robert became Bob, but Clarence was called Bill, Billy, or Sonny. The girls acquired more mysterious names: Dorothea became Tis, Gertrude became Toots, and Margaret became Audie. It is these nicknames that Louise uses when she refers to her siblings in the diaries.

The family was musical. Albert was an excellent violinist and also played clarinet. Louise and her sisters all played the violin, piano, and organ; the boys played clarinet and violin. The Wegner family was often called upon to play for socials in Marshfield. Albert and Louise also provided the background music for silent movies in Marshfield theaters. Louise recalled that usually she had not seen the movie in advance and had to improvise suitable mood music as she watched the screen. When the scene changed, she changed the music accordingly. It was an artistic challenge calling for an extensive repertoire. Sometimes other musicians joined in, and the ensemble had to somehow coordinate their parts. Music was always important in Louise's life. She played a variety of musical styles on the violin, from classical to Irish reels and American-style fiddling. When she lived in Ladysmith during her years as county supervisor she usually carried her violin with her, and because she frequently provided

Children from the Cox School relax in the Jump River during recess, 1910. Louise is waving to the camera.

music for local parties and dances, she says, she generally did not get much opportunity to dance.

The Wegner children all attended a small country school near Marshfield and then went on to Marshfield High School. In that era, many young people did not complete a high school education; most entered the workplace in their early teens. The Wegner parents, however, valued education and encouraged all of their children to finish high school.

Louise graduated valedictorian of her high school class in the spring of 1910. Shortly after, she boarded the train in Marshfield and left for Stevens Point, where she spent the summer at the Normal School to prepare for a career in teaching. At the end of the summer session, she passed her exams and obtained her teaching permit. And at the age of seventeen, she boarded a train and traveled north about eighty miles from Marshfield to take a job teaching at Cox School—later called Riverside—just west of Sheldon, Wisconsin. Louise had learned of the position from her aunt Eda Pickering, who was also a teacher. Eda's husband, David Pickering, owned a sawmill on the Little Jump River, north of Sheldon. Cox School was about six miles from the Pickering home—too far to walk each day—so from her salary of forty-five dollars a month, Louise paid room and board to live with a farm family, the Coxes, near the school. She developed a lasting friendship with the Cox family. As we shall see, Lawrence Cox ("Law"), Dan, and several other members of the family appear repeatedly in her diary, even eight or nine years after she lived with them. Except for occasional visits with the Pickerings, Louise was quite isolated from her family in Marshfield, but kept in contact with them by writing letters and post cards.

In the fall of 1911 Louise gained a position a little closer to family, a rare luxury for most of the teachers

The Wegner homestead at Sheldon, with some fields cleared and the first house and barn erected, 1915.

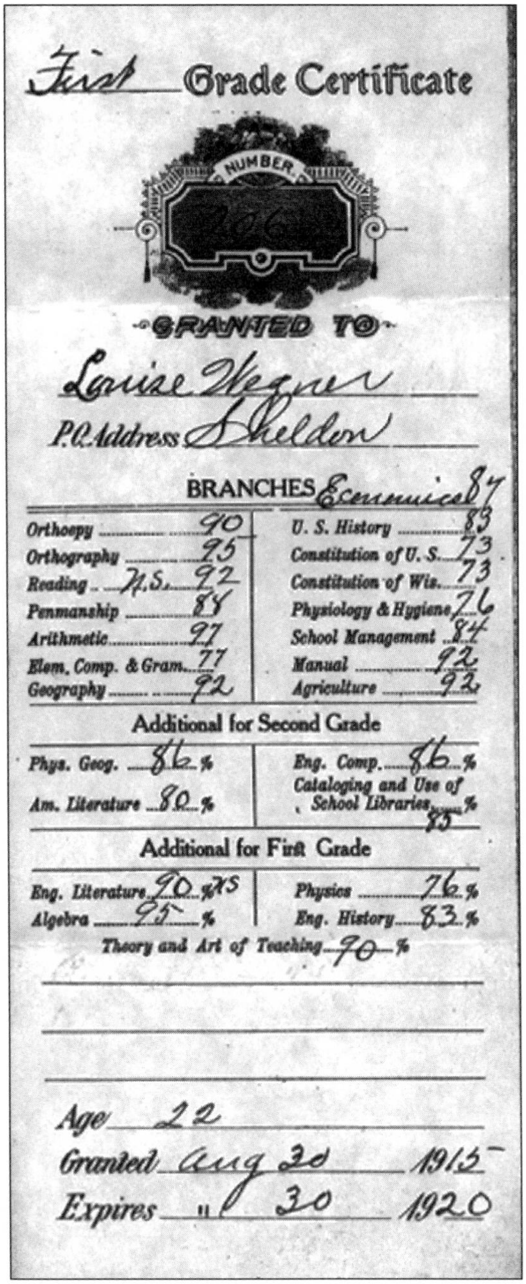

First **Grade Certificate**

NUMBER

GRANTED TO

Louise Wegner

P.O. Address *Sheldon*

BRANCHES *Economics 84*

Orthoepy	90	U. S. History	83
Orthography	95	Constitution of U. S.	73
Reading H.S.	92	Constitution of Wis.	73
Penmanship	88	Physiology & Hygiene	76
Arithmetic	97	School Management	84
Elem. Comp. & Gram.	77	Manual	92
Geography	92	Agriculture	92

Additional for Second Grade

Phys. Geog.	86 %	Eng. Comp.	86 %
Am. Literature	80 %	Cataloging and Use of School Libraries	85 %

Additional for First Grade

Eng. Literature	90 % HS	Physics	76 %
Algebra	95 %	Eng. History	83 %

Theory and Art of Teaching 90 %

Age 22

Granted Aug 30 1915

Expires " 30 1920

"First Grade" indicates the highest level of certification.

in the Wisconsin wilderness, when she began teaching at Linden School, north of Sheldon and not far from her uncle's sawmill. She took this opportunity to live with the Pickerings, an experience that developed strong and enduring ties with the couple and their children, Leon and Dorathea.

The next school year, 1912–1913, found Louise on her own again. She was transferred to the Town of Atlanta District No. 6 School, which was about six miles north of the village of Weyerhaeuser in the western part of Rusk County, about thirty miles from Sheldon. Again, she boarded with a local farm family and was almost totally isolated from her own family in Marshfield for most of the year. She returned home only at Christmas, taking the train from Weyerhaeuser to Ladysmith and then on to Marshfield. These long periods of isolation from her family helped hone her letter-writing abilities and may have prompted her to

Louise's sisters, Gertrude, Margaret, and Dorothea, at a teacher's conference in Ladysmith in 1917.

Louise, with an armful of folders, walks along a road in the remote parts of Rusk County, 1916. Her caption for this photo was "The Lonesome Road."

start journal writing as well. At the end of that rather lonely year, Louise was transferred back to Linden School near the Pickerings when the No. 6 School and another school were consolidated.

That year, 1913, Louise's father bought a choice wooded eighty acres along the Little Jump River a few miles south of Linden School, and in 1914 he began the task of clearing the land, building a house and barn, and making a home out of the wilderness. The Wegners moved to the new farm site, and after several years of near isolation from her family, Louise welcomed the opportunity to spend time with her brothers and sisters again. Louise continued teaching in rural schools for the next few years, but she was now able to see her family more often and she devoted much of her free time to helping her family clear stumps from the fields and build the house and barn. The homesteading process was hard physical work, and the men and women of the family shared it equally. By the spring of 1915 there were patches of clearing that served as the first fields on the farm. The Wegners lived in a temporary house consisting of four or five rooms until the permanent home was built in 1918.

In the fall of 1914, Louise moved again, this time to Murry in the far northern part of the county. It was her first opportunity to teach at a larger school, with more than one teacher, and she enjoyed the experience very much. After Christmas, however, she was transferred to the State Graded School at Sheldon to serve as principal and one of three teachers. This proximity to the family farm again enabled her to spend time helping her family.

Louise had begun her career with a teaching permit after only one summer of post-secondary education. She continued her education, however, by attending summer school nearly every summer and progressing in her quest for a permanent teaching license. After each summer session she received an update of her teaching certification.

Louise's three sisters all followed in her footsteps. Dorothea graduated from Marshfield High School in 1912, earned her teaching license from Rusk County Normal School at Ladysmith, and taught in various rural schools in Rusk County for about six years. Gertrude graduated from Marshfield High School in 1914 and from Rusk County Normal School in 1915, and taught in Rusk County until 1922. Margaret graduated from

Louise on the steps of the State Capitol in Madison in 1916.

Marshfield High School in 1916, from Rusk County Normal School in 1917, and taught for about five years.

After five years of teaching in the rural schools, Louise decided to apply for the newly created position of county supervisor. She passed the qualifying exam for the job, beating out two other applicants, and assumed her duties on October 5, 1915. As supervising teacher she was required to visit each of the more than one hundred rural schools in the county at least twice each year. The schools were far-flung throughout the county; some were near towns, while others were in remote areas. For the most part Louise relied upon train travel during the 1915–1916 school year, her first year as supervisor, but some of the more remote schools necessitated walking many miles along primitive roads through the cutover forests. Roads were merely places where the dirt had been leveled; ditches were rudimentary, and the brush crowded in from the roadsides. Louise hired a horse and buggy for some of her longer trips, but a majority of her travels were on foot. Many trips lasted several days, so Louise stayed in hotels in the various towns along the railroad lines. The more remote areas had no hotels, however, so she had to find lodging wherever she could. Often, if an invitation was extended, she stayed overnight with one of the teachers—usually sharing the bed—in the farm home where the teacher boarded. From these overnight visits developed close, long-lasting friendships between Louise and the teachers. Travel in the fall and spring was generally rather pleasant, except for the occasional rainstorm. As winter set in, however, travel became much more difficult. The roads were unplowed, and though Louise occasionally hired a horse and cutter to reach the schools, walking was still her main means of travel, even in deep snow or bitter cold.

The weather was not the only danger one might encounter on these remote trails. One of the stories Louise recounts illustrates this point well. Having

Louise's horse, Coley, and buggy in 1916.

concluded visits to several schools some miles north of Ladysmith, she began the long walk home on a late fall evening. As she walked along the brush-lined road in the gathering dusk, she noticed an animal in the road some distance ahead. She continued walking, wondering what the animal was, for it stood still, watching her approach. As she got closer, she saw that it was a rather large wolf. Alone and armed with nothing but a few books and folders, Louise had only a few minutes to review her options. She could not turn around and return to the school some miles back, and besides, she had to reach Ladysmith that evening. In desperation she picked up a stick and kept walking toward the wolf, hoping that it would run off. But the wolf stood stock still, staring at her as she approached. She walked to the opposite side of the road from the wolf and passed within about ten feet of the shaggy gray animal, which never took its eyes off her. Throughout the entire episode the wolf had not moved a muscle. It watched her intently as she walked past and continued down the road. Immensely relieved as the distance between herself and the wolf increased, she glanced back over her shoulder every few steps to see what the animal was doing. It continued to watch her for some distance, and then ran off into the brush. The rest of the trip to Ladysmith was, fortunately, without incident.

In September 1916, Louise made her first trip to Madison to attend the first convention of supervising teachers. The meeting was held in the new capitol, lasted two weeks, and was under the direction and supervision of the state superintendent and his assistants. The trip was nearly a full day's train ride from Sheldon and must have been a memorable experience for a young woman from northern Wisconsin. While in Madison, Louise took exams in several subjects to continue her progress toward certification for her permanent teaching license. Although she had obtained a permit to teach in 1910 and had attended summer

Louise and Victor Wegner, with Sophie, at their grandparents' farm near Neillsville in 1917.

255

1918

Little Flivver :— Last year your account, so carefully begun, dwindled down to nothing, as the preceding pages will testify. But whatever your cost, you were worth it all, dear little car! Now once more I begin your account. How long will it continue thus?

License	10 —	✓
Gasoline — 5 gal.	1 30	✓
Gasoline — 5 gal	1 30	✓
(Two new Tires — A Christmas Present.) —		
Apr. 12 1 Can Radiator Comp.	75	
" 13 1 inner Tube .	3 75	
" 11 4 gal. gas.	1 00	✓
4 gal gas.	1 04	
7 gal. gas	1 85	
7 gal. gas.	1 95	
5 gal. gas.	1 40	
4 gal. gas.	1 12	
Storage for April	3 00	

Louise's ledger documents the purchase and expenses of her Model T Ford for 1917 and 1918.

251

Sophie's Account				
	Sophie	# 373	—	
	License	5	—	
Apr. 21	7 gal. Gasoline	1	75	
" "	1 gal. Oil		60	
" "	1 set Chains	2	65	
May 4	5 gal. Gasoline	1	25	
" 5	Parts	2	16	
" 5	4½ gal. Gasoline	1	13	
" 13	5 gal. Gasoline	1	35	
" 14	4 gal. Gasoline	1	08	
" 15	3 gal. Gasoline		81	
" 18	6 gal. Gasoline	1	62	
" 23	6 gal. Gasoline	1	62	
" 23	Labor & parts		80	
" 26	Labor & material	2	08	
" 27	Inner Tube	3	45	
" 27	Two patches	1	10	
" 28	Sponge		25	
" 28	Chamois		35	
" 16	Labor	3	59	
" 16	Material		65	
" 26	5 gal. Gasoline	1	35	
	Storage – one month	5	00	

classes for several years, she still needed additional credits to qualify for a permanent license. Louise made a second trip to Madison for another convention at the end of December 1916.

In the fall of 1916 she bought a horse and buggy, which enabled her to visit more schools in one day and eliminated at least some of the long walks. She boarded her horse, Coley, at Dr. Kinyon's livery in Ladysmith, and on overnight trips she rented livery space in other towns. When the roads were filled with snow, she took a cutter instead of a buggy, wrapping up in fur robes for the long, cold journeys from school to school. In the depths of winter, however, she could not leave the horse standing outdoors for hours while she visited schools, so on the coldest days she still walked many miles through the snow.

Although Coley and her buggy or cutter expedited her travels about the county, Louise was never fond of driving or riding behind the horse. Consequently, in 1917, she did an almost unthinkable thing for a young woman of her time and purchased a new Model T Ford. Unfortunately the diary that recounts the story of this event has been lost, but some details survive in record books and letters. Louise's secondary journal—primarily a ledger of her school visits and expenses—gives some information about the Model T. Louise paid $373 for the car and $5 for the license. She first saw the "shining black beauty" on April 21, although the car had been stored in the garage at a pea canning factory in Ladysmith since the first of January. On April 23 and 24, Louise received her only two lessons on how to operate the car, and on April 30 she

A picnic at Amacoy Lake made possible by Sophie and another Model T Ford, in July 1917.

took her first solo trip. On May 5, she and her sister Gertrude made the fifteen-mile trip home to show their parents the new car, down narrow rutted roads, steering around the worst of the bumps and ruts. Louise wrote, "May 5: Toots and I went home with her, a long trip for the first one, but the experience was a very valuable one in every way and I gained more in real knowledge than in any other way." The flivver enabled Louise to get around the county much more easily to visit the many schools. Walking, she could travel about two to three miles in an hour; with Coley she could average perhaps seven or eight miles per hour. But the Model T could go an amazing fifteen to twenty miles per hour, perhaps even twenty-five on good stretches of road. Furthermore, it greatly increased mobility for socializing, and Louise and her sisters definitely took advantage of this. They named the car Sophie, and when school was out they spent a delightful summer of joy riding and trips that would have been out of the question with a horse and buggy. Recorded only in the photo albums from that summer, the trips included

a picnic on Amacoy Lake, about twenty miles from Sheldon, and a visit to their childhood homes, the farm near Neillsville and the house in Marshfield, some eighty miles away.

In August of 1917, Louise returned to Madison by train for another convention of supervising teachers. As usual, the meetings were held in the capitol, so she stayed at a hotel near Capitol Square in Madison and was much impressed by the luxury of life in the city. It is upon her return from this trip that the journals can finally take up the story. In the first three entries (October 29–31), Louise is at the family farm in Sheldon, but on November 1 she returns to the suite of rooms she rents above Fritz's Dry Goods Store. Both Toots and Audie stay here with Louise on occasion, and her young brother Bob and cousin Leon Pickering live with her here while they attend high school in town. At this time, Toots is teaching at the Pepper School, about four miles northeast of town, and boarding with the Pepper family at their farm. Audie, meanwhile, is teaching at the Cloverleaf School, about five miles

The streets of Ladysmith were still dirt, and boardwalks served as sidewalks, when Louise lived there from 1915 to 1920.

south of Ladysmith, and boarding with the Leighty family but is still near enough to see her sisters regularly. Tis, however, is teaching at the Horseman School in the far northwestern part of the county, is boarding with the Bittle family, and is somewhat isolated. Louise's brother Vic is working at the garage of his uncles Max and Otto Wegner in Marshfield, and her brother Bill (Sonny) is only eight years old and living primarily at the Sheldon farm.

Louise also has two good friends, Ruth and Laura LaBerge, who are schoolteachers and sisters from a large French Canadian family in the area. Two of their brothers, Fred and Archie, also appear in Louise's journals. Archie is a particularly significant figure; he would eventually become Louise Wegner's husband. A great many other names appear in the journals as Louise travels the county, encountering friends, family,

acquaintances, and teachers. Most are mentioned in passing, but some names recur: Leon is her cousin and friend to young brother Bob; Ernie is one of the young men in town, and he and his father, Orville, help Louise keep Sophie running. Ernie also plays a romantic role later on. Mr. Dresden, Mr. Householder, Miss Jenkins, and Miss Biggs are all teachers and friends from the Rusk County Training School. The school, housed in a two-story red brick building in Ladysmith, trains teachers to work in rural schools. Louise often goes there on Saturdays to do her paperwork. Mr. Rice is the county superintendent.

Archie, or Arthur, LaBerge, the intense and handsome young man who would eventually marry Louise, is the fifth of nine children, born February 7, 1891, to Ludger (pronounced "loo-share") and Elizabeth LaBerge. The family is one of the first to settle in the

Fritz's Dry Goods, where Louise rented a room on the second floor. It was located on the southeast corner of the present Miner Avenue and West Second Street, where the current city hall now stands.

area, and their third child, Eugene, is the first white child born near Ladysmith. Ludger LaBerge was from Chataguay, a small town north of Montreal, Quebec. He graduated from the Montreal Business College in 1878, then moved to Winnipeg and later to Chippewa Falls, where he met and married Elizabeth Beranek in 1883. The couple had their first two children, Louise and George, in Chippewa Falls before they moved to Flambeau Falls (later to become Ladysmith) in 1885, where Ludger took a job as a scaler and timekeeper for the Daniel Shaw Lumber Company. They bought an "eighty" of land along the Flambeau River east of town and built a log home. Eventually they had nine children: Louise, George, Eugene, Leon, Arthur (Archie), Fred, Laura, Ruth, and Allan. All the LaBerge sons would also be employed by the lumber companies as lumberjacks. Archie was a particularly agile young man who mainly worked on the log drives on the Flambeau River as a logdriver, an extremely hazardous occupation. Having been raised in the wilderness of early Ladysmith, Archie was at home in the woods. He and his brothers were adept and avid outdoorsmen, rather like the frontiersmen of early American history, even keeping a pet deer and pet fox. After 1910, however, as the logging industry began to decline in the area, Archie returned to civilization to help clear land on his parents' farm. His love for the great outdoors, however, remained undiminished, and, as we shall see in Louise's journals, he is a powerful figure, a "man's man," and a little intimidating to the young schoolteacher as such.

But let Louise tell the story in her own words, for she was remarkably adept at painting word pictures of scenes that make you feel as though you are living the experience yourself. With her talent for capturing details in writing and her discernment in photographing events, the story comes alive again after more than eighty years. Except for minor changes in punctuation and spelling, the journal is presented exactly as Louise wrote it. While we can only guess at the stories the lost journals might contain, the ones that have survived tell of a way of life that was common a century ago but now lives only in memoirs such as Louise's journal. Here is her story.

Louise's friends Laura and Ruth LaBerge with their horse and buggy in 1917.

Louise (right) and her three sisters, Dorothea (Tis), Gertrude (Toots), and Margaret (Audie) on their way to a "social" in the fall of 1917.

Fall 1917

Monday, October 29, 1917   You begin with a Monday, Little Book, and I hope that you will show, when you are completed, that something has been accomplished during your little life.

The day dawned cold and blustery. I walked down to the crossing with Bob and then turned toward Marie's school. Short cuts always bring surprises, and this one was no exception. It was only a short distance from the railroad bridge to the road corner, but I came to two little open streams. The first one I was able to jump, but the second one almost made me say, "I came to a river and I couldn't get across." Other people had crossed, however, and I followed their footsteps as well as I could, now on a log, now on a treacherous-looking bit of ice, and then for a little ways on bunch grass. I reached the other side with dry feet. Bravo!

Marie is doing well for her first year of teaching. Primary work is very plainly her forte. I had made up my mind to ask her about the money she owed me, but I just couldn't do it. I suppose I'll simply have to lose it. Lending money has its disadvantages the same as borrowing it.

Tuesday, October 30   I helped Mother and Dad clear land down in the south end this morning. My fingers simply itch to get rid of the brush and logs, and how I do love to see the piles of "poverty wood" grow and grow!! I don't suppose I did very much, but I at least had the satisfaction of being with Mother and Dad and helping a little.

In the afternoon I went up to call on Mabel Bailey. She belongs to a type of personalities all her own, fiery, quick, a, perfect chatterbox, but very likable all the same. Her teaching in a school suited to her temperament would be very good, but here, with some of these slow-thinking children, she is very much out of her element.

She came home with me and spent the night with us. She is jolly company, surely, and can coax laughter from almost anyone and anything.

Wednesday, October 31   Dad went up to help Uncle Dave haul poles for wood. I had planned to visit the Cox school today, but when Dad said he was going up to help Uncle Dave, I threw all those plans aside and stayed at home to visit with Mother. She would have been alone all day if I had gone, and it isn't good for anyone to be alone very much. It makes you broody, and attacks of the blues come upon you very easily. Even if you have work enough to keep you busy, your mind will take long journeys off in any old direction, and sometimes you won't be the same person when it comes back again.

The sun came out bright and beautiful, and the cold scurried away to the North Pole. It thawed and was quite warm outside.

Mother and I didn't go out into the woods and cut poverty wood but stayed in the house and talked and talked and made a million plans, at least. The new house receives the most attention, just now. I wonder how long it will take us to have it all as complete as our imagination has pictured it.

Thursday, November 1   Came back to Ladysmith this morning. The boys were mighty glad to see me because it relieved them of the great responsibility of getting dinner. I took Sophie out in the afternoon and went to visit Toots. The roads were hard and quite rough, but traveled considerably.

We had supper out tonight at the Hospital Bazaar. A dandy supper, too! I wonder how many pieces of pie the boys disposed of? At any rate, it didn't make them sick, and we are all glad we went.

Friday, November 2 I met Zelda Breed on the street this morning and she gave me quite a surprise. Her brother is very sick and her father telephoned her to come home—Poor girlie!

I buzzed out to Susan Siglin's and Ora Deerwester's schools in the afternoon. The roads were slippery and I did some fancy skidding in places, but nothing frightened me or the car, not even the deep ruts.

Ora has some mulatto children in his school that cause him a great deal of needless worry. He dislikes them because of racial hatred and cannot conceal his dislikes. They are not the most desirable children, perhaps, but all the same they are just as good as the other children in school, and should receive the same time and attention.

The boys had already left when Toots and I got home. The Training School had invited us both to attend a Hallowe'en party. I felt devilish, but Toots wasn't in a similar mood. However, we made a flying trip down to Thompson's and Robelia's, in search of clothes for witches to wear. The witches wouldn't materialize, but with red handkerchiefs and some burned cork we became pretty fair witches. We took our hair down and snarled it and when we were "dressed" we called on Jordan's. They really couldn't recognize us, and we felt repaid for the energy expended in our make-up.

We decided not to wear many wraps to the school, but when we reached the foot of the stairs, all courage failed us and we couldn't let ourselves be seen on the street. It was a busy time of the evening, with many people on the street. After many attempts and wild scurrying to cover again, we skipped across the street and

The Wegner family clearing stumps and brush to create fields on the family farm in 1916.

ran all the way to the Training School, across vacant lots and wherever it was dark.

The building was crowded with ghosts and goblins, with an old witch as hostess. Miss Biggs and Miss Jenkins couldn't recognize me, and not until I laughed did they know who I was.

I felt like a fool, and when Mr. C.S. Arnold came in and after him Mr. and Mrs. Rice and Mrs. Dresden, all in "society" clothes, I could have crawled into a shoe box. Even winning the prize as the best impersonation did not improve my state of mind.

We played games down in the gymnasium and enjoyed ourselves. Toots won the most points in all the games and received a big horn as a prize. We had a nice lunch and after most of the girls had danced a little upstairs (to my poor music) we went home. We were both very glad that we went, but next time I'm going to prove to people that I *do* own a party gown.

Saturday, November 3 The usual office day. Audie came up to have some dental work done, but went back with Leighty's again, and Toots went home on the scoot.

This was my expense-report day, and, as usual, Mr. Rice made me dreadfully angry. He is so very unwilling to be the least bit fair in the matter of allowing expenses. Nearly every month of my work I have had to insist on what I was sure were my rights, and this time it was the new tire that broke the camel's back. I had paid for the other tire myself and I thought it was only right that a part of the second tire should be allowed me. Mr. Rice had strong opinions to the contrary and I had to strike out the tire. I was mad clear way through, just plain American Mad, and I cried like a baby, but I really couldn't help it.

Mr. Rice did his best to smooth over the affair and suggested that I send "a respectful letter" to the Board and humbly ask that they allow me some credit for the tires used. I most certainly will not do it, and neither will I use the car again!

I was too angry to think clearly and even resolved to hand in my resignation that night. I knew I was foolish, but after a while, when my anger cooled, I realized how foolish that resolution was. "All things are for the best," they say, but I can see no best in this; perhaps I may discover it later.

I met Therese Diederich on my way home from the office and she took pity on me in my mental anguish, and took me home with her for supper. I was very glad to go, because the Blue Devils would have almost devoured me had I been alone that night.

From Diederich's I went down to Robelia's to give Clare his music lesson, and then stopped at Thompson's to take Harriet with me to spend the night. I simply couldn't bear the thought of being alone.

My anger was gone now and I began to see that even this question had two sides, same as any other.

Sunday, November 4 Toots came back on the scoot and then the three of of us went down to Thompson's for dinner! Um-yum, oyster stew, and it surely was good.

We took Sophie out and went down to call on Audie. It was almost three when we got there and they were still in house gowns, with the dinner dishes still unwashed. We had a dandy supper, and then after a tea-fortune session, in which I really felt quite inspired, we "motored" back to town. I phoned Audie later in the week and she told me that all my fortunes had come wonderfully true, and that they were all anxious to have me tell tea-fortunes again. My luck doesn't usually last for two tellings, so I won't promise to tell them again.

Monday, November 5 Zelda Breed came back on the early morning train. While she was gone they fumigated her school and all her belongings. Poor child! She seems to have no end of troubles. I had promised to take her down to the schoolhouse, but the hour was rather early and, as I could hardly wait very long for her, she decided to hire a livery later in the morning. Her

10

Schools visited.

Date	Name				
Oct. 1	Sunday.				
Oct. 2	Office (Ladysmith)				
" 3	Lillian Solberg	Grant.	1	½ da.	
" 3	Terna Schweiger	"	6	½ da.	
" 4	Ruby Dakins	Flam.	2	½ da.	
" 4	Gertrude Wegner	"	1	½ da.	
" 5	Anne Christman	Flam.	11	½ da.	
" 5	Mamie Stevens	Flam.	2	"	
" 6	Rose Klopfenstein	"	"	"	
" 6	Dorathea Wegner	"	4	"	
" 7	Office (Ladysmith)				
" 8	Sunday.				
" 9	Albena Plante	Hub.	3	½ da.	
" 9	Ruby Kepner	"	7	"	
" 10	Laura LaBerge	Grow.	2	"	
" 10	Office			½ da.	
" 11	School Board Convention.				
" 12	Julia Nelson	B.B.	7	½ da.	
" 12	Elmer Chickering	B.B.	4	½ da.	
" 13	Esther Kehl.	Stubbs	5	½ da.	
" 13	W. B. Graham	St.& B.B.	8	"	
" 14	Office. (Ladysmith)				
" 15	Sunday.				

Ledger pages show Louise's expenses and school visits in October 1917.

11

Oct.	16	Office (Ladysmith)				
"	17	Mrs. Althea Davis	Grant.	3	½ da.	
"	17	Mrs. Mary McCabe	Grow.	1	} ½ da.	
"	17	Lula B. Cruse	"	"		
"	18	Wanda Formella	Will.	4	½ da.	
"	18	Gladys M. Kaiser	Marsh	3	"	
"	19	Alice West	"	4	½ da.	
"	20	Lottie North	"	5	1 da.	
"	21	Office (Ladysmith)				
"	22	Sunday				
"	23	Office (Ladysmith)				
"	24	George Bartelt	Marsh	2	½ da.	
"	24	Mrs. Earl Loper	Will	2	½ da.	
"	25	(Rain)				
"	26	Mrs. Eleanor Arnold	Will	3	1 da.	
"	27	Lenore McFarland	Will	1	1 da.	
"	28	Office (Ladysmith)				
"	29	Sunday				
"	30	Viva Bollman	Grant	1	½ da.	II
"	31	Martha Finnegan	"	1	½ da.	
"	31	Mrs. M. G. Musselman	Thorn	4	½ da.	

younger brother has had an operation and is very sick. The poor child worries so about him. I hope she'll write to us some time and let us know how everything is. Good-bye, Zelda, come back again sometime.

Tuesday, November 6   I made arrangements yesterday to take Miss Jenkins and Miss Biggs out on an inspection trip. Miss Jenkins went out with me to-day. We took our lunch and planned to spend a whole day out in the country. Anna Riley's was the first school. We arrived just at nine o'clock. Miss Jenkins commented favorably on the general order and the industrious spirit of the pupils. We stayed until recess and then took a new road over to the Bell School. All short-cuts are alike, poorly traveled and narrow, and there is always a strong probability of not getting through. However, as bad as the roads were, we came right through, tho'

I am sure not many cars had gone along that road since it was made.

Susan Siglin always had a good little school. There was quite a difference in clocks, and we reached her school at the same time as we had left Anna Riley's. We had our lunch here and talked until almost one, and then rode along on fairly good roads up to the Laurel Hill School.

We found the most upset school I ever went into. There was perfect bedlam in the room until I opened the door. Nora W. had punished a little girl by slapping her and then locking her up in a closet. She was sobbing at the very limit of her ability to make noise. It had a very disquieting effect on the school, and made both of us so nervous I could hardly stand or sit quietly. Finally, my patience reached the end of its rope—Miss Wilber seemed determined to let the child cry until it

Interior of one of the larger rural schools that Louise visited. Note the double desks for the children.

fell asleep—so I walked quickly to the closet, opened the door and, before the teacher could think of resisting, took the child outside to the well. I bathed her face and talked to her and she finally stopped her sobbing. I took her back into the schoolroom and sent her to her seat, and in less than two minutes she had fallen asleep, thoroughly exhausted.

Miss Jenkins had taken charge of the class and was telling them the story of the Bishop of Bingen. They had memorized the "Children"s Hour" and seemed to know nothing about any of the references in it.

We stayed there until recess time, and then, after a serious talk with the teacher, we decided that our nerves would appreciate a change. I cannot endure seeing such wretchedly poor teaching as goes on in this school. This is the third "official" visit Nora has had and, though I can see some improvement, she is far from coming up to any kind of standard.

We stopped for a moment to visit Mae Carter and to see some good teaching. Though I could never like her personally, I must admit that she does very good work. She has certainly wrought a marvelous change in that school in the few months she has been there.

It was almost four o'clock when we left and I hurried over to Toots' school, hardly expecting to get there in time to see any school work. She was just about ready to dismiss when we came, but we inspected the work on display and all her decorations for the Social which is coming up on Friday—no, Thursday, I believe, because Friday and Saturday are Institute days. I helped get some decorations by going down to the spruce swamp and getting some trees for her stage settings. I nearly chopped off several toes! When we got up to the school with our trees, she had swept and was ready to go home. So was I, Little Book, and I'm sure Miss Jenkins was tired, too. It had been a perfectly glorious day and we had enjoyed ourselves, but it was strenuous all the same. Five schools in one day is a record I have never before equaled.

Wednesday, November 7 Miss Biggs' visiting day was not nearly so ideal as yesterday. It was cold and very foggy and seemed much darker.

Our first school was Beldenville, and we saw some very poor work. Miss Biggs is right up and coming when any suggestions are needed, and Violet S. was surely in need of suggestions when it comes to handling children. We left a list of suggestions with her and then hurried off to some of the schools in Atlanta.

Atlanta village was the first on the list, and Miss Biggs could not speak favorably enough of Isobel Stenson's work. She is a little dandy. We stayed until nearly eleven and then with the promise of coming back for dinner, to have a little chat, we went up to Anna Sed.'s school, which is also in excellent condition. Of course, I do not like her at all, and never will, but all the same she is a good teacher and doing better every year it seems.

We came back and had dinner with Isobel Stenson and then left just about one o'clock, bound for Amacoy. Viva Bollman's work is stiff and she doesn't make the least effort to make the work pleasant for the children. Miss Biggs made some very decided criticisms on her work and left her some suggestions, which I don't think she will follow. I'd be surprised if she would.

We were both cold and when we reached Bruce on our way back home we decided to have a lunch at McArthur's. Mrs. Mac finished up a dandy little lunch, and we felt up to facing the cold until we reached Ladysmith.

I went out again to get Toots but never reached the school. She was already on Pepper's hill walking, and when we asked her to ride back to town with us she graciously consented.

Thursday, November 8 A very foggy day, and too damp to enjoy riding.

I visited the Training School in the morning and went to the office in the afternoon. Hardly enough penmanship specimens came back to me to make it worth while to prepare the exhibit.

Audie had promised to phone at about 4:45 and tell me whether we should come after her, but 5:30 came and she still hadn't sent any message. I phoned twice and she hadn't come home. Then she phoned and told me to send the boys down after her, and about five minutes later, when Bob and Leon were just ready to start from the garage, she phoned again and said that we didn't need to come. Of course, I had to send a hurry-up call to the garage and nearly scared Ernie to death by my frantic order to "Tell the boys not to take the car out of the garage." Effects of the scare were still to be seen after supper when they demanded a written order before they would allow them to take the car. I was almost angry, though they were justified, of course.

Miss Jenkins and Miss Biggs and Therese Diederich were going with us and all three were up at the rooms when Audie finally came up. She had had some trouble with her biggest boy and she was still so nervous and excited that she hardly knew what she was doing.

It was the foggiest ride I ever had that evening. The fog was so thick along the river that we could see only a few feet ahead of us and corners were almost out of sight. I was very glad that the road was so very familiar to me, I could have gone over it in pale moonlight, knowing every spot in it.

Audie came out with Ed Hanson and Orville. Toots had sent Ernie a special invitation and just before the program he walked in. There was quite a row of cars standing outside.

The program was very good. "The Land of Nod" was the main feature, and it was just fine. I never have seen a program quite so pretty or so well carried out. The costuming was quite elaborate, considering

The Wegner sisters en route to a social at a rural school, 1917.

how inexpensive it was, but it made all the difference in the world.

Miss Biggs had a friend who was coming on the limited at 9:23, and she had asked Bob and Leon to go with her back to Ladysmith to meet her and bring her back out to the Social. They left late, the limited had already whistled for Ladysmith when they started, but it was only a little ways and I knew they would hurry all they could.

The "pounds" were sold just after the program and the method was far from satisfactory. Each box was numbered, and numbers corresponding to these were sold. No one knew whose box they were getting or even what it looked like. It worked out fairly well, but I'm afraid that some of the boys would rather have had the privilege of exchanging boxes in the background.

The boxes were all sold. Mr. Pepper got mine, Archie got Toots' and Mr. Shukar got Audie's, but she wouldn't eat with him. The boys hadn't come back and I was beginning to worry. We ate our lunches and still no boys. After supper we played games, but as often as I went to the door to watch and listen, all was dark and quiet. What could be keeping them so long?

After nearly an hour's waiting while we played games and tried to be gay and happy the four paraded into the room and almost their first words were, "Sophie's on the bum entirely. We left her at the foot of Pepper's hill." It was a perfect thunderbolt from a

The Wegner & Pirwitz garage in Marshfield where Vic repaired and maintained the unpredictable Model T's. On the back of this photo he wrote, "Glad that you got home safe and sound. How are the blueberries? My draft no. is 1710. Vic," and sent it to Louise as a post card in 1917.

clear sky, because she had been running so beautifully only about an hour before. I was ready to weep, and I must have looked ready to begin, but everyone seemed so confident that she was only balky, and Ernie's "We'll fix her up alright" brought back enough hope to carry me through the evening.

The crowd went home at eleven o'clock. I packed Miss Biggs and her friend, Miss Jenkins and Bob and Leon in Ernie's car, and the kind-hearted fellow took them all back to town. The rest of our bunch went over to Pepper's and danced a while. As usual, when I am the principal musician, I have very little opportunity to dance. To-night, however, I really could not enjoy dancing, the car at the foot of the hill was in my thoughts every minute.

When we were ready to go everyone deserted me except Therese Diederich, dear girl. Toots went with Archie, Ernie and Ed left and Orville and Audie stayed behind we two brave and reckless beings. Sophie surely was "on the bum." She seemed to buzz fairly well and we managed to slide down the hill and across the swamp, but she could not climb the next swamp. We both got out and Orville picked us up in his car. When we were almost within sight of town I remembered that I had not drained the radiator, and by morning it surely would be frozen up solid. Orville very obligingly turned around and went back, and just as we reached Sophie, I heard Ernie coming back. There was no need for Orville to stay, so he left. Ernie had no flashlight, and only a few matches, and he very soon decided that it would be best to let Sophie here until morning and then come out and get her. I had to agree, there was nothing else to do, so we hurried back to town. This was Ernie's sixth trip over the same road that night and it was one of the fastest and bumpiest rides I ever took. I could hardly stay down on the seat.

We were a blue-feeling bunch that night, or early morning.

Friday, November 9   Institute today. I always hate Institutes, because I must act so "supervising-teach-ery"! I do not belong with the teachers as a teacher. My writing exhibit didn't look as well as I wanted it to.

Toots and Audie left early and went down to get Audie's school order. They had a dreadful time with Sophie. I was blue enough before they came home, but when they came into the rooms with their tale of woe, it was too much for me, and like a big baby, I just cried for hours. I felt better after that, but the whole family absorbed some of my feelings.

Saturday, November 10   The second day of Institute was much brighter than the first. I almost enjoyed it. We left rather early and went over to the garage after Sophie. We made two "trial trips" and brought her back, sputtering and coughing and acting up perfectly awful. We were almost afraid that she would blow up right in the middle of town.

Then Ernie came to our rescue and after one glance, put in a new timer, and lo' and behold! she was O.K. Oh, what a joy and peace of mind to know that she was in running order and would really *go* again. I was so happy I could have sung for joy!

We cleaned up the schoolhouse, and when we went by Pepper's, Mrs. Pepper made us stay and have supper with her. It was a dandy supper, too. Louis Wagner (our "way-back cousin") called and entertained us for nearly an hour. Executing people by cutting off their heads was his main topic, and I had to stuff up my ears or it would have sickened me. He's quite a character!

We were late in reaching Ladysmith, but we had planned to go to a dance at Sheldon and tho' we had premonitions of trouble ahead, we all donned our prettiest clothes and went.

None of our Ladysmith friends were there and everyone at Sheldon must have eaten "grouch-pudding" for supper. We had a rotten time. Lawrence wouldn't even speak and went home after a few dances. Roy sat in a corner. We tried to be jolly with the two Shephard boys, but I hardly knew them.

Audie's bunions were nearly killing her and Toots' soft corn was on fire and to make a trio of misery, I fell from Dietze's porch and almost broke my leg. I could hardly walk. I danced twice after supper, but my ankle was so numb, I thought better of it and sat in a corner.

How were we to get home? None of us could walk, and there was no one to take us home! We had almost decided to wait for the limited and go back to Ladysmith, when Roy offered to take us. We were mighty glad to accept. Roy's not so bad after all. We were a most miserable bunch of cripples when we reached home at nearly three o'clock. I could scarcely walk.

Sunday, November 11   Bob took us down to the depot, because a Sunday morning return is so much easier than early Monday morning. Sheldon was as dead as usual after a dance the night before.

When the scoot came, just imagine our surprise when Vicy stepped off. We could hardly believe our eyes. The cranky brakeman wouldn't let us talk even a minute, but we learned that he had taken the wrong train at Marshfield and had come from Abbotsford on the scoot. We were so glad to see him, and we hastily resolved to come back with Sophie in time for dinner. We usually carry out our resolutions with enough speed to make most people gasp.

Within fifteen minutes after reaching Ladysmith we were on our way home again, Toots driving. The roads were fairly good and the day was perfectly beautiful. Vicy hadn't taken our statement very seriously and so there was no dinner left for us. We didn't care very much, Sunday at home is always jolly.

Mother, Dad and Bob took the horses out for a plowing lesson, and I saw for myself how Belle acts up when she is in harness. Heavens above! I was nearly ready to run for cover every minute. Pete and Johnny Yaeger came over to see what was up, and finally got one of their horses, Queen, and put her with Belle. There was very little improvement, and Billy got so wild that he jumped right on top of the pig pen and turned a complete somersault and tore his strap and dashed over to Belle. It was a perfect wonder to me that he didn't kill himself.

Vicy went hunting for a few hours and saw a "horned rabbit" and got a shot at it. Hunting talk just makes me eager to get out into the woods myself.

Leon and our crowd were all going back to Ladysmith that night, but Sophie acted so queer when we started, she stopped dead several times. We were worried. We stopped for Leon and then started for the "bad road," with Sophie sputtering and balking. At Niepow's we stopped and told Harry there would be no school for another week. Ed Hanson had the Mumps. Here our courage failed us and we decided to go around the gates. We turned, and from then on Sophie went perfectly. We never stopped once, went right by home, hoping that no one saw or thought of us just then (vain hope!) and reached Ladysmith about eight.

After a hurried supper we took Audie down to Leighty's and had quite an exciting time getting our two fellows home where they belonged. It was ten when we finally got back home again, tired as could be.

Monday, November 12   I took a long trip with Sophie to-day, down to the Boyer and Roi Schools. With a horse the trip would have been nearly impossible, but with a car it was not at all bad.

Coming back I passed a man and a woman driving toward Ladysmith. They hailed me and asked for a ride, and thinking that perhaps something on the buggy had broken, I stopped as soon as I could and the man came running toward the car, while the woman turned back. In my conversation with him on the way to Ladysmith,

I learned that he works nights in the "fire hole" at the Menasha Wooden Ware, then walks home seven and one-half miles, works several hours during the day on his farm, sleeping about three hours and then walks back to Ladysmith in time to work all night. He told me that he had been doing that all summer, but that as soon as he could no longer work on the farm, he would stay in town. His ability to work and work hard is beyond comprehension. It is no wonder that Bohemian and Polish succeed where Americans fail.

I took Miss Biggs out for her first lesson in driving a car. Perhaps I am a poor teacher, but she learns slowly about the simple processes of starting and stopping a car. However, although we ran into a sand bank and once into a ditch, nothing serious happened, and we reached Ladysmith with a whole car and whole passengers.

Tuesday, November 13   I spent the morning in attending to my own reports and correspondence. Aunt Eda and Uncle Dave surprised me by coming up just before dinner. She fixed up a dandy dinner, seemed good to have a real meal for a change.

In the afternoon I took a quick little spin out to Emma Fond's school. The poor child is having all manner of trouble with discipline. Expulsion of one or more pupils is the only end to the trouble, as I see it.

Wednesday, November 14   Island Lake was my destination to-day, and everything went beautifully until I was about two miles south of Bruce, when suddenly the car "spewed" down and I had just time to turn slightly out of the road when it stopped completely. I knew instantly what was wrong—no gas—but there were telephones within walking distance and I set out right away towards the nearest one, about a quarter mile. "We'll be down right away," said the man at the garage, and almost as soon as I got back to the car, I saw the garage flivver coming. In all, I believe I only

lost about a half an hour. While the man was filling the tank, old Mr. Stevens came along and had a good laugh at me.

I visited three schools in spite of the morning's delay, Soft Maple, Bessie Clark's and the Island Lake school. How I would like to condemn that old building! It's one of the poorest in the county.

The ride back was long and cold and I felt nearly frozen when I got back to Ladysmith. I felt a little bit scary about driving so far alone, at night especially.

Thursday, November 15   Another long trip to-day. I went away down into the corner of Washington, the sand barrens of Rusk County. The day was warm and sunny and I couldn't help but enjoy every minute of the drive. Even the drive home in the dark wasn't nearly as bad as usual.

Marie and Chrystella came up this evening—Chrystella went to a party given by the Eastern Star—and Marie, after buying a suit at Fritz's, came up and spent the evening with us. We had a very enjoyable visit with her, quite like old times.

Friday, November 16   It seems almost as though I'm trying to reach the very outermost parts of the county this week. Blue Hills isn't quite on the edge of the county, but seven miles beyond Bruce, and being in among those dreadful hills always make it seem almost like seventeen miles from nowhere.

The stony hills are hard to climb, and the last one, just before the school, taxed the power of the car almost to the limit.

On the way back, I stopped at Mattison's for a little while and when I was leaving I joked with Minnie Mattison about going back to Ladysmith with me "just for a ride." She took my joke seriously and accepted before I realized what was happening. I wasn't unwilling to take her, but the question of what to do with her when I got home was a problem. She was ready within a few minutes, and I inspected the car and found a broken fan belt. I couldn't fix it so I decided to wait until I reached Bruce. I wasn't sure whether we'd have trouble without a fan belt, but I was willing to risk it.

Nothing happened and the ride was beautiful. I had a new fan belt put on in Bruce and we hurried on toward Ladysmith. Unexpected company was a surprise to the boys especially and when Bob went down after Audie, he readily accepted an invitation to have supper with Leighty's, to avoid having to eat with "that teacher."

Audie and I took her back after supper over the little hills in the new road to Bruce. We found three teachers waiting for the limited, and in the goodness of our hearts, we took them all back with us. Of course, Sophie had to show how naughty she could be, and was balky all the way home, climbed every hill on three cylinders, and not all the careful adjusting I tried to do helped a bit. She didn't stop completely, however, and we reached Ladysmith before the limited. Toots went to a social out at Laura LaBerge's school, and I would dearly love to have gone, but because it was a dance, I hated to go and run into trouble with Mr. Rice. I know we missed a good time.

Saturday, November 17 A busy office day as usual. I came home shortly after five and we got in the flivver and packed in our belongings. Joey and Ed were down at the car when we were ready to leave and we came nearly having to take them home with us. Both had been at Tony that afternoon, I am sure.

Max was there when we got home and both Vicy and Max were in hunting togs and could only talk hunting. We were also planning for *our* hunting trip next Sunday.

Sunday, November 18 Toots and I took the boys, Max, Vicy and Bob, up to their hunting camp this morning. We put on the most outlandish things we could find, in order to look as much like hunters as possible. With all the blankets and robes, guns and ammunition, and "grub" and cooking utensils, the load was all the three could carry. We took Sophie up to the beginning of the logging road and then followed that for over two miles, up as far as Sergeant's old camp. Here Vicy said we must turn back, because they were going through the woods and we would never be able to find our way back. We *did* so want to help them pitch the tent, so that we could really see what it looked like, but Vicy's orders were to be obeyed, so we went back. At a fork in the logging road, we couldn't decide which was the one we had taken, and quite naturally we chose the wrong one. We noticed it almost immediately, but we found such beautiful evergreens along the road that we followed it almost half a mile, before we turned back.

The flivver was still standing by the side of the road when we got there, but I just hated to leave the woods. I could just stand there and breathe and breathe and never get enough of the woodsy air in my lungs.

We were home in time for dinner, and that afternoon we went "calling," like ladies of leisure. We only planned to go for a ride "around the square," but we stopped for a short call on Mrs. Clara Cox, incidentally to see the new house. The house was already full when we got there, but tho' our call was short, we had a jolly time.

When we got home "teacher dear" was there, had arrived only a short time before. We packed hurriedly and left for Ladysmith before supper. Wow! the ride was *some* cold!!

Monday, November 19 Stayed home until noon to-day and then took the noon train over to Weyerhaeuser, and walked out to Kief. Sophie was being repaired to-day. Ernie is gone but Eben Thompson will do in a pinch. The "knocks" in the engine have been getting worse every day until I really couldn't stand it any longer.

Tuesday, November 20   Used the train again to-day. Went to Bruce and tried to hire a car, but the great number of hunters have almost filled the town. No car was to be had, so I took the motor car, and went up to Anna Ward's school, but the hoodoo still followed and the man on the first team I met told me that Miss Ward had been hurt in an auto accident, and there was no school.

It was too late to reach another school and the motor car had already turned back so I had to spend the time in any old fashion, until it came back after me. I called on Mrs. Cornell and then went over to the crossing and crocheted on my gray cap. Before long Mr. Tatro came along in his car and asked me to ride along. I didn't say no, but before we reached Bruce we met a car bringing out his hunters. The two cars exchanged loads and I finished my ride in a Buick about a block long. Some car!!

For the second night I came home on the limited. These late hours are beginning to tire me.

Wednesday, November 21   A cold foggy day, threatening to rain almost any minute. Sophie is O.K., at least I can't hear any more "knocks." I took a trip down to Flambeau, and on the way picked up my hard-working Bohemian friend. I promised him I'd come back that way in the afternoon.

I came to some very rough places in the road after I left the Gates road, nearly shook me out of the car. Both the schools I visited, Flambeau and Mud Brook, are in good condition. I'm very glad I have both these schools behind me now, they are both so far from Ladysmith, they hardly seem to belong to our county.

My Bohemian didn't wait for me, and when I came back, I passed him, just in Ladysmith. There were dozens of hunters on the road and most of them were trudging many weary miles back to Ladysmith. I decided not to pick up any of them, tho' I could see that some were very tired.

Thursday, November 22   Twenty degrees below zero, it seemed to-day. The roads were hard as glass. I went over toward Weyerhaeuser, and had to stop at the garage and have them find a dreadful squeak. It was in one front wheel, as I thought. Ladysmith is completely out of gas, so I filled the tank here, in hopes that when it was all gone Ladysmith might have a new supply. Visited Blanche Nelson in the morning, and had to travel over some poor roads. I splashed the car with mud and water, and while I was at the school, it formed a perfect case of armor about the wheels and lower part. When I was ready to start, I thought for a minute that something would break before I could get the wheels to move. Really, I nearly froze to-day; winter driving is no pleasure.

When I came to Mr. Graham's school, I found that Mr. Rice had spent the morning there, so I left again very soon. I never saw as noisy a school as his. I pity his successor, if the district ever wakes up to the fact of his poor work and hires a new teacher. It will require some months of severe disciplining to bring the school back to anywhere near normal.

I spent the rest of the afternoon at Apollonia, not much of a visit, but I saw some of their work.

I was careful not to get any more water on Sophie, because at Mr. Graham's school I had quite a time again, to break the ice on the wheels. It's a wonder I didn't tear the tires when I started.

Sunday we are going hunting. Archie and Irwin Prindle are going to take us. I can hardly think or plan anything else. Here we are, scared to shoot a gun, and trying to pose as experienced hunters. Archie will laugh all day at our foolish mistakes.

Sunday, November 25   We nearly overslept—fact is, it was seven o'clock when we looked closely at the clock, and Heavens! Archie had told us he would be here at seven. Had he been here and we were still sleeping!? The thought nearly drove us frantic. Our lunch had to be packed, breakfast cooked and eaten. The breakfast cooked itself and Toots and I ate it while we dressed and packed the lunch between bites. Oh, it was a grand scramble! Our luck held through it all, and we even had the red cloth on over our caps and coats when Archie came up.

Our boots and socks were the niftiest part of our outfit; they gave us the real atmosphere. We had had a great time getting them the day before, and after trying nearly every store in town got two pair at the Fair Store.

I bandaged my ankle as tightly as I could and earnestly hoped it would not ache. It was still swollen and not very strong.

After going out to meet Irwin, we whizzed through town and away toward Tony. Mercy! it was cold.

Louise practicing her marksmanship with a rifle.

Our coats were suited for walking, and in the car they were very little protection. From Tony on, the roads were rough and narrow, and at the river, the road ends on the bridge, with the steepest hill I ever saw right before the bridge. We put the car in the old shed and then prepared our ammunition. I was scared to death of the rifle Archie gave me, and really did not know how to shoot it. I am positive that if a deer had run right in front of me, I would have been afraid to point the gun at it.

We tramped across the bridge and climbed the high banks on the other side. All four of us straggled out in "Indian file," ready for anything, and I for one was shaking like a leaf with cold and nervousness. On the top of the bank we spread out "easy-like" and Archie shot at a rabbit with the .22. Suddenly toward the left something jumped in the brush. Archie gave one quick glance and then yelled, "Shoot, Cheesy, shoot!" Irwin wasn't ready and the deer was bounding away. Archie turned savagely on me—"Christ! Give me that big gun." He fairly hissed the words, and I made the most speed I could to get the gun to him. Of course, after all this commotion, though it took only a few seconds, the deer was out of sight, and our only chance, and a slim one, was to try to scare it up again, or come upon another in one of the little swamps.

I followed Archie for a while, and then when we four came together again, they led us over toward "Look Out Mountain." It was rather easy walking, on the ridges and thru a stretch of woods, where we came upon a "porky" and I gathered up enough courage to shoot at it. Needless to say, I didn't kill it. On the "Mountain" we had a beautiful view of the country. We could see the river, and away north of us, the little log house where "Calamity Jane" lived. We saw some hunters across the river, nearly a mile away. Archie now planned a drive. We were to go down and watch on a run-way and he was going to tramp across the "flat" and drive out the deer. We followed an old logging road for almost half a mile and then perched on another hill.

We sat there a long time, listening and watching and waiting, but no deer came "bounding up the pathway." Finally we saw Archie coming; scrambling over the tops, puffing and panting. He had come upon fresh "beds" several times but the deer had circled around behind him. No luck again.

I was cold now and we all felt like dinner, so we camped in the first cozy little hollow we came to. Archie built a lovely fire, and we all perched around it and ate our dinner. Toots and I each had eight slices of bread, and I know I could have eaten more. My appetite was perfectly horrifying. We ate some of the boys' dinner, only an apple, but it was good, all the same.

After dinner, I went with Irwin and Toots followed Archie. We were all four to cross a swamp and then meet on a hill about a half mile away. It was a dreadful place to cross—logs, windfall, holes and hummocks—and I was afraid to step on any spot that Irwin hadn't tested. Suddenly, Bang! Bang!—Bang! Bang! My gun went up and my eyes tried to take in the whole swamp. I listened intently, but no shout came from Archie's direction, and as the seconds went by we knew the shots had been without effect. Irwin and I reached the hill first and we waited for Toots and Archie. At first we could only catch an occasional flash of red, and finally we made out the two "hunters." Archie had "jumped" the deer (perhaps we had "jumped" it), at any rate, he got four shots at it, but the doe was running for her life and escaped unscathed. The excitement warmed us and our hopes of seeing something to shoot at went sky-high.

The afternoon was passing and it was getting colder. The boys said the early morning was the best time for hunting. It must have been, because we saw nothing more that day. From the hilltop, we followed an old logging road to Crooked Creek, which we crossed about six times, each time a thriller, with slippery logs and stones and swift water below. I lagged farther and farther behind, my ankle was all tired out.

At one crossing we all drank, lying flat on our "tummies." I believe I got more water in my nose than I drank. The road finally brought us to the river. Here we shot at target across the river, and at a tin can on a log. My marksmanship wasn't so very punk, in fact, I was almost proud of some shots.

It was rapidly growing dark, so we began to walk back to the bridge, across Crooked Creek again, this time in the water, and up a hill so steep, I could hardly breathe when I reached the top. From here we followed a trail, thru Ernie Mitchell's barnyard, down a hill again, and then across the new bridge.

Some other hunters were having trouble with their car, couldn't start it, and for nearly two hours, Archie and Irwin worked to find and fix the trouble. As the last resort, they towed the car and started it that way. Then they sent the other car ahead, and were at last on our way home, with curtains up this time. At Tony Archie insisted on stopping for supper, and we had to consent, though we girls surely hated to be seen in public. No one arrested us, however, and the hot coffee was certainly good. I drove from Tony out to Pepper's to take Irwin home and then home for us.

It had been one grand, glorious day, and I enjoyed every minute of it. I don't care a snap about not bringing home a deer, the tramping and woodsiness of it all is almost enough for me. I'm going to practice shooting at living things in the woods, and perhaps sometime I will get a deer all myself.

Wednesday, November 28   I am ashamed to say it, Little Book, but the after-effects of hunting, and the anxiety of our "proposed trip to Horseman" after Tis, has nearly worn me to a frazzle. Monday, I missed the way-freight, and so spoiled a proposed visit to Glen Flora. So I spent the time on my charts and tabulations, and early Wednesday morning, I began to look for Vicy, and think, "I wonder what he is doing now?" I couldn't settle my thoughts on anything but Vicy. I watched at the window until my eyes ached. "Would he come?" was my one worry. Just as the noon whistle blew, I glanced out of the window, and there—Vicy went by. My heart beat a perfect tattoo of joy and I wanted to run down and hug him. In a few minutes he came upstairs and after a hurried lunch, we were ready to leave, at about 12:30. Mother had put in enough robes and shawls to keep a dozen old women warm.

Away we sped thru Bruce, stopping a moment to ask for Isla MacArthur, but she was at school, thru Weyerhaeuser, Strickland and out of the county. Here we came upon the "ruts," but though they were very deep and all over the road, we got thru beautifully. I could have driven the car thru these places myself, but all the same, I was very glad to let Vicy do the driving. We got off the road twice, but not far, and after jogging over an exceptionally bad stretch of road, we reached Bittles a few minutes before four. Tis wasn't

home from school, so we went to meet her. 'Twas a joyful meeting, we were too happy to say very much. We went back to Bittles again and Mrs. Bittles made supper for us, a perfect treat. Both she and Tis encouraged us to try the short-cut. It had been fixed, they said, and with the roads as hard as pavement, we finally decided to try our luck. It was dark when we left, but the snow helped to make the woods light. It was a terribly rough ride and twice we girls had to get out, the tires pinched in the ruts, but all went well and almost before we realized it, the dreadful swamp, the Devil's Elbow, and the steep hills were all behind us and we were speeding away toward Ladysmith.

It hardly seemed possible that the road was the same one we had traveled with Mr. Householder about a month ago; no water, or mudholes, the clean snow now covered it all, and I didn't even know when we crossed the swamp.

The interior of the Horseman School in 1917. Note the ornate desks.

It was 7:30 when we reached Ladysmith. Toots wasn't looking for us yet and when I phoned to Audie, she could hardly believe that we were back to Ladysmith. After a few minutes of Thanksgiving shopping and some quick packing, we left for Leighty's—cranberries and grapes, oysters and etc. etc. on our feet and in our laps and a tire around my neck, plus a carload of robes and shawls. We were *some* load!!

From Leighty's, after Audie got in, we were the happiest, most packed-in bunch of travelers that ever traveled those roads. We sang and laughed and chatted. I'm sure Mother heard us fully two miles from home, and just at 9:00 the hilarious crowd drove into the driveway. The house already had quite an atmosphere of Thanksgiving, cranberries on the stove, and duck half picked, on the table.

Thursday, November 29   Thanksgiving!! A real one, too! A fat duck roasting in the oven and an appetizing odor about the whole house that made one ravenously hungry long before the dinner hour. Paul was still hunting and our Thanksgiving table stretched across the whole kitchen, almost. Of course, the boys didn't hunt very much that morning and they were careful not to be late for dinner.

We spent the afternoon talking and planning with a generous sprinkling of music over the whole day. It's so good to be all together for a few days. We are all watching the weather with anxious eyes because we want Tis to stay until Sunday and then Vicy will drive her back.

Dorothea Wegner (Tis) outside the home where she rented a room near the Horseman School, 1917.

The Wegners at a family gathering in 1917, one of the last times they all were together. Left to right: Tis, Vic, Bill, Bob, Mother, Audie, Dad, Louise, and Toots.

The limited, stranded in Ladysmith by a major snowstorm in March 1917. Note that there are two engines to enable it to break through the deep drifts.

Winter 1917–1918

Saturday, December 1 These two days have been so very out of the ordinary that I hardly feel like my old self. We've all donned old clothes and have cut poverty wood and piled up brush just like the Polacks do. Then when the out-door work tired us we came in and either the kids would play or talk and I tried to sew a little. I'm making a new dress out of my blue poplin, a nice, warm, heavy dress. All thoughts of school and plans have vanished for these few days, and I'm a different being entirely from the serious-minded supervisor. A change of occupation, they say, is good for everyone.

Sunday, December 2 The family scattered today—Audie back to Leighty's, Bob and Toots to Ladysmith and Tis away off to Horseman. They left early, before ten, planning to reach Horseman about two and leaving again before it was dark. Ed was coming back with Vicy.

My thoughts traveled with them—now they must surely be at Bittles, and so on, all day. I tried to sew but I could hardly force myself to it and again and again I found myself watching at the window. As supper-time came and it grew dark, Mother joined me in my watching. Supper was nearly ready when we spied a light, coming from the opposite direction, but it was Ed and Vicy.

I had to ask a dozen questions when they came in, and in due course of time I got fairly satisfactory answers to them all. Yes, the trip had been very pleasant, no mishaps, they had had a splendid dinner, had brought Ethyl Blowers back with them, had nearly lost their way around Dan Cox's, but had finally found the road to Sheldon and now, here they were, and I was satisfied. Tis was back and no great trouble to get her there and Toots and Bob were in Ladysmith all ready for Monday's work.

Monday, December 3 I gathered up all the surplus courage I could get my hands on this morning and started out for Vallee. It was cold, but not very severe, and with a whole day before me and a good car under me, I could have gone almost anywhere.

A part of the road was perfectly strange to me, but lonely as it was, I found my way, though several times I was almost lost and traveling in the wrong direction. Even the worst roads have an end sometime, and the last three miles into Walwrath, as it should be called, were long enough for me. I had to follow the deep ruts all the way, and almost continually "on low." When I reached the school, there was no teacher or pupils so I went over to the store and found Mr. Rietz. The teacher had gone home for Thanksgiving and would not be back until noon. I had to wait for her and finally went up to the school house again and built a fire. Then I had dinner at the Boarding House, and incidentally met someone I had seen once last summer. She was a Miss Sergeant, who had been with Law when he came to ask us to play for the Royal Neighbors dance. My gauntlets were a clue, she said. I also met Mrs. Walwrath, she's a *lady*, too.

Finally, Miss Cosgrove came, at about 1:30, and gathering her small flock about her, we went back to the school house and I supervised the rest of the afternoon. This is the school that Audie nearly got this year and wants to have next year. They are intending to build a new building, a two-roomed structure, as modern as they can afford to make it. The community is fine and I know I would enjoy teaching here myself.

I left at 4:30 with about thirty miles before me. I buzzed right along, thru the Range Line district, thru Tony, and then along the "bad road." At one place in the woods—it was dark now—I saw two eyes blazing at me from the darkness, and my heart almost choked me. But whatever it was crept to one side as I went by. Home was a mighty welcome sight, my nerves were all aquiver, because I do not like to drive alone at night. I had to talk away my nervousness that evening, for another long trip loomed up before me to-morrow.

My new dress is all done, Mother worked all day on it to finish it for to-morrow.

Tuesday, December 4   We woke up this morning to find the ground covered with four inches of snow and more still coming down. For a few minutes I was afraid to attempt the trip, afraid of being stalled in a snow drift, but Vicy made fun of my fears and spunk came to my rescue. With Mother I wouldn't be afraid of anything.

When we went by the school house, there was Ed, sweeping away like fury. It does seem queer to see a man sweeping or even teaching.

The road was good in spite of the snow, and it wasn't a bit bad. Before we reached Conrath, we picked up Mr. Fischer, clerk of the Mercer school, and at Conrath, Mary McKnight joined us. The two of them perched upon the sack of potatoes and other junk that we had piled in the back seat. It was a cold drive for all of us and my poor hands nearly froze. The closer we came to Ladysmith the more traveled the roads were and everything went beautifully.

The convention was nothing out of the ordinary. Mr. A. A. Thomson was there and was quite his usual affable self. We had the usual rush and confusion about the certificates of attendance. Mr. Thomson became angry and said some really sharp things about this needless waste of precious time. I don't blame him— it is needless and worse than that.

After the meeting the "big people" adjourned to the office and discussed topics too deep(?) for the laity. I knew Mother was waiting most anxiously for me to come home and I grew more nervous and fidgety every minute. It was five before I broke away and by 5:30 we

were ready to start. The car was already at the door, and changing shoes was the longest item. Poor Audie and Toots both have such very sore feet. They can hardly wear any ordinary shoes.

It was quite dark when Mother and I started for home and Cold!! Wow!! I knew later that my nose was frozen that night. The wind was from the east and almost took my eyes out.

We reached home at last to find Dad and Sonny bravely beginning supper. We all had to talk like magpies and eat like campers. It seems as though I am always hungry.

Wednesday, December 5   The thermometer read 22 below this morning and I wasn't very willing to take the car out, but I do hate to waste a day, so I braved the cold. The only real worry I had was that the radiator might freeze and burst or that the engine would get so cold that I wouldn't be able to start it.

The Cox school was my first stop and I carefully covered up the engine. The school house was dreadfully cold, almost too cold to put one's feet upon the floor. Chrystella is doing good work, as she naturally would, but she does not like the school, and is quite discouraged. I hope I left her somewhat cheered up.

I went out once to "buzz" the engine, and found it still quite warm, and when I started her at noon, there was no trouble. I tried to turn in the "Y" but nearly got stuck in the ruts. I had to go to the lane in the bend and turn around there. The French school was my second stop, and I reached it very nicely, and again tucked Sophie snugly in.

When I came to leave here, the car was cold and I had some trouble in starting, but after a little coaxing, she buzzed and away we went. The engine began to heat soon, without any apparent reason, and before I reached Dan Cox's it was boiling hot and the radiator was ready to blow up. It almost blew up when I took off the cap. The steam and water flew all over me. I got some water at Dan's and after it stopped boiling so fiercely I went on again. Before another half mile was covered the radiator was boiling again, and when I got out to investigate, the water was coming out of the drain pipe like water from a faucet. Before I could close the pet-cock with a pliers, nearly all of the water was out and my gloves were all soaked. I stopped again at McCann's and carried about six pails of water to fill the radiator. I really was afraid of it by this time.

I went after the mail at Sheldon, and by the time I got there my fingers were nipped by Jack Frost and hurt like fury. Clarence B. (darn him, anyway!) held my hands until they were warmed. When I left Sheldon nothing more happened to either Sophie or me until we were almost home, when the steam began to hiss from the radiator again, but I wasn't going to stop and adjust the little curtain again, so we kept right on. I had a soft, unspoken, little fear that one or two of the little tubes in the radiator might be frozen, but everything seemed right, so the fear vanished.

I have hereby resolved that this is my last visit with Sophie. It is too cold, and the fear of freezing up takes every bit of pleasure out of the trip. I suppose I'll soon be using Coley, though I'd rather walk than ride behind him.

Thursday, December 6   Came back to Ladysmith on the scoot and spent the afternoon at the office. There is very little to do.

Saturday, December 8   Colder than ever! And this is our Library Institute day. I'm afraid this cold has prevented many teachers from coming. At least those who must drive a considerable distance will find it hardly worth while to come. The city teachers made up the greater part of the enrollment, and one thing above all that impressed me most was their knitting and crocheting during almost every minute of the meeting. During the School Board Convention there was a little group of teachers in one corner who crocheted and tatted, but their idea was rather covert. Here it seemed almost impudent to me. Knitting for the soldiers will pass but crocheting while someone is talking

Louise's sisters on the steps of the library in Ladysmith during a teachers' convention, 1917.

does not look very well. I know how I dislike inattention during a little talk, and I am sure other people have the same feeling.

As far as gaining any new ideas, I can not say very much. Other teachers thought and said the same thing. However, the idea of permitting country teachers to draw books from the public library for their people received some very favorable discussion, and to Mr. O.S. Rice it was a new idea.

Toots went home on the scoot, and about 2:30 Audie came in, with one cheek frosted. A spot about the size of a dollar was covered with tiny blisters. I was quite concerned about her long drive back.

The Caley Lake Social Center had a meeting scheduled for to-night and Mr. H., Mr. Dresden and I were going. I knew it was almost too cold for that seventeen mile drive, but I wasn't going to show the white feather just because it was below zero. Audie went back about 6:00, with my muff, and at 7:00 I was at Dresden's. We waited most patiently until nearly 8:30 for Mr. H., and were almost ready to say he had forgotten us, when his car squawked, before the door. We assembled at the garage and made speedy preparations for a fast and cold ride. It only took us forty-five minutes to get there, not time enuf to get cold. It was as fast a ride as I would ever wish for, at night.

The meeting was good, though I spoiled part of it by getting up and pretending to make a speech. I really thought Mr. H. was joking when he said he was going to call on me for one. But the joke was on me, alright.

Our drive home was almost as fast, but not as cold. The town clock showed 12:00 when we drove thru town. 'Twas some night, and *some* cold!

Sunday, December 9   The wind came from the wrong direction, to heat our rooms, and we actually suffered from the cold. I did not get up until the scoot was almost due, and when Toots came we did very little except rage about poor janitor service. Sundays here are very lonesome days.

Just before supper Mrs. Anderson came to the door and invited us over to a "musical evening." Mr. Woody and his wife came to help, and we spent a lovely evening, with songs and violin and Mrs. A's victrola. It was just grand! I felt filled with music for once. Mr. Woody sings well and with all the feeling and expression that make it a pleasure to listen to him.

Monday, December 10   Mother sent me such a "blue" letter, and I'm down in the very depths myself. Toots signed up for a correspondence course without really consulting anyone who would advise her, and Mother feels just dreadfully about it. She wants her to try and secure her release and recover the money. I myself think that $150 is quite a price for a course, especially when it does not fit you for anything in particular, only prepares you to take a civil service examination, and then all the uncertainty of a government appointment.

When Toots came home I let her read the letter and then we both felt as blue and down-hearted as perhaps Mother had when she wrote it. Toots wrote immediately to the Co., and now I wonder what will happen.

Tuesday, December 11   I am desperate to-day and hired a car to take me to the Toepfer School. It's the first time I've hired a car from Ladysmith. It beats driving your own car, when you are going, but there is always the fact that you are dependent upon someone else, and I abhor being dependent. Everything went beautifully to-day. The Toepfer School is almost a school this year, getting along very nicely. At noon I walked over to Shaw's Dam. Quite a walk, considering how much out of practice I am.

Nora Wilber isn't making much improvement, though conditions are not as bad as the last visit I made with Miss Jenkins.

The car came back after me, and considering all things, the day wasn't bad, though the weather was cold and blizzardy.

Thursday, December 13 A very cold day, but I've lost one day this week, and I cannot lose another. I went to Bruce on the limited, but it was so late, I had barely time to eat a hasty breakfast and then run to catch the motor car. We just started when I missed my purse, but it was only a few steps from the spot where the car had been standing. It gave me quite a thrill to think of being stranded without any money. Truly, the day was beginning rather unpleasantly. At Atlanta, I learned that the motor car would not go up the line, but I managed to secure passage on the logging train. The bumps I received in that caboose were ten times worse than the worst ones I ever felt in the way-freight.

They very obligingly stopped for me at the crossing and at about 10:00 I reached the school, good time, considering all the delays.

Miss Ward made me share her lunch and at 12:30 I was on my way again. The day was bright and beautiful and though the road was new and part of the way poor for walking, I really enjoyed the walk. When I am hiking along a road, the time always passes too quickly in my imagination and I usually imagine it is several hours later than it is. Even my shadow does not give a very accurate estimate of the time.

My visit at Bertha Norstrom's school was rather short. When I eat dinner at the first school and then walk three or four miles to the next one, a good part of the afternoon is gone. However, I make up for that loss of time by talking until nearly five. I visited with Miss Norstrom until about 4:40, and then my uneasiness

The motor car, basically a motorized platform, that carried people along railroad lines. Louise waited for a car similar to this. (Photo courtesy of the Rusk County Historical Society)

about the car would not allow me to stay any longer. I walked as fast as I could, the mile and a half between the school and the crossing, my nerves alive to the least put-put of the motor car. I was almost sure I was too late, and when I reached the track, I listened long and carefully but there wasn't the least sound. My heart was going pit-a-pat with sheer nervousness, because I really did not know what I would do if I had missed it. I had to *know* whether the car had come before I could decide anything, so I went up to the nearest house and asked. "Yes," they told me, "the car came up about fifteen minutes ago and waited about three or four minutes and then went back." Tears of anger and disappointment came to my eyes. I was stranded, eight miles from Bruce, on a bitterly cold night. I turned away, just barely able to say, "Thank you," and walked to the gate. I would walk to the nearest house with a phone, which I guessed was about a mile away, and telephone for the car to come out and get me. It was perfectly dark now, and I was just a bit frightened to go through a little wooded stretch before the corner. It had to be done, however, so I put all fear and anger in my pocket and forgot I had any.

I wonder what the people at the corner thought when a rather wild-eyed, red-faced girl stood at the door and asked if they had a phone. I was so glad to find one here and the livery man said, "Yes, I'll send a car out after you." I was too nervous and hungry to rest, and when the minutes went by and no car came, I began to grow uneasy. At last we saw a light coming, but they speeded right by! Surely they must have understood my directions! I called up the barn again. "Yes, the car left about twenty minutes ago." Then I called up two families living north, hoping to have them stop the car and send it back. No one had seen it, so all I could do was to wait until the driver was tired of looking for me, and start back for Bruce. I believe every window in that house had at least one pair of eyes anxiously peering out toward the road, and some had four pair. Nearly half

an hour went by and then the look-out suddenly announced, "A car's coming down the road." They stopped at the corner, and with scarf and mittens in one hand, my purse in the other, I did a marathon to get to the road before the car would leave. It was my car, alright. The boy had gone two miles further north and not finding or seeing anyone, had turned back. It was dreadfully cold and the car was steaming, so we could hardly see ahead of us, but I was at least on my way back to Bruce.

It surely had been a day of near-adventures, and for once, I must confess, I was dead tired. I had supper at 8:00 and it wasn't much later when I went to bed.

Friday, December 14 Yesterday's experience with the motor car made me sick of the sight of it, and I hired the same car again. I went out to Helen Haasl's school and then had the car come after me again at noon. I spent the afternoon at Apollonia and incidentally enjoyed some products of the Domestic Science class, some fudge that wouldn't fudge, and had to be eaten with a spoon. Both schools I visited to-day were good schools, and I wasn't so tired as yesterday. Both Apollonia teachers went to Bruce with me and we had a lovely car ride, part way.

I came home on the limited, ready for any rest I could get on Saturday or Sunday.

Sunday, December 16 Yesterday was a very busy office day, reports had been stacking up until there was a truly formidable number, but we cleaned them all up, and the table was clear for the next week. Audie came up and we had our weekly gathering that night.

Audie stayed over until Sunday and then the question arose, how was she to get back? Her feet wouldn't permit walking, so it was a case of finding a way to get her down to Leighty's. We couldn't find anyone in Maple Center to come up and get her, so as a second hope I went over to Kinyon's to try to get a horse, but the barn was empty. Mr. H. seemed our only hope and it seemed impossible to locate him, but when we found his car at the garage, we were sure he wasn't out of Ladysmith. Finally I found him at Dresden's, and he very obligingly said yes when I asked to borrow the car. His was a "professional flivver" and when I saw how much different it was from Sophie, we asked Eddie Fults to drive us down. He was only too willing, and we really had quite a joy-ride. He told us that Ernie and Ray Hanson had both enlisted and had been gone several days. It was such sudden news, it gave me rather an unpleasant thrill. We came back a-flying and just as we left the garage, Ed Hanson went by, in Ernie's car, and he picked us up to give us a ride. Something was wrong with the car, it had a dreadful knock, and our ride ended in a few blocks. The car stopped while he was turning around and wouldn't start again. So we all walked back. Poor Ed was at a loss about

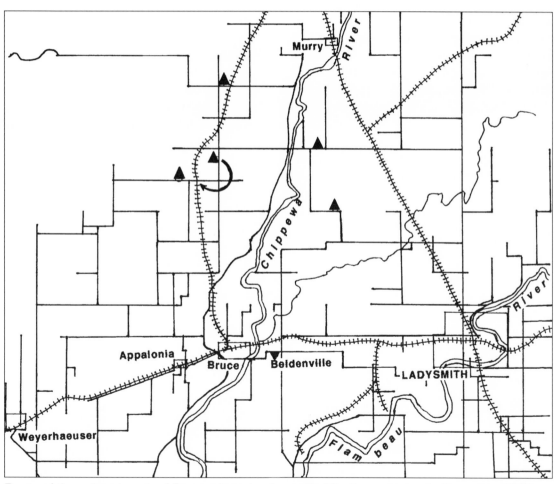

Route of the railroad north of Bruce where Louise waited for the motor car in December 1917.

what to do and I suppose he had to have the car pulled to the garage.

The next thing was a trip we had decided to take out to LaBerge's to see the head that Archie had promised. We donned our rubbers and hiked out, and gave them a little surprise. Laura had almost a wagon-load of Christmas socks ready for her program and Ruth had just taken hers over to her school that afternoon.

The head was all we had dreamed it would be, the horns were glorious and when we looked at the deer itself, it seemed almost impossible to realize that two men had carried it over three miles through the woods. The two deer each weighed around two hundred fifty pounds, the weight of a very large man. We gave Archie instructions as to just how the hide should be cut and then we started back for town. Archie walked part way with us and met Fred LaB. coming with the car. He had a ride home and we finished our walk as we had begun it, on foot.

The day had been no exception to our rule of "thrillers every Sunday" and we felt genuinely tired.

Tuesday, December 18   Yesterday I walked out to the Kiefer School, and after being rather stern and cranky for a morning—for I gave one little boy a real shaking—I walked on down to Port Arthur. There is too much Christmas program in the air to make visiting really worth while and all I saw here was a rehearsal of the whole program. It is well prepared and Esther ought to have a very good entertainment.

I had made plans to stay overnight with Esther, but unless people give me an opening to ask if I may stay, I can never ask that question, and so five o'clock found me walking back to Ladysmith. I called on Mrs. Taggart and wasted a few precious minutes in visiting. It was rather a long walk and I was truly tired when I got home, to find the supper all vanished, though I managed to find enough to eat. Of course, no one knew that I was coming back, so I couldn't be angry.

To-day I hired a car to take me to Gladys Kaiser's school and then at noon I walked over to Virginia Tate's school. I surprised them both. Gladys had a brand new building and things are not yet quite complete, but she will have a very nice building when it *is* done.

Virginia is so fussy, and in some ways so slow that she makes me nervous. However, she is trying to do her very best, and one must give her credit for that.

I wouldn't have walked back to Ladysmith that night for anything, and when Virginia asked me to stay with her, there was no thought of refusal in my mind.

I met Mrs. Summerville for the first time and like her very much. Mr. Summ. is a splendid man, though he looks as though he could get very angry when things went very wrong.

We spent the evening talking of roads and traveling generally, and after we got to bed, Virginia and I talked for several hours on every subject dear to the hearts of all girls.

Wednesday, December 19   I left Summerville's with Virginia and kept right on walking toward the dam. The day was cloudy but not a bit cold. I had never been over this dam and was rather timid about crossing it. There is a narrow little foot bridge over the dam, and when the water is rushing over it, I would hardly have nerve enough to walk across. No water was visible now and I reached the mill in perfect safety. Here a new difficulty came up. I did not know the way through the mill, and I hated to act and look like a lost chicken. I walked as fast as business would allow and luckily walked in the right direction. I saw one of the Girard boys and he recognized me. Out of the mill at last, I followed the railroad tracks up to the crossing and then I was in familiar territory, with the school house in sight.

The building still had all the stage and stage setting of the recent program and it required a good high step to get onto the stage. The morning's work was hurried through in order to have time for practicing the program. I left early, and had dinner at Girard's. I found the whole family in the "blues"—Art has enlisted in the Marines and Mrs. Girard is nearly heart-broken over it. She gave me all his letters to read. It was hard to be sympathetic and cheerful at the same time. Agnes has had a near-attack of pneumonia, and that also worries Mrs. Girard. She is so changed from her usual jolly self that she doesn't seem like the same person. Poor, dear woman!!

The walk from Girard's to Beldenville was the longest walk, it seems, that I have taken this year. It was a long straight road that stretched out for miles ahead of me, and seemed almost without end. I was really tired when I reached the little Beldenville School. There was no school in session to-day, the boys were getting the tree ready and the girls were putting up the decorations. I was an audience of one to another Christmas program and later on helped with the decorating all I could. It was fun.

Mr. Stewart was late in coming after Violet and we had almost reached the big bridge when he overtook us.

I was dead tired to-night and the wait for the limited seemed much longer than usual.

Thursday, December 20 I spent the morning at the office, answering reports and getting the January plans ready. These simply must be finished before I go home for Christmas, because some of the schools will be in session before I come back to work.

The Training School had a program this afternoon and I went, of course. The children of the Model Department made me a present of a very pretty desk blotter. The program was simple but good and we all had some hearty laughs at the presents Miss Biggs and Miss Jenkins got.

Friday, December 21 I came home from the office at just five and after giving the boys hurried instruc-tions about supper, I walked out to Toots' school. This morning we had packed all the candy sacks in a tub, hoping that someone from the district would come after them. At noon they were still by the door, but at night when I came home, they were gone, so I knew some-one had been to get them.

The walk out was lovely and Toots was waiting for me at Carmain's for supper.

She had new lamps for this program and the improvement was great. Clyde Bennett was there with his new wifey. She's cute, but is too much of a city girl to be a success on the farm.

Of course Toots' program was good, it always is. It was short but the children all did very nicely. One number was a "Selection by the Orchestra." The orches-tra was the whole school with a very competent little director, Earl Carmain. Combs and horns and a drum and a little piano were the instruments, and I played "On, Wisconsin" as loud as I could play. Really, it was was one of the most effective little things I have ever heard and it received most generous applause.

We had a great time with Frank Parks. We certainly impose on his kindheartedness, but then we aren't the only ones. Toots and some of the other teasers had wrapped up a little caramel cookie and when Frank hes-itated about opening the package, quite sure that it was a joke, the whole crowd got around him and coaxed him to unwrap it. No, Frank would not. Finally, Toots gave him his choice. "Frank, do you want to take me to town tonight?" "You bet, I do." said Frank. "Alright, then open it." It was dreadful, but Frank had to do it, and slowly and carefully he took off one paper after another. At last "something" was reached, but before anyone saw it, his great hand crunched it into a mass of crumbs.

But Frank took us home! Proud as a big boy, he sat at the wheel. "Gee, but it's fun to drive a car. Let's go for a joy-ride." "Oh, no, Frank," we said, "it's too cold." But the ride to town was enough of a joy-ride for us.

Gracious! how he did drive! The car almost wobbled it went so fast. I was almost afraid, but I knew that Toots would shut off the gas when he was going too fast, especially at the corners. Our lives were insured, so we needn't have worried.

At the rooms Frank said, "Well, as long as I can take one of you girls to the show, it's alright." We'll have to live in seclusion for the rest of the winter, because neither of us will go with Frank, even if we never go to the show. Not with *that* fellow. Really, I almost hate him at times. Brains! Brains!! He has nix. Hints slide off from his fat shoulders like water off a duck's back, and nothing but a point-blank statement will affect him and then he's usually mad. Even if he is a great friend of Archie's, he is no great friend of mine.

Tis will come to-morrow. She also had her program to-night. How I want to see her!

Saturday, December 22   Saturday!! Audie's program to-night!! I am satiated with Christmas songs, drills, dialogs and pieces. It's really worse than if I were preparing a program myself. Still, I enjoyed watching the rehearsals.

There was a large amount of work at the office and so many people came in that we hardly got anything done until close to five o'clock. I saw Tis shortly after she came. Audie was also in town, doing her last bit of Christmas shopping. Vicy came up later in the afternoon, and what with work and worry and nervousness, we were a cranky and irritable bunch. One little delay after another only made matters worse. Audie's program was also a basket social and packing up the boxes is a miserable job.

Well, at last we were all ready and had the luggage in the car. There was barely room for us and our feet when all the apples and candy sacks were stored in the tonneau. Being on the way made us feel happier again and when we discovered that Vicy had had a cut-out put on the car, we felt positively hilarious.

Even though it was late, we were about the first people at the social, but I, for one, had such a headache, I couldn't enjoy anything, and I felt cross and cranky at everybody. The program was short but fairly good and then came the selling of the baskets. I know I swore off on all basket socials and really this was as bad as any I've gone to. I guess I won't write anything more about this night, Little Book. Norman Hoff got my basket and I had a nice time eating with him.

It snowed several inches before we were ready to go home and we had to sweep out the snow in Sophie. At twelve we were ready to go home, after solemnly promising Audie to come back to get her Sunday morning. Amid a chorus of "Good nights," Vicy speeded away for home.

Sunday, December 23   Vicy, Tis and Sonny went on a tree-hunting expedition early this morning and a little later Toots and I took Sophie out and started off for Ladysmith to "tote" home all our junk. We stopped for Darcy and took her along with us. She ought to get out more than she does, poor girl!

The junk! Yes, the *JUNK*! Toots and Darcy settled themselves in the back seat and then we piled suitcases and boxes, bundles and packages, around them, under them, over them and all over them. They couldn't have moved for love or money, after we were ready to start. On top of all was the deer head that we had stored at Thompsons, and Toots had a big bunch of holly in her arms. When we reached Leighty's and Audie got in with her suitcase we were loaded, both front and back seat.

We filled the house almost to overflowing with the junk but before very long it was packed away here and there and Tis and I were upstairs wrapping up Christmas parcels. There is no pleasure I know equal to that of wrapping and labeling presents. I wish I had a trunk full of things to wrap up.

Monday, December 24 Christmas Eve! A little shadowed by the great economic wave that has swept over the country, but Christmas all the same. The girls gave me a beautiful white ivory comb, the first piece of my white ivory set. Tis had a manicure file and a cuticle knife, Audie had a hair receiver and Toots a pincushion—all in French Ivory. Mother and Dad are going to get me two new tires, and I certainly appreciate them.

Christmas can be filled with the real Christmas spirit even if the presents are few and small. I would rather give ten things and get one than give one thing and get ten things in return. Next year we plan to give our presents to the house, but I for one, won't wait until December to give my presents. Only I'll have to begin to save before the Christmas shopping begins.

Tuesday, December 25 I donned skates to-day for the first time in my life. I was scared to death of falling and made as much or more commotion as an elephant on skates. After a few scrambles and valiant efforts I managed to make a few strokes that seemed like skating. It was fun and I know that if I could skate only 5% better I would be as crazy about it as Toots and Audie are. If I live long enough and skate as much as this each year, perhaps I may sometimes learn to skate. Here's hoping!!

Directly after supper we four pals left for Ladysmith so that I might take the early morning train for Madison. The car was equipped for the cold ride, and as cold as it was, none of us were frozen and the radiator was still O.K. when we drove into the garage. It was rather fun driving, the moon was beautiful and the roads the greater part of the way were smooth and hard as pavement. We four are always a jolly crowd and were in high spirits every minute of the way.

Wednesday, December 26 I was awake at 4:30, dressed and went over to the depot, to find that the train was four hours late. I came back and went to sleep again, and even had breakfast with the girls. Some premonition that the train might come earlier made me get ready about half an hour before the four hours were up and sure enough—the train came and I had to make a run to catch it. People came running from every direction, puffing and panting and—I am sure—almost ready to swear at the agent.

Gene and Booth and the baby were on the train and I talked with her all the way to Cameron. It's been so long since I saw her and talked with her. Gene does not look very well, or very happy, it seems to me. The baby is the cutest little scamp I ever saw and is the liveliest little fellow for his age you can imagine. He seems to have inherited all of his father's and his mother's impishness. I wonder what he'll be like when he grows up.

Of course, with the train nearly four hours late, we missed connections at Cameron, and to our utter and absolute dismay we discovered that the next train was not due for nearly twelve hours. Twelve hours in Cameron!! To one who has never experienced a long wait in a miserable little junction, those words mean very little, but to those who know Cameron, they mean worlds. I wrote letters until I was tired, crocheted until I was sick of it and wrote in my diary until I could write no more. Then I sat and sat. Others were in the same fix as I so I had company in my misery. But even the longest, most wearisome day will finally pass, and twelve o'clock came at last. This train was also late, but being on it and knowing that I was moving toward Madison helped matters a great deal. I slept very little on the train. It was crowded and almost unbearably warm.

Thursday, December 27 'Twas nearly eight o'clock when I reached Madison and the examinations were to start at nine. I left the depot and walked bravely up the street to the Capitol Hotel. I tried to be a grand lady from "Somewhere" but I was scared as could be and

I'm sure I looked as green as grass. My room is 106 and is the nicest room I ever saw, hot and cold water, telephone, comfortable chairs and two beautiful mirrors. This is worth coming to Madison for. I tidied up and then went out to breakfast. And it was some breakfast, too! Rusk County can show nothing anywhere near it.

Then I hurried off to the Capitol to find the examining room. My soul! I finally located the Department of Education and they showed me where the Senate Gallery was, across the Rotunda, but reaching it was another matter and I believe I would be looking for it to this very day if I had not been escorted to the very doors. I introduced myself to one of the examiners and was given an application sheet to fill out. That wasn't bad. Then I received my first set of questions—Arithmetic. The questions were all catchy, but I proved and double-proved every one and they ought to be nearly all correct. It was hard to keep awake and my eyes wanted to droop.

At noon I had dinner at the hotel and also phoned Miss Spence. I know I surprised her. She asked me to have supper with her at the Capitol Cafe.

I was sure I could never find my way back to the Senate Chamber, but by blindly following my sense of direction I came to the doors and actually reached it. Some guardian angel must have guided me because I could not tell one direction from another in the Capitol. It is the easiest place to lose your way I ever saw.

I wrote on Manual and Geography in the afternoon. The questions were hard alright but I answered them to the best of my ability and I hope that is sufficient.

I was dead tired at the close of this writing period and my room was a very restful place. At six the phone rang and Miss Spence was talking to me from the lobby. She was knitting when I came out to meet her, and to me she looks as she did—let me see—fully six years ago. We talked and asked questions about this and that and had a real reunion over our supper. The Capitol Cafe is a most pleasant place. I believe I'll come down here and have my dinner tomorrow.

After supper we went to see Geraldine Farrar in "The Woman God Forgot," and I met a very nice little friend of Miss Spence's. I'm very glad that I saw her and had this talk with her.

Friday, December 28   More exams and harder, if anything, than those of yesterday. I actually found my way to the Senate Chamber again, all alone, too. I had dinner down at the Capitol Cafe with another teacher from Fifield—she knows Zelda Breed.

I shopped on my way home this afternoon. Bought a Georgette waist and a camisole. I've wanted one for so long and this one is a beauty, dark blue with embroidery down the fronts. I put it on as soon as I got to the hotel and enjoyed its beauty for a while.

Saturday, December 29   This is the homestretch day, and I'm very thankful, because the nervous tension is almost too much. English History, this afternoon, was my Bunkerloo—I failed flat. If I got thirty in that, I'll consider myself lucky. I wrote in School Law and Supervision, just to test myself, and really enjoyed that subject. I wasn't sure about several questions, but I wrote something and I hope it's correct.

I am not as careful as I was on the first day, and I know my standings will show it. But I'm going home to-night and that is the biggest thought in my mind right now. I went down to the depot quite early—the shock of knowing my hotel bill was so pleasant that I could almost have flown. Only $4.50 for three days in that beautiful place! I had set $10.00 as the limit and having so much more money left than I expected was almost too much for me.

Sunday, December 30   Sunday came in without me knowing it. I read and wrote until 1:45 when the train came in. It was crowded, as all trains have been, but I did not mind it. I fell asleep once and woke up to find the car as cold as a barn. Something had gone wrong with the heating system. At 4:45 we reached Merillan, to find that no trains were running on the Omaha line. There was a freight due about noon and that was all. There was nothing to do but wait, and I was much more sorry for a soldier boy home on a furlough than I was for myself. One whole day wasted in this miserable dump.

Noon came and went and four o'clock came at last. Finally, at five minutes to five the train came in sight, with a miserable coach, hot as an oven and no ventilation. I met a girl from Neillsville on the train, a Miss Miller, who knew Aunt Cal and Uncle Abbie and all the rest. We became quite well acquainted with the soldier boy, though I did not learn his name. He is from Nasonville and knew lots of Lynn, Granton and Chili people. It was very pleasant to ask each other, "Do you know _____?" and then the answer, "Oh, yes, she's married now, you know."

The hour and a half spent in going the fifteen miles or so to Neillsville were the shortest part of the day. The lights of the little old city came into sight at last and we both said goodbye to the lad in khaki, and wished him good luck.

I gave Aunt Emma one grand surprise when I knocked at the door. They were half expecting me, but had no idea when or from which direction I would come. Only a few hours remained before limited time, and we tried to ask and tell everything that could be told. The girls took me over to Grandma's, and we surprised her and Aunt Cal, and talked some more.

The depot at Sheldon was a welcome sight after a long trip. This photo is from a post card that Louise sent from Sheldon to her mother in Marshfield, not long after she began her first year of teaching in 1910.

Twelve o'clock came all too soon and we four, Aunt Emma,Theo and Ella, went down to the depot. There were promises galore and then the train came and I was on my way to Marshfield.

Monday December 31   I saw very little of our "old home town"— I took the bus to the Soo depot and as it was night, nothing much was to be seen. At 2:15 I was on the train bound for Sheldon. I fell asleep before we were out of Spencer and had to be wakened as we neared Sheldon.

Sheldon was dead and deserted and I waited at the hotel, sleeping every few minutes. I was nearly dead for lack of sleep. At last I saw Vicy and the flivver, and it surely was a good sight. Dad went to Ladysmith to-day. I went over to the store and saw Lawrence for a minute. They want us all to go to Holcombe for a dance to-night, but we have made other plans.

Home at last! Talked and talked, and then talked some more, but my sleepiness had vanished. After supper we went down to skate for a while, but I didn't put the skates on at all—I was almost too dead-tired to be jolly.

The New Year came in quietly this year—no one but we'uns and Ed Hanson to watch it in at our house. One whole year has been recorded in you, Little Book, and I wonder much what the New Year will bring. Will we all be together next year? Who knows? We hope to be in the new house next year and feel almost "at home" in it. May the New Year be as good to me as the old year has been!

Tuesday, January 1   This has been a queer New Year so far. I woke up at about three o'clock, as sick as I have ever been before. I really thought I was going to die, and I aroused the whole house. I came downstairs and tried to get warm by the fire and Mother soon had me warm with hot compresses and warm shawls. The spasms or convulsions or appendicitis (whatever it was)

relieved somewhat so I was packed to bed with a hot water bottle. I slept then, but poor Eddie got no more sleep. As punishment for being bad I was kept in bed all day, which was simply unbearable by evening. I rolled and turned and had the bed almost upside down by the time the girls came up to bed. Oh! we are some silly bunch! Wonder what Eddie thinks of us!

Thursday, January 3   Came back to Ladysmith to-day. There is very little to do and the mailing out of the plans and our County Survey sheets is about all I have done, except to wish that the kids would come. I think foolishly and too much when I am alone. Ernie is on my mind constantly, though I suppose he never gives little me a second thought. If I had his address, I'd write to him, because I'm sure letters, no matter from whom, are worth getting to the boys who have a homesick feeling. I'm going to try to get the address from Eddie.

This certainly has been a lonesome two days without Toots and Audie.

Saturday, January 5   Mr. Summerville gave me a great surprise to-day. He came into the office and said he wanted to speak to me, and my first thought was — "Here's where I get a calling-down for something I've done or haven't done." But instead he apologized for "some things" he *thought* and said about me not doing enough in my work, and said he had heard some things from Mrs. Munroe and then he referred to the old sore of my expense account. "If Mr. Rice ever refuses to O.K. your account, just hand it to us and Mr. Spears and I will see that it is O.K'd." Well! I was almost taken off my feet! He made some allusions to helping me, if I ever needed help, and then said something about "matters we needn't talk about just yet." I was so surprised, I could hardly act natural and I was happy as a king. I have always admired Mr. S. and have been almost a bit afraid of him at times, but I like him better than ever now.

Well, Toots and Audie came up and I am as happy as ever. I've been living on a milk and toast diet for three days and I am very ready to quit. I'm not a bit sick any more.

Tuesday, January 8 My standings came to-day! I could hardly wait to open the letter and when I saw how splendid they were, I could have sung for joy! The only failure was in English History and at that, it is three points more than I expected—33%. School Law and Supervision is my triumph—95%, and all the rest range around 84 and 85%, with two 70's—two that I was almost sure would be failures. Yes, I'm proud of them, and I'm going to work as hard as I can to finish the limited Certificate and then earn a Life Certificate—it's worth all the energy. I wrote right home to tell Mother the good news, but I'm not going to tell many others.

Wednesday, January 9 To Weyerhaeuser on the morning limited—for my first walking trip. I have my rubbers and heavy socks with me. Mr. A.A. Thompson was at breakfast when I went in and we had a few minutes' conversation before his train left.

I find the rubbers very tiring and my toes feel very sore, as though the rubbers are too short, but even at that I made fairly good time down to the Mansky schools. I spent the whole day with Mabel Harmon—had dinner at Mansky's (though I couldn't eat very much) and then after school I hiked back to town. I was dead tired—really more than usually tired—my knees and ankles seemed to feel it most.

I met all the Weyerhaeuser teachers at supper, but I do not like any of them particularly well. Perhaps I might, if I knew them better.

I had a very nice visit with Grace McGee after supper, talked on quite elevated subjects—retardation and child psychology and Eliot's five-foot list of books—but I enjoyed it very much. She is a girl who

Train Terms

Even after Louise acquired Sophie, she often had to depend on various forms of train travel—local, limited, scoot, way-freight, and motor car—to make her way around the county.

The *local* train stopped at every town and milk platform. The *limited* made few stops.

The *scoot* was a local train, sometimes merely a freight train with a combination car (passenger compartment and express/mail compartment) on the rear end. Sometimes passengers rode in the caboose if no passenger car was available.

The *way-freight* was a local freight train that stopped and switched at every town, setting out and picking up freight cars at all the local industries. Passengers could ride in the caboose if no other accommodations were available. All the switching made riding the way-freight a bumpy experience.

The *motor car* was a four-wheeled gasoline-powered vehicle used by short lines and logging railroads to haul passengers and small freight packages to the villages and camps along the line.

The principal railroad serving Ladysmith was the Soo—the Minneapolis, St. Paul & Sault Ste. Marie Railway.

Soo service in Ladysmith consisted of a limited each way, a local each way, a regularly scheduled freight each way, and a regularly scheduled way-freight each way. In 1918, No. 7, the westbound limited, arrived in Ladysmith at 5:20 a.m., and No. 8, eastbound, arrived at 11:05 p.m. The westbound local, No. 85, arrived at 12:01 p.m., and the eastbound, No. 84, at 2:40 p.m. The scheduled westbound freight came at 11:05 p.m. and the eastbound at 8:02 a.m. The scheduled way-freights came at 3:15 p.m. and 8:38 a.m., respectively.

wants to be entirely independent, no matter what people say or think.

Thursday, January 10   They called me at 5:00 this morning, so that I might go to Strickland on the way-freight. I had breakfast all alone in the big dining-room and before 6:00, I was on the train. They usually wait for the morning limited, but it was late—as usual—and we left on time. It was still dark when we reached Strickland and I waited for nearly an hour, before starting out on my first spasm—over four miles, I was told. I enjoyed walking, as all my yesterday's stiffness had vanished.

I reached the first school almost before the teacher did, so I made a very complete visit. It's really an awful school—the children are so rough and noisy I believe I would have nervous prostration within a week. I was actually glad to get away at noon.

The afternoon visit at Tommy Daniel's school was shorter, but much more pleasant. I have a warm spot in my heart for Tommy D., he's alright.

The whole day had been cold and windy and later in the afternoon it actually turned into a blizzard. Tommy walked with me for a mile and in my zeal to prove myself a good walker I nearly walked beyond my strength. In fact, I ran down every hill, and there were several in that mile.

No walking for me to-morrow—I'm ready for a rest. I fell asleep after supper, and while a Victrola downstairs played all my favorite songs, I dozed, half asleep, but hearing all the music. I awoke with a start, sure that I had overslept and missed my train, but I still had half an hour's time. It was a great relief, you may be sure.

I was mighty glad to reach Ladysmith and curl up to sleep away my tiredness.

Friday, January 11   I had one of the greatest surprises of my life this morning, so great that it was more of a shock than a surprise. I'll tell you about it, Little Book.

It was a blowy, blustery morning, but I decided to make one visit in the morning at least, so I went out to the Vance Miller school to see how O. J. Melby was getting along. I came into the hall and listened for a few minutes, as I always do, but I listened in vain for Mr. Melby's masculine voice. "That's queer," I thought. "Is he one of those teachers who teach without talking?" I listened again, but heard only the children's voices, as I thought, so I opened the the door and walked in, and there—Oh my Soul! there was my _least_ beloved friend—Alice West!! I had barely strength enough left to carry me to the chair near the stove. I had recovered sufficiently by the time she looked directly at me, to smile at her. We chatted quite amiably at recess and again at noon, but all the same, I love her not. She is certainly getting some order out of chaos in this school, but she has had to fight for every bit of it. I wouldn't trade places with her even if my job sometimes disgusts me. I'll give the kids some thrill when I tell them my morning's experience.

Saturday, January 12   I left the office early this afternoon, in order to go home on the scoot; the limited is too late for comfort. Toots stayed up here alone and the miserable old scoot never left Ladysmith until close to six o'clock. I couldn't find either Dad or Vic in Sheldon, but Mr. Dietze told me he had seen Vic only a short time before. I saw the suitcase in the hotel, so I decided to wait for someone to come and get me. I had supper and then knit on my new scarf until almost train time. No one came after me and finally the limited came and went and still no one came. I wanted to walk home, but the weather was too dreadful, snowing and windy and desperately cold. I made up my mind to wait until morning and _then_ walk home.

Sunday, January 13   When I went to bed last night, Little Book, I thought I was escaping a very cold walk, but my room was so miserably cold I nearly froze to death. To tell the honest truth, I slept with nearly all my clothes on, but I could not get warm, which is really unusual because I can almost always get warm even in the coldest bed. But last night—well, I vow I will never spend another night at Dietze's [hotel], unless I must.

The walk home wasn't at all bad. I donned my rubbers and tripped lightly out of town. I was hungry as a lion when I got home, but no one was really expecting me at this hour.

We had to get the suitcase from the hotel somehow, and we all hate to drive behind a horse, so in sheer bravado, we decided to try the car for a change. Vic drove and Bob and Sonny came along. There were several places where the boys had to push good and hard, and in going out of the yard, the whole family had to come to the rescue, and even at that there was hard pushing for all of us. Talk about a cold drive— Waugh!!! Sonny and I crouched down on the floor of the car to get away from the wind. From the cemetery corner traveling was good and we drove into Sheldon, right through a deep drift, almost after the fashion of a snow plow. But as Vicy says, "We simply *must* not get stuck right in town, with dozens of people watching us." So we hit the drift with every bit of Sophie power and we got through. Going back we had to make another dive through the drift, but, with Vicy driving, Sophie is capable of amazing stunts, and no one in Sheldon saw us get stuck. The whole trip took us less than forty-five minutes, less than one trip to town with a horse would have been. And except for an occasional hard push, it was thrilling fun.

I've knit all the spare time to-day and my scarf is nearly done. It's a perfect beauty, too, and won't it be nice and warm, cuddling around my neck! Dear me—Yes!

Monday, January 14   Bob and Leon and I came back to Ladysmith. My plans were to stop at Conrath and visit schools that day, but the scoot came so suddenly,

I became excited and bought my ticket to Ladysmith. The local and limited were very late that morning and so perhaps it was well that I did so. At any rate I had time and opportunity to pay the last installment on my Liberty Bond and have that load off my mind. Twenty dollars cuts a big hole in a half- month's salary, and I'm thankful that this is the last payment.

Over at the depot that night someone at my elbow spoke to me and for an instant I didn't recognize Pat. The dear boy!!(?) We chatted all the way down to Conrath, and he said he was sorry I wasn't going further. He's on his way to Stevens Point to get another job, says he's been home for two weeks with sore eyes (I doubt that story). Of course, he was very nice to me, seeing that his Edna was nowhere in sight, but Oh!! how I despise him. I *hate* him more than words can tell. I was *very* glad when I reached Conrath.

Tuesday, January 15   I spent the whole day at the Polish school and I enjoyed the Polish classes most of all. An unknown language always seems to fascinate me.

This evening Mrs. Knaack and I called on Miss Sabean. She came down on the same train that I did last night and she was a very sick lady. She's been in bed all day, but seems better to-night.

Wednesday, January 16   I started out bright and early this morning for I knew that a long walk was in store for me to-day. My first spasm was about four miles, with the first stop at Bessie Tate's. It was the coldest, most uncomfortable school I was ever in. I just went after the fire and when we had almost filled the stove and fixed the dampers, the room was soon *HOT*. Bessie is one of those teachers of whom Mr. Cary says, "They do not know how to build a fire or to keep it going." She is fussy, too, which I detest in a teacher. Sympathy and patience are so much more admirable, and they *get results*.

I left the school at one o'clock, with about five miles ahead of me before I would reach Marie's school. A talk with Mr. Beveridge delayed me a little longer and it was nearly time for dismissal when I arrived. Though I saw very little school work I was in time for a birthday party for Pansy McCann "aged 7 years" as the birthday cake showed. She was the most pleased little girl I have seen for a long time and the generous piece of cake she took home to her mother was worth its weight in gold, judging by the care she bestowed upon it.

We chatted for a while after the children went home and then I started out, through the short-cut and down the railroad to the crossing, hoping that I might be fortunate enough to meet a home-coming train. A mile and a half is a ride worth watching for and as I neared the crossing I looked most anxiously toward the hill. I caught one glimpse of a white horse and something seemed to tell me it was Vicy. Yes, I was right, and for once my luck could not have been better.

Mother was half expecting me, though as usual, if I do not come, no one is surprised.

We had music galore that evening. Eddie sang and we all played. It was fine and I'm sure every one felt better for it. There's nothing like music!

Saturday, January 19   I was home for only one night and next day went to Bruce and spent the afternoon with Isobel Stenson.

On Saturday (to-day) I found quite a few surveys and "it made my heart rejoice." I hope we won't have much trouble to get them.

Marie and Chrystella had dinner with us and it seemed almost like old times to have Marie with us. I wonder if she will ever pay me for last year's board. I really wonder.

Sunday, January 20   Housecleaning! and I enjoy it, too. A change of work is good for anyone. We shampooed our hair and pressed our clothes and brushed the cobwebs of week-day work from our minds.

Monday, January 21   I went to Bruce this morning. The limited was so late it almost spoiled the morning for me but by walking as fast as I could I managed to reach the Abbey School at about ten o'clock. This is where Audie should have been teaching if things had turned out differently. The building is entirely new, and is certainly splendid. The room is very large and very pleasant.

During the noon hour I walked to Beldenville, and had a nice cutter ride with a man who enjoys "war talk," which I do not, but I had to say something occasionally.

Violet S is about the poorest teacher in the county, and after school she had pupils "stay-in" until nearly five o'clock. She is very willing to take suggestions, but I wish she had a little more pep and self-confidence about her.

I came back to Bruce in the mailman's "box"— three of us, and of all the awful rides I ever had that was by far the worst. The box is small and we were piled in three deep, the roads were tippy and the driver made the horse gallop. Oh, Heavens! I was sure we would tip over. My knees were lame for almost a week after the ride from the terrible tensions of bracing myself for each threatened tip. I'll walk before I ever ride in that thing again.

Tuesday, January 22   I made my longest walk to-day—almost fifteen miles and I'm dead tired to say the least. Each spasm was about five miles, but the last one seemed twice as long as the first. I took a short-cut, hoping to make the distance less, but for almost two miles I waded through soft snow and I was almost ready to drop. Finally I came to where some teams had been hauling wood and I was most thankful. I could hardly have walked through the snow the rest of the way. A short-cut is always a failure, it seems.

Wednesday, January 23 Another walk to-day, not quite so far, but still close to nine miles. The children in school gave my rubbers many queer glances, but I don't mind them any more.

I had dinner at Sam Johnson's and met both Mr. and Mrs. J. They certainly have a beautiful house.

I have found a new little friend at the Maple Center school—Ernie's youngest brother, Clarence. He has a smile like Eddie's and he gave me several sweet ones. I like him.

Thursday, January 24 I was the only woman at a Patriotic Conference this morning. Prof. James of Madison talked to us on the problem of labor, sending the boys out to work on the farms before the close of school. Leon and Bob are very much interested in the result of the conference because both are much needed at home. Nothing was done, of course, but I hope the idea suggested is carried out in this county. Another survey is advised—and I shudder to think of what the teachers will think when they receive the blanks.

Friday, January 25 When I rushed home from the office at noon I found Eda preparing dinner. Lee says that's one time we had a real dinner, and I guess he's right.

Mr. Rice didn't appear all day and I prepared my Tony talk. The subject is Heating and Ventilating Systems and I have reports on the systems of twelve schools, scattered throughout the county, to show what conditions actually are. These are tabulated and look very well on a large piece of cardboard. On another sheet I have a diagram of a Heating and Ventilating System, and an explanation of the method of operating it is part of the talk. For once I have a topic I like and I hope I will be able to do justice to it.

Toots and I have formed a wild plan with Ruth and Laura LaBerge—we're going to walk to Tony and hope to get there before the way-freight.

Audie phoned that night and wanted us to come down after her and we said yes. I got a horse from Kinyon's Barn and we started out for a cutter ride. Evidently the horse considered us great jokes because he refused to take our "clucks" and "giddaps" seriously and set his own pace. The moonlight was beautiful and if the horse had only been a mite faster everything would have been lovely. But coming back!! Massy-me! We had to face a cold north wind nearly all the way and the horse—we knew his name now, Maje—lost all interest and love for the barn at Kinyon's and absolutely refused to move faster than a slow plod. On Hanson's hill the wind was almost more than we could endure, but here we changed places and I became the wind-break, my plush coat being nearly one-hundred per cent wind-proof. We "clucked," we "giddaped," we whistled, we yelled at Maje, we did everything we had ever seen anyone do or try to make a horse travel, but Maje was immovable. He has killed all of my love for horses—I never want to ride behind such a creature again. It was the coldest ride I have ever had or ever hope to have.

Saturday, January 26 We had promised Ruth and Laura to be out there by 8:30, which meant that we must start not much later than 7:45. I donned my Georgette waist, which was just a bit foolish because the thermometer showed 20 below, with a fairly brisk wind. But nothing could dampen our resolution, and at a few minutes past 8:30 we were at LaBerge's. Ruth was the only one who had planned to go with us but Laura decided to join us and both were ready by nine. Laura and Toots led the party and at first Ruth and I tried hard to keep up with them, but the distance gradually increased and we let them go. We walked fast and kept ourselves warm, in fact, I became almost too warm. The last mile, with Tony in sight, was really the worst. The wind came straight from the east and we walked right against it. It was almost too much and another half mile would have finished me. I believe I would have dropped and Ruth was as all-in as I was. Toots and Laura had reached the school at 10:00, twenty minutes before we got there. We changed our footwear and tried to get the wind-blown look out of our faces, but mine was beyond hope. My eyes were blood-shot and my nose a bright vermilion. Some sight I must have been.

The dinner was the rosy spot of the day—a perfect feast. We selected our crowd, and with Mr. Dresden at the head of the table there was constant laughter between courses. The dishes were all refilled some several times and we did our best to empty them all before we left the table. We four were desperately hungry and the rest of the table were not far behind in eating capacity.

My speech went as well as I could wish it to. I "talked" and did not read anything. My charts were interesting and I know I held everyone's attention. The condition of my face made me self-conscious—just a bit—but what care I.

To prove we were completely American, and therefore "full of devilment," we decided to walk back to Ladysmith. Both Mr. Rice and Mr. Dresden tried to persuade us to take the way-freight, but when we learned that it was two hours late, not even the offer of having our fare paid could tempt us, and we set out with a sympathetic crowd waving at us from the windows. The trip back was much pleasanter than our morning's walk, no wind to face, no bitter cold, nothing to carry this time and most of all, no speeding. We took our time and reached LaBerge's without feeling so very tired.

We stayed there for supper and it was a worthy follower of the dinner at Tony. Venison steak and tame strawberries! Um-Yum!!

Archie took us into town and then followed a series of rapid fire telephone calls between Mae Carter and myself and twenty minutes later found me on my way to a "Pie Social," as "game supervisor." The way-freight came in at eight o'clock, five hours late from Tony, and then to think that they pitied us!

The Social crowd was small but jolly and we played games until nearly eleven, and just as we were settling down to eat our pies, who should come in but Toots and Archie! They didn't have much to enjoy of the Social but I was glad they had come. Archie ordered a car to come after us, and we finished up a very eventful day with a flivver ride.

I like such days—when we can do things that others are afraid to do. I wasn't so very tired but still the bed looked good to me and we *slept*.

Sunday, January 27   A lonely day. Toots walked down to Leighty's with Audie and I enjoyed the Sunday by myself.

I wrote the letter I have thought of for so long. I wonder how foolish it was. I tried to make it very sedate and serious but I am not always thus, and there might have been one or two streaks in the letter. I wonder whether it will bring an answer. I *hope* so.

Monday, January 28   This is my first real experience with Monday closing, though it is the second heatless Monday. I could hardly get matches in the morning and after 12:00 noon you could not get a thing but bread and rolls from the bakery. We had heat today, but last Monday Toots says they even Hooverized on that. I wanted to do some shopping, but not so! Everything is closed.

Tuesday, January 29   To Bruce at last, though the train was about five hours late. I wanted to hire a livery to take me the first part of my way, but every time I called it was out and in my stubborn pride I decided to walk. I reached Amacoy just at noon and couldn't eat my dinner because it was frozen. I stayed until recess and then walked on down to Soft Maple. I ate part of my lunch, but I felt too blue to care whether I had dinner or not. I managed to see about three quarters of an hour of school at Soft Maple. Visiting two schools in a half day is pretty good work, especially so.

When I left Bruce that morning, I did not know where I would stay that night and had almost decided it would be at Stevens's, but when I planned out my circuit, I saw that I must get farther that night, to Island Lake, if possible.

From Soft Maple, straight south, I walked right into a stinging wind with snow. How long the road seemed! The ten-mile walk was beginning to make itself felt. I was so afraid of being late for supper, so I walked with all the speed I had left, and succeeded in reaching Burpee's after six o'clock. They were so good to me, gave me some slippers to rest my feet, and tried to make me feel as comfortable and homelike as possible. The snow was still falling and the wind still blowing, but I tried to forget them both. No use borrowing trouble and I had need of a good night's rest. I slept as soundly as a log that night, too.

Wednesday, January 30   It was perhaps for the best that I paid no attention to the storm last night, for the morning showed an unbroken whiteness over the road, no tracks to be seen. I decided I would try walking and if I couldn't make it, I'd come back to Island Lake again. The wind was still blowing when I left the house, and the mile or less, around the end of the lake was almost the worst walk of my whole life. The wind caught my coat and at times almost blew me about and the drifts went above my knees. I puffed and plowed my way through the snow and my breath was soon only a little gasp now and then. I thought once or twice of going back to Burpee's, but that would be acknowledging that the day was too much for me and my stubborn pride carried me on. In about half an hour the wind grew less and the clouds promised to part and let the sunshine through. Some children, four or five, had also broken a path and now the walking was easier. I almost began to enjoy my walk.

I had a nice visit that morning with Ruth Miller and I have not often seen a school as neat and pleasant as hers.

I left at noon with Rusk Farm my destination for the night. The sun was now out, bright as could be, but the snow showed no desire to thaw. I struck out steadily but the first long hill was a damper on my gait. I had to rest several times and walked backwards part of the way up. The rubbers seem to put your foot in an unnatural angle and they pull the cords in my leg so much that I cannot endure it to walk up a long hill without resting, facing the foot of the hill. Funny I must look, but the fact cannot be denied. The hills became steeper and closer together as I came nearer to Rusk Farm until they seemed like this [sketch of hills]. The whole road looks something like this:

Some of the Polish people kept very ugly dogs and I made it a point to be as small and unobtrusive as possible when I went by a house with a snarling dog prowling about the gate.

I was *really* tired when the big buildings of the farm were at last visible, and after finding Mrs. Olson—in the "Rag House"—I only needed a hint, to stay and rest and postpone my school visit until the next day. Mrs. Olson is such a dear kind-hearted soul and does love to talk. When Mildred Calkins and Miss Malloy came home from school I had on Mildred's comfy slippers and was quite at home in the big rocker. We had a nice evening and talked about every subject under the sun it seems. Everybody at the Farm is knitting—Mrs. Olson has knit fourteen slip-on sweaters, besides several pairs of socks. I watched her knit for a while, and I do not wonder at the amount she has accomplished when I see the speed her needles have.

Mildred and I slept together and talked an hour or more, just things that girls always talk about—daydreams and visionary stuff, you know. I like Mildred.

Thursday, January 31   It was cold this morning, but no one told me just how cold, and so it did not seem as bad as some mornings I have known. I was just a bit stiff from yesterday's hill-climbing, but the walk to-day was just long enough to be nice, about three miles or a little less. I stepped along, almost singing. The school-house was dreadfully cold and though the fire was burning nicely and the stove red hot, the room would not warm up, even with my energetic firing. I made the children march and exercise by jumping and it helped some. By noon time it was becoming fairly warm.

I walked briskly back to the farm for dinner but I was late and hardly deserved the good dinner Mrs. Olson made for me.

I spent the afternoon at the Rusk Farm School, almost the first graded school I have visited this year.

The evening was most enjoyable. Mildred and I went out to the "Rag House" and had a nice dash through the cold and snow. They are planning a House Party for June, sometime, and I have been invited. Isn't that fine, Little Book ? The summer cottage is on a lake and there is opportunity for rowing and swimming and fishing, sports, however, at which I am rather inexperienced. I know I could have a good time in spite of that fact.

The thermometer was slowly but steadily falling and when we went to bed that night it had gone down to 32 below. It meant at least 40 below by morning if not more, but Mildred and I curled close together and tried to shut out the howling of the wind, by talking about the House Party.

Friday, February 1   Our expectations of a *cold* day were completely realized next morning. Before I was up, reports were coming in by phone and some said it was as low as 45 below. My heart almost froze. But I could not stay—I must get to Chetek and I swallowed down all my fear and forebodings.

The air was still and cold in the morning and with the tucking-in Mrs. Olson gave me, I did not mind the cold at all. I found Nina Barnett and her pupils huddled about the stove—a good fire but no noticeable heat. We fed the stove all the dry wood it could hold and the thermometer was gradually coaxed up to normal. I felt miserable and should have been in bed or in a warm spot near a stove, instead of battling with the wind and cold. My cheeks were hot but my hands were like ice.

I had to reach Chetek at about 4:15 or near that and six long, cold miles lay between me and Chetek. I counted on about three hours for the trip and so at one I left Nina and started. I had seen the wind drifting the snow and whirling it around the school house, but I had no idea how dreadful it was until I got out in it. Every unprotected stretch of road was drifted knee-deep with snow that gave no footing. The first quarter mile almost finished me and my heart sank when I realized what was before me. Now and then, where the road was protected by trees or brush on the west, the snow had not drifted and I would have a few rods of easy walking. The wind was blowing a perfect gale and I almost had to throw myself into it. Before I had gone a mile I realized how foolish I had been to attempt a walk like this. I knew I could not make it and I felt ready to cry with sheer anger at Fate. Why should this day, of all days, be so dreadful, when I was the least fit to cope with the wind and cold?

At last I saw a team of horses ahead of me preparing to start with a load of wood. There was only one destination that I could imagine it to have and I made up my mind to get a ride, even if it was on a load of wood. I passed them while they were doping a cut on one of the horse's fore feet and down in a swamp they caught up with me and the man asked, "Going to town?" Of course, I was and soon I was perched on the end of the load with two horse blankets to keep me warm. I turned my back to the wind and snow, and now, come what would, I was at least better off than walking through the dreadful drifts. The man had three horses to pull his load and "Maud" was the leader. We went up some dreadfully steep hills, so steep that the horses had to rest two and three times, and again we would have a brisk run on the down-hill, sometimes almost a quarter of a mile.

I grew stiff and numb with cold as mile after mile rolled away behind us, and though I did not think my nose or feet were freezing, my whole body was chilled. The last few miles near Chetek were the worst of all. I can hardly find words to describe the raw, stinging nipping, cold wind that blew from Chetek Lake. It went through all my wraps, almost to my very heart.

When the man stopped in town for me to get off, I was too cold and stiff to know where I put my feet, and I rolled rather than climbed down to the ground. My knees were stiff and had no feeling and my whole body felt like it did not belong to me. I looked for a restaurant and found one in the same block but when I asked for hot cocoa, I found that they had only coffee. Well, even hot coffee will warm you, but though I stood beside the stove, as close as I dared, I could not stop shivering. I almost rattled, I trembled so, and for more than two hours I shook. It must be Nature's way of getting up circulation in a half-frozen body.

The train was a few minutes late, and soon I was on my way to Cameron, not actually suffering any more from the cold. At Cameron, several hours' interval before train time, but I was too tired and worn out to

A sleighload of logs, similar to the one Louise rode on to Chetek on that bitterly cold February day. (Photo courtesy of the Barron County Historical Society)

care about anything. Even the thought of waiting three or four hours did not annoy me.

The train from the north came in at about nine o'clock and Ray Smith entertained me from then on with his lively chatter. Rather a bit too much brag about him to suit me, but perhaps he means well enough.

My one greatest reason for wanting to get back to Ladysmith was to see Tis before she went back to Horseman. Something almost drove me to be there Friday night. I knew that Toots would not come in, at least not very early, because Carmains were going to have a party that night. Perhaps she might not see Tis at all before she left.

After dallying along the way for an extra hour, our train finally came in and a few minutes past twelve I came up to the rooms, to find Tis all alone and rather lonesome. "Gee, I'm glad you came!" was her first greeting. You might imagine that we had a lot to say. She had been alone since scoot time and I know how it feels to be all alone even for a few hours. At one-thirty

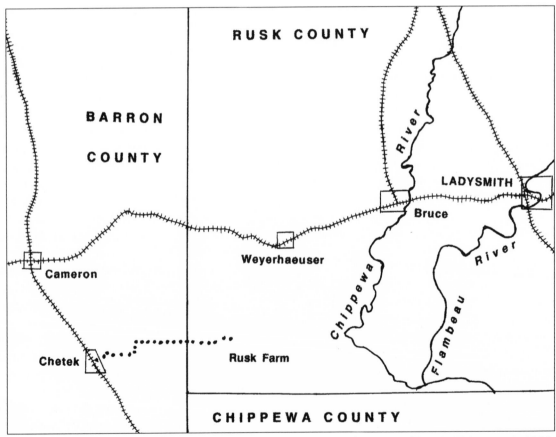

The route of Louise's epic nine-mile walk from the Rusk Farm School to Chetek, February 1, 1918.

Toots came running up the stairs, all full of excitement and happiness from the party, and we had to begin all over again in our conversation. At 3:30 we decided that we must go to sleep and though we were all more than tired, our nerves were so tense, that I, for one, barely slept at all.

At 4:30 the alarm rang and Tis got up and dressed. But on going over to the depot, she found out that the train was about two hours late, so she came back and slept a little longer. At seven o'clock she went over to the depot again and soon we saw the train come and take her away. For five long months she will hibernate in Horseman, though perhaps during the last month we may be able to run up and see her. Here's hoping!!

Saturday, February 2 At eight I was in the dentist's chair and for one hour he did his best to make me cry out. At any rate several bothersome cavities are filled and with several more sittings my teeth may be brought back to decent condition again.

At nine I was speeding up to the office, to find Mr. Dresden, Miss Jenkins, Biggs and Hawes, preparing to do some carding of questionnaires for Mr. Munroe. All of us were inexperienced, and the work was new and strange, so the fact that the first card took almost an hour to fill out is not so bad, when you remember that it had *only* forty-six items on it. In spite of all this, it was rather interesting work.

In order to make a complete day, Toots and I went to a dance with Archie that night, a Woodman Dance. I should have been in bed, but a dance will call me from anything, so I shook off my fatigue and deadness, and had a dandy time. Audie came up with Orville and Mabel and Ed Hanson. I half expected to see her there, so her arrival was no great surprise.

Archie skipped home after bidding us good night at the foot of the stairway and then Eddie insisted that we come and have an oyster stew with them. It was a late hour but the stew was too great a temptation to resist and so we tramped over to Kings. That also was right good!

Mrs. Diederich had invited us to come down for supper and we gladly accepted. Invitations to dinner or supper are always welcome to us.

The clock said 2:00 a.m. when we two finally turned out the light. To say that we were tired is too mild —I was tired almost beyond the point of feeling. My head ached dully and my eyes had a wild, blood-shot look. I seemed like another person.

Sunday, February 3 In an effort to make up lost sleep, we slept until almost noon, and then only the afternoon's call urged us out of bed.

We made some splendid fudge before we went down to feed it to Archie when he came up that evening. I made it and it was just splendid.

We stopped for a short "How-de-do" at Thompson's and then hopped over to Diederich's. The afternoon was different than most that we usually spend. The two little girls are cute and Gertrude can play and sing very well for a little girl. They also had some candy, but the supper! Um! It went right to my heart or rather the warm spot in my tummy. I can't remember when anything tasted so splendidly, or perhaps I was so genuinely hungry. Salad and gloriously fried potatoes, cold roast pork and cheese, canned crab apples and lovely cake! and ever so much more, I can't remember all now, but they made the supper complete and then some.

At a little after seven we hurried home and got here just a few minutes before Archie. The show was a rather sad story—a mother-love theme—and Archie could only say, Punk! Toots shed a few sympathetic tears, but my eyes were dry. I liked the story because everything ended as it should, happily.

And thus passed another Sunday, quite happily, though I wish it were summer and the roads were good!!

Monday, February 4   As usual when you have cast all care to the winds for a day or so, the scattered ends are hard to find and arrange in order again.

Until scoot time, I worked like a fiend to mail all the February plans, and Bob came in almost before I realized that it was time for the scoot. Lee didn't come up this morning. I wonder if they are moving.

At last I was half-way ready and the scoot was still waiting for me so I hurried into my boots and away I went, with my knitting under my arm. I was the only woman on the train and it seemed very unpleasant. But I knit busily without hardly glancing up. There was a soldier-boy on the train, sent home from Waco, Texas, because of inflammatory rheumatism.

At Murry I got off, and with only a glance or two to see if any of my one-time friends were in sight I started for Lucy's school, walking as rapidly as my moccasins would take me. I can almost run with them on my feet, they are so light and easy.

I surprised Lucy, of course, but I had a very nice half-day with her. Poor Child! She has been suffering for almost a week with an aching tooth, and has my sincerest sympathy.

My plans always grow out of circumstances, so I was not discomfited when I found out that it would not be convenient to stay with Lucy that night. Serley's was only about three miles away, so I decided to walk there after school. Lucy and I talked a long time after school, about old times and events and shortly after five I left. When I finally came upon good roads, I almost ran. It was growing dark and the woods were lonely and gave me a spooky feeling. I came upon some dreadful drifts where no team has been over, and only a faint trail, Lida Berg's, I suppose, was visible.

My moccasins are so soft that I can walk with almost no sound, and even the dogs at Serley's did not notice my approach. I surprised Mayme considerably when I opened the door and said, "Hello, Mayme." I was in the dark and she couldn't see me at first. Ida came in soon and also had a surprise. They were both so good to me and are both such dear girls. Later on I went in to see Mrs. Serley. Dear me! She doesn't look very well and coughs almost constantly. Her "cold" is always with her and wears away her strength bit by bit. I sometimes wonder how she can manage to hang onto life with such intensity. Mother has often said that the Norwegian people, of all nations, seem to have the greatest love for home and family, and this seems to be one example of a pure case. Her love for her children, even though all are grown up, seems to be her anchor in this world.

I slept with Ida and, of course, we didn't go to sleep for some time, talking of everything.

Tuesday, February 5   I spent the whole day with Lida Berg in her school. Dear me! How much one's personality is reflected in the school. Lida is *so* impatient and cranky, I could almost shake her, but I know it would not change her own self.

That evening I spent several hours with Mrs. Serley and incidentally knit all my yarn. The sweater is growing rapidly and if I only had the other ball of yarn I could almost finish it before I return to Ladysmith.

The one great piece of news I learned to-day is that Palmer Serley is married, in fact, has been for several days. And to whom do you think he is married? You could never guess, Little Book! To our own little Zelda and none other! I wonder why she never said a word about it to us, though for that matter, Zelda was never so very talkative concerning herself or anyone else either. I wish them joy and happiness, and all the good luck possible. But sometimes, I wonder and doubt—!??

Wednesday, February 6   A heavy bank of clouds made the morning seem rather dark and dreary, but I walked down the track to Klinger's crossing and had fine walking all the way.

My main thought on the day's visit is that I do not like Miss Radtkke and I feel that she returns the compliment. Nothing seems to suit her in these northern wilds, and that always angers me, to complain about conditions around us. Nothing will ever be made better by growling, and each one of us can improve at least one little corner of this old world.

After school I walked to Old Murry, rather a stiff walk and I was truly tired when I reached Kittleson's. Most of the road was poor, hardly any trail at all and only the last quarter mile was good.

Thursday, February 7 Every spot around Murry brings back old memories—every turn in the road, every house recalls some particular incident, and somehow I always feel a little bit homesick when I visit my old school in Murry 6. The children have all changed so much that I would not feel at home with them now. My little ones then will soon be ready to graduate and my big boys and girls are young men and women now.

Edmund LeBlanc came down to Kittleson's in the evening and I had to look and think hard before I could realize that this tall young man was the little boy of my Murry days.

I believe I have met the champion tease in Louis Serley. Nothing escapes him and nothing can stop him. If I was not absolutely tease-proof he might have provoked me, but teasing is not one of my worries.

Friday, February 8 From Kittleson's I walked to Jessie Sergeant's school, and then at noon, to Crane, spending almost an hour in the Crane School. Here my mind is always divided, rather unevenly, too. Three-fourths of it is listening for the train and one fourth or less is observing the classwork. A freight gave me a little run but when the two blacks did not appear at the end of the train I came back to the school and had the thrill of running all over again when the scoot *did* come about fifteen minutes later.

The thought of getting back to Ladysmith and reading all the letters had been a sustaining hope all week, but when I saw no letter from Ernie and read a "blue" one from Mother, I was in the dumps myself. Vicy has been called to Marshfield for his physical examination and, of course, Mother has worried a great deal about his leaving so suddenly. The boys were gone and Toots did not come in for supper, so I ate a lonely meal, feeling more unhappy every minute.

I wonder why Ernie hasn't written?

Saturday, February 9 Carding again! Only Mr. Dresden and the Training School squad worked in the afternoon, so I had a splendid opportunity to slip away and go home on the scoot. Audie had come up and all three of us were going home. Vicy's sudden departure had taken the starch out of all of us and somehow the most natural thing for us to do was to hurry home to Mother.

Vicy's last letter contained one phrase that almost made my heart thump, it was so thrilling—"I am leaving Marshfield to-night and *I do not know what my future address will be."* Our first thought was that he had enlisted and had been sent to some cantonment. But why hadn't he said something? We could only wonder and think and wait for his next letter.

Toots and I received our Liberty Bonds to-day— after months of waiting. Mother has put them away with the other "papers" for safe keeping.

Sunday, February 10 I broke the sabbath and sewed all morning on my new green dress. I need some new clothes very much, but I would rather buy them ready-made instead of spending the time on them myself or having Mother sew on them.

Toots and Audie set out shortly after dinner with Old Bill, and Eddie will come home with him tonight. I don't envy them their long slow drive.

Poor dear Mother! She has more and greater worries than any of us really imagine. I did my best to cheer her, but when our pet slogan, "It's all for the best, even when we can't see it now," is all that's left to fall back on, encouragement isn't easy. I hope with all my heart and soul that home matters do brighten up, when the new house is ready to move into.

Eddie came in about nine o'clock, very sleepy from his long drive. I think he slept during part of the drive, at least. Old Bill is so slow and pokey.

Monday, February 11   Mr Rice was rather annoyed when I came late this morning, in fact, he was as angry at me as I have ever seen him. Of course, I had to be meek and humble for the rest of the day, but I can't see why he should have been so cranky. Another score laid up for you, my dear sir!!

Tuesday, February 12   Audie's birthday to-day and I cannot reach her by telephone. I'd like to wish her a happy birthday, at least.

I went to Glen Flora on the way-freight, after a hurried scramble to get some valentines for all my little proteges.

Joey Forchette got on the train just before they started and I had interesting though perhaps not the most desirable company until we reached Glen Flora.

I couldn't find anyone in the livery barn so I decided to walk out to the north school, the Red School, I believe it is called. Joey tried his best to coax me to go to Ingram and hire a livery from there to Mr. Simond's school, because he wanted to ride out to the camp. But he found a team from camp in Glen Flora, so my pity didn't amount to very much. Joey never changes and is never any older, but in spite of all his faults and weaknesses, and he has many, I like him. You really can't help but like him. He and Ed. Sass are true pals, quite inseparable.

Wednesday, February 13   I made a long circuit to-day, from Glen Flora to the Range Line, then to the Sievertsen School and from there back to Glen Flora.

A wild impulse seized me to go home on the way-freight and I asked at the depot about the way-freight. "It will be here in about ten minutes," the agent told me. Great luck!! I had ample time to go and pay my bill, gather up my belongings, and even eat a little lunch that Mrs. Wilson fixed up for me, when someone called, "Here she comes!" I swallowed the last mouthful of cake and ran.

I was the only girl on the train, as per usual, but I didn't care much. I knit every minute of the time, though the light was very poor. At Tony almost everyone left the caboose for an important errand and I secretly hoped that some of our red-nosed passengers would become too interested to watch the train and would miss it. But everyone was back on when the train left, and all brought with them the "perfume" of Tony. I very nearly suffocated before we reached Ladysmith.

My first question when the flat was reached was, "Any news from Mother?" "Not a thing," was the comforting report. Why doesn't Vicy write? I know that Mother is thinking of him every minute of the day.

Thursday, February 14   My desire to get home was explained when we woke up this morning. A young but healthy blizzard was raging and evidently meant business. Toots prepared for a tough walk but I know she was thoroughly worn out from fighting the wind and snow, by the time she reached school. Poor child! I wish now that she hadn't gone out.

I didn't do a thing to-day but watch the storm. I ventured out to get some things for dinner and the wind nearly blew me off the stairway. The drifts grew deeper and deeper, even paths couldn't be found anymore. The wind blew a perfect gale from the north. This is almost like our blizzards of last March, when even the trains couldn't get through the snow. The boys battled their way to and from school, but they were literally covered with snow each time.

Saturday, February 16   Toots came in last night and told me all about her experience with the storm. She only got as far as Carmain's and there she simply dropped upon the porch, completely exhausted, and in pity, they hitched up the horses and took her the rest of the way. That night she only got as far as Pepper's. Even Audie didn't walk to school in this terrible weather.

We carded again to-day, and so many people came up to work, to each of whom I had to explain the entire process, that by evening I was all "nerves." We carded until after three and then I worked at our own Saturday's work.

Toots was going to a party that evening, a farewell for Bennett's, and at five o'clock she and Lizzie came up and persuaded me to go with them. I went.

We had supper at Carmain's and then drove over to Bennett's. The little house was completely packed with people, but we played some jolly games and had a fine time. It was almost a puzzle to think of games to play in the little kitchen, but we managed. I felt too tired to play very much but I guess I laughed as much as anyone. I met several new people, though most of them I have known for a long time.

It was after two o'clock when we finally went to bed. I was almost too tired to sleep and to make matters worse, Lizzie had taken a red-hot flat iron to bed with her and my foot came in contact with an exposed spot. I *just* touched it, my toe didn't wait any longer, but I felt it long enough. I was in mortal fear of getting my foot on it again and went to sleep curled up like a bear.

Sunday, February 17   Of course Carmain's took us to church with them. I didn't feel like going, and during Sunday School I became so sick that I had to leave. I almost cried, my side hurt me so. When I got up to the rooms I got warm as quickly as I could and soon the pains stopped.

It seems as though my Georgette waist is a hoodoo. Each time I have worn it (almost) I have become sick.

We spent the afternoon with Thompson's and Robelia's and Mrs. Robelia asked us to stay for supper. She fed me tomato soup and made me feel almost well again. She's been so good to us this winter.

Gertrude Wegner (Toots) leaving for her four-mile walk through the snowdrifts to the Pepper School.

Eddie came up before limited time and we had a nice little visit with him. I don't envy him his walk when he gets to Sheldon. He startled us by hinting that he might not stay the entire year. I hope the fancy leaves him because I want him to stay.

Monday, February 18 I went to Weyerhaeuser on the noon train to-day. I wanted to go on the morning limited, but it was hours late, in fact, it did not come until about 3:00 that afternoon.

Eben Thompson was on the train and I had a nice visit with him until the train stopped at Weyerhaeuser. Of course, he talked a great deal about Ernie and most of all about his new work. Evidently he likes it and it pays. I wonder what Carrie Carmain would have said if she had seen Eben talking to me. Nothing pleasant, I fear.

I was just ready to leave the train when someone caught me by the arm and I turned to look right at Ida Serley and her sister, Mrs Alvey. I had another little visit with them during the stop for dinner. Ida is going to Minneapolis and has promised to write to me from there.

I became quite well acquainted with one of the Weyerhaeuser teachers, Ruth Blinston, and after supper, I walked with her to her rooms and visited for a while. Personally I do not like her, but she has ideas and is a character worth studying. She is very capable when it comes to designing and making her own clothes. She had some of the most beautiful Georgette crepe waists, made by herself, that I ever saw. My fingers just itch to make some myself, because I know I can.

Tuesday, February 19 I left Weyerhaeuser early in the morning, with a wind blowing and small flakes falling, but as I had the wind at my back all the way, I didn't mind it a bit. During the morning, however, it began to snow harder and harder and by noon we were almost having a blizzard. I had to face it all the way back and

with the deep snow and my rubbers, hat and scarf full of snow, I really had a fine time. Every few rods I would stop and turn my back to the wind and catch my breath again. I was so tired I could hardly walk, and as I came within sight of Weyerhaeuser, I heard a train whistle that sounded exactly like the afternoon train. My heart almost stopped beating and I began to run, but it proved to be a freight, pulling into a side track. I had time enough to get dinner at the hotel, and incidentally shake the snow from my clothes. My feet were wet and I was cold, likewise the dinner, though I ate every bit of it.

The train was very late and at Ladysmith, the scoot was just about ready to leave. I had to change my shoes, so, of course, I missed it. I wanted very much to go home and coax Mother to come up to Ladysmith for a "Food Conservation Demonstration" and also to be home for my birthday. But I knew that Dad wouldn't come to Sheldon in such a blizzard and I didn't want to walk.

The storm quieted down by six o'clock and by nine the moon was out, beautiful and bright. I decided suddenly that I would go home after all and I went. I knew that I would have to walk the two miles from Sheldon, but the night was almost as light as day, and I pushed all my fears aside and went.

It really wasn't so bad after all, though several times along the track I was almost sure I heard voices, but each time, when I stopped and listened, my own heart beating was all I could hear. Even the wind had died down completely and only the occasional snapping of a tree "broke the silence of the night." At the crossing I walked as softly as I could so that the dogs wouldn't hear me. Luck was in my favor, because they didn't even whimper.

Near Lukinick's hill, the wolf scare that Aunt Eda and Leon had, several years ago, suddenly popped into my mind and I became so nervous I could hardly breathe. I glanced from side to side and behind me every few steps, but not even a shadow moved.

Evidently the bears and wolves were dreaming sweet dreams, and didn't care to bother me. I didn't object.

At Petrick's again I was very quiet, hoping to get by without arousing the dogs, and again, luck was good to me. Not a single living thing had I seen or heard since leaving Sheldon, and that, too, had been dead.

The lights at home were a protection as soon as I could see them and from then on, I was no longer in a panicky state of mind. I guess Mother heard me as soon as I came in, and of course, she knew who it was, too. Almost her first words were, "We know where Vicy is!" and to my excited question "Where?" she told me that he was in Detroit, working for the Dodge Motor Co. Here we have been making a soldier-hero of him, all for nothing. But perhaps the time will yet come, who knows. At any rate, we girls will all write to Vicy at once. He's been gone almost two weeks and that's an age when you don't get any letters from home.

My nerves soon relaxed and I went to bed and slept a well-earned sleep.

Wednesday, February 20 To-day is my birthday, Little Book, I am twenty (—). There, that is sufficient. At any rate, I do not feel as old as I am, and I hope I never will. I want my heart to always stay young.

I visited Eddie this morning and was very favorably impressed with his work, considering that he is only a boy(?). At any rate, he has good discipline, which counts a whole lot.

Mother had the blues this afternoon and in trying to be cheerful, I nearly gave way myself and we both shed a few tears in sympathy. There are some things that are unexplainable to us now, but I hope so much that sometime we will see that "All is for the best after all."

I had dinner with Aunt Eda in their new "bungalow." There—I ought not make fun of their new home. They are living in the auto-shed at present, and are a little bit more than crowded. As Uncle Dave told Eddie the other

night, "Why, man, when you get in you couldn't turn around, you had to back out!" It is much better now, but nothing can be much worse than a hasty moving.

We just reveled in music this evening. Eddie and I played for several hours, every reel and jig and quadrille that I could remember, and I really feel that the music comforted Mother more than any words I could have said.

Thursday, February 21 I hiked down to Sheldon, with my dainty footwear—moccasins—caught the train back to Ladysmith, and promptly after dinner, started out for Toots' school—to attend her "Mother's Meeting," or rather the meeting of the sewing circle. The little program was very good and a little "take-off" that she had composed on the "Priscilla Club" was the best of all.

Mrs. Pepper and I went back to the house to make the cocoa and I had a rough-and-tumble time with Wilber. I *did* wash his face, but what he all did to me is beyond words! He's too rough to be any fair match for me.

The whole meeting was a success, though Toots was quite disappointed because so few of the mothers were there.

Since to-morrow is Washington's birthday and a legal holiday, both Toots and the boys went home to-night. I was really tired after my third spasm of walking, and would hardly have been able to walk out from Sheldon, even if I had been allowed to go.

Friday, February 22 I only worked at the office during the morning, and at noon Mr. Rice very kindly told me I was free to take the afternoon off. I would almost rather have worked, because the rooms were so lonesome, I could hardly endure the silence. But there was work enough to keep me busy, at least my hands, though my thoughts went traveling as per usual. I swept and dusted, cleaned the shelves and put new paper on them and generally house cleaned. The meals are lonesomest of all when I am alone, and I wish then that I could dispense with eating entirely.

I wrote another letter to Ernie this evening. Perhaps he didn't receive the first one. At any rate, if he is like the great majority of people, he may not care about answering them. My thoughts go to him so often that I simply must write this letter.

Saturday, February 23   Our Bruce Institute. I am not the least bit interested in it, but I feel that I must go, in order to prove that I have professional spirit.

The program was much the same as the one we did at Tony, and several of the same people were on the program. I barely succeeded in keeping my attention on what was being said.

Miss Jenkins and I whiled away the long hours until limited time by writing letters. I wrote three long ones, the first and longest one, of course, went to Vicy.

Sunday, February 24   The lonesomest day I ever spent. Audie came up yesterday and left a little note for me. Toots said she *might* come up on the local on Saturday night, but when I opened the door, no one was there, and my feelings went down, down —! I didn't know what to do with myself and nothing seemed natural. I was almost ready to go anywhere, when (about 5:30) I heard heavy footsteps coming down the hall, and someone knocked. Imagine my surprise when I opened the door and saw Toots and Bob standing there, but my surprise almost reached consternation when they said that they had *walked* up. Think of it—fifteen miles!!! I could hardly believe it, but with their packs, they looked quite genuine. The day had been so beautiful and warm, they had bravely started out at about 2:20 and here they were in Ladysmith at 5:30 or a little better, hungry, but not unusually tired. The rubbers had hurt Toots' feet but she could still walk.

Mrs. Anderson asked us to come and play that evening, and we had a musical climax for a long day with a very pleasant ending.

Monday, February 25   To-day's weather was the very opposite of yesterday's. It rained and then snowed and all the while the wind blew a perfect gale. Toots had to resort to all sorts of devices to keep herself dry during her walk to school. Several pieces of oil cloth helped to make her tam water-proof and an old old raincoat covered her shoulders. Why is Monday morning so often a wild and stormy time?

Tuesday, February 26   I made a circuit to-day—first to Susan Siglin's school, then a walk to Anna Riley's and home with her. Here in town the streets are almost bare and for a considerable distance out in the country there is hardly enough snow to cover the ground, but when we turned west from Flunker's Cheese Factory, we came upon snow so deep that long stretches had been plowed open, and had the pleasure of a tip-over. It wasn't a sudden tip, but I fell out, all the same. I'm thankful that the horse didn't run away.

This evening I washed and scrubbed, which ought to make a fairly complete day for one person.

Wednesday, February 27   Another visiting day! The team that took me out to-day was unusually slow and I felt that it must be nearly noon when I came to Doris Connors school. It wasn't nearly as bad as I imagined, of course, only 10:15, but how I hate a slow horse!!

Doris is a character that I enjoy studying. She has a personality of her own and no one can be just like her, and she will never be just like anyone else. She is doing good work, too.

At noon I walked to Shaw's Dam and had another nice visit. Mrs. Howell has had a marked effect on this school. Order is coming out of chaos, and an altogether different spirit seems to exist among these rough, coarse Slavish people.

I was fortunate enough to get a ride of over two miles with some people who had attended an auction sale in the district. And again at the Novelty Works, Mr. Sinclair offered me a ride. I came into town in grand style in his big car and wasn't nearly as tired to-night as I had expected to be.

I very nearly went to a party out at Spiegelberg's to-night, with Bob and Lee, but mid-week affairs are against my policy and we decided not to go. The last party at Bennett's had such unpleasant effects upon me that I will think twice before going to another, during the winter, especially.

Sunday, March 3   Toots and I spent the afternoon at Thompson's. The day was too beautiful to think of spending it all at the rooms. On our way back we saw Eddie and Mabel and they called us in for a little while and then we, in turn, asked them to come and have supper with us. Eddie generously got almost everything we needed, dear boy! We made oyster stew and also a batch of fudge and just as supper was nearly ready, in walked Bob, fresh from another tramp of fifteen miles from home. Audie walked from home to Leighty's, about nine miles, and I wonder how she feels.

After supper we had music and dancing and fudge galore! Yes indeed, it was a right jolly evening. I hope they come again.

We have two more names to add to our list on the table. How I do like to see it grow.

Thursday, March 7   I've been at the office all week and life goes on in the same old groove as usual. Toots fell on the ice, coming home from school to-night, and hurt her knee. I hope it won't be as bad as my lame knee was.

Friday, March 8   Poor Toots didn't sleep a wink all night and groaned and tossed continually. She kept me awake nearly the whole night, too. She simply wasn't able to walk and I persuaded her to stay home to-day. I phoned to Mrs. Pepper and told her that Toots couldn't come. It's too bad to have all the children come to school, only to be told that "teacher" wasn't coming.

This evening Toots used liniment and hot water on her knee, but it will be awhile before the stiffness leaves, I fear.

Saturday, March 9   We awoke this morning to face a white blizzardy storm, a raging, swirling snow-storm. I have never seen anything like it. The storms of last March were bad but were tame compared with this. At noon I fought my way through drifts and was a snow-covered image when I finally struggled up the steps at the office. Paths were blown shut so quickly that one could hardly be sure of keeping on the sidewalks. Around the corners, the wind came with such violence that small people were helplessly whirled round and round.

Nervy people continued to use cars until noon, and after that only the foolhardy ones dared to attempt to drive a car through the streets. In one place the street was so filled with snow that a car backed onto the sidewalk and ran a whole block on it. One car after another got stuck in the snow and had to be pulled out. In front of the Baker Hotel a big car attempted to fight its way through the drifts, but after pushing a mass of snow almost as high as the car itself, in front of the radiator, it gave up the battle and backed out. The wheels spun the snow into perfect clouds, but all its power availed nothing against the huge drifts.

Toward the close of the day the wind went down and the snow almost ceased to fall and soon the snow shovelers were busy making paths through the snow. I never saw the snow come down as it did to-day, in some places the drifts were over four feet high, and people estimated that two feet, on the level, had fallen in less than twelve hours.

Sunday, March 10   This morning Audie phoned and said they were all coming up, so we put on a kettle of candy. They were so long in coming that we almost gave up looking for company, but at last Audie came tramping in, and after an interval, Orville and Eddie also came up. The candy was nearly ready to pull and we had a wild time pulling it. I burned my hands, and how it stuck! Finally, after dropping some and painting my hands with butter, it began to pull. But the time was going, and almost before the candy was cut it was limited time, and with his mouth full of candy, and hands and pockets ditto, Eddie made a wild dash for the train. We watched him from the window and we know he got there on time because he didn't come back.

Mrs. Leighty came up soon and after enjoying (?) some of the still-warm taffy, she marshaled Audie and Orville over to Kinyon's barn, while Toots and I arranged for a livery to take her out to Pepper's (No— Carmain's). Her knee is still too lame to use for a hike that distance through the snow we have to-night. Within a few minutes I was all alone, except for my thoughts and, of course, they went straight to one particular spot and to one particular person (——!).

Monday, March 11   The snow is simply evaporating under the warm coaxing sun. Water, water everywhere, under the soft snow.

Wednesday, March 13   This noon I encountered some posters informing us of a "Patriotic Meeting— Important matters will be discussed." That sounded interesting and mysterious, so all alone I found my way into the high school gymnasium and took a seat in the rear row. Mr. Householder joined me and I was very glad he came, because I was beginning to feel like a lost lamb among so many men.

Some spirited songs and intensely patriotic talks began the program and then Mr. McGill dropped the bomb by introducing a resolution condemning the act of V. V. Miller in voting against the resolution introduced against [Wisconsin's U.S. Senator Robert] La Follette. I voted in favor of the resolution, but I really believe the enthusiasm of the meeting carried me along with it. Somehow, I cannot and will not believe all the evidence that has been woven about La Follette. I have spoken to him and have shaken his hand and I will stand behind him until all this is proven.

I came home with my nerves in a state of high tension that drove away sleep for several hours.

Saturday, March 16   All four—Toots, Audie, Bob, and Lee—went home last night and I spent another weekend alone.

This morning a letter from Great Lakes came in the mail and one glance at it sent my pulse up to 160 and my heart even higher. I could hardly wait to get up to the rooms to read it. I'm so very glad he answered my letter. The thought that it would never be answered had been growing, but it is dead now, and won't easily come back to life again.

Sunday, March 17   Toots and Audie aroused me from my slumbers at 5:00, or thereabouts, and after an artillery fire of questions and answers, we all curled up and slept until nearly noon.

Spring 1918

Louise and Gertrude stand atop Neillsville Mound near their childhood home. They made the trip to Neillsville on one of their "travels with Sophie."

Spring 1918

Thursday, March 21 The first day of spring!! I wore neither hat nor coat when I went to the Training School to take part in their Literary Program. This is the first program this year that I have really attended, and woe unto me—they appointed me critic. I really feel that I did much better than last year. Even the poorest among us can improve a little.

This evening we had very impromptu plans to attend a patriotic Social at the Kiefer School. They were impromptu in the truest sense of the word. We rushed around like frantic hens, watching the clock's hands slowly (?) moving around to 7:30, but with all the hindrance that haste can cause, and with all the other little delays, we were ready when Miss Biggs and Miss Jenkins came up. The car was punctual, as livery cars go, and after some scrambling to comfortably seat ourselves, we were off.

The road was splendid until we reached the corner one-half mile north of the school house, and then ^^^^^^^^^!!! I was scared stiff that we would dash off the road or turn completely about, or (least dreadful of all) get stuck in one of the dreadful holes. But our driver kept right on moving and was as unconcerned as though we were driving through the streets of Ladysmith. I was stiff with nervousness and I don't believe I took one whole breath all that awful half-mile. I don't know what I would have done if I had been driving myself, for I am a different person entirely when responsibility rests on my own shoulders. I can even summon up some little show of recklessness then.

I worried all evening about the chances of the car being able to come back after us. I won't say much about the program—Mr. Rice spoke and spoke and spoke as per his usual custom, Mr. Dresden gave a short but good talk, and the pupils sang two songs. Then the baskets were sold and after more than an hour's auctioneering (which I fairly hate) we ate our lunch. Mr. Scott had my basket.

I expected the crowd to remain and play games, but they began to gather up coats and wraps, chairs, lamps and lanterns, and before very long we four were all alone in the big school room, waiting for the car. Eleven o'clock came and went—eleven-fifteen ditto, and still no car. We sang and talked and then sang some more, and still no lights to be seen. We had almost begun to express the thought that our driver's courage had failed him, and he had deserted us. Eleven-thirty came and our outlook reported a light on the hill. "The car," of course, but the minutes went by and the light came no nearer. "He's stuck." We waited and waited, and finally, in desperation, locked the door and set out to meet him. He was much nearer this time, caught in a rut and we saw him kill the engine again and again in an effort to get out. When the lights shone upon us, coming down the road, he managed to back out and turn around by the time we got up to him. He *had* been stuck twice coming the last half mile, he told us, and we did not doubt his word.

The ground was frozen a little, but hardly enough to hold up the car, but we managed to navigate until we reached the lowest place and then the car stopped. We all got out, and Toots, who is champion "cranker," started the car and with four of us pushing, we finally ground our way out. One other bad spot almost had a similar effect on the car but we all held our breath, and with almost its last ounce of power the flivver crawled onto solid road, and we were safe. By twelve we were home and not very many minutes after we were in dreamland.

Friday, March 22 Mr. Rice kindly allowed me a few days at home. Office work is slack and I am wild to go home and boil sap. Maple sap season has really arrived, so we four all went home together, Friday night. The boys tried to scare us along the track, and succeeded quite beyond their expectations. We were really the silliest, noisiest bunch that ever traveled that road, and it was fortunate that few people lived along the way, or they might have sent the constable after us.

Saturday, March 23 Sophie crawled out of her shed this morning and Toots and Mother, Billie and I went to Sheldon. For being in the shed all winter, she was all O.K. and we had no trouble in starting her. The roads are fair, but we buzzed right along. Oh, there's no joy like joy-riding! Watch us this summer!

We boiled sap until almost eleven, Mother and Toots and I. The moon was out beautifully clear and the woods were lovely. There is no woods like ours, especially our "Park."

Sunday, March 24 The "snap-shot" bug bit us and we finished taking a roll of pictures. All of them are "woodsy" pictures and I want them to carry a bit of Wisconsin to Vicy. We developed them this evening and consider them fairly good. I'm glad.

The sap ran gloriously to-day. Dad and Bob had to gather it twice, and almost everything is full. Yesterday the gathering was quite a bit of fun, but I'm glad that Bob is here to help to-day. My arms are considerably longer from yesterday's carrying, than they were when I came home.

Our logs are being sawed at Lacy's Mill. Another bit of evidence of "our new house." The brick is piled up on the "lawn"—Fireplace—hurrah!!

Monday, March 25 Eddie came in so softly last night that hardly a soul heard him, and in marked contrast to him, we woke up at three o'clock and made preparations to take the kids to the limited. We tried to be quiet, but five people made considerably more noise than

Eddie. Our time was all carefully planned, but the car caused a few minutes delay, and when we left it was only a few minutes before four, with the limited due at 4:10. Verily, I say unto you, I drove like a "deuvel," where the roads were smooth enough. But as usual, when *we* are on time the limited is late, and for nearly

Toots (left) Louise, and Audie (right) and friends at the sugar shanty in March 1918.

an hour, our anxious eyes kept watch "for the light" and we had almost reached the point of "seein' things" when the headlight suddenly flashed out from behind the curve. A limited always makes me quiver with excitement, it is like a living monster. The kids were gone and Mother and I buzzed home again.

At seven I made another trip to Sheldon, with Dad, Henry Yager and Mr. Bollom. It was light enough then to see how rough the roads really were. I don't hardly see how I managed to get over them so quickly in the dark, but it must be a case of "what you don't know won't harm you."

Mother and I gathered sap alone this afternoon. It wasn't an extraordinarily good day but even at that, it was too much for us and we quit before all was gathered. Eddie might like to gather the remaining trees, and the guess was correct, too.

At six I went after the "mill crew" and almost got down into the mud, but with three men to push (though all were supper-less), Sophie got through alright, but the engine heated—!!! Our logs are all sawed and as soon as he can get in and out of the mill yard, Dad will start to haul.

Eddie and I boiled sap to-night, and had a first rate fine time. He is some jolly boy. He helped me wash the dishes in order that we might all go down to the shanty at the same time. I wanted very much to talk to him about Ernie, but I couldn't do it, so that subject was untouched by both of us.

Tuesday, March 26   We had a lovely candy fete to-night, and ate enough to make an ordinary person sick. Eddie stirred like a Trojan, but the last pan of candy, Mother's, was just perfect. Creamy and soft!! This is to go to Vicy for his Easter feast and he'll love it!

Wednesday, March 27   It took me all day to reach Ladysmith, although the kids have walked it in less than four hours. I missed the scoot after the hottest, fastest walk that I can remember and then walked back home again. Immediately after dinner I went down with Dad, in order to be there in time for the local. But like all freight trains, it has its own time, and I finally reached Ladysmith in time for supper.

We printed pictures this evening and had good luck, in spite of a dozen or more obstacles. The developer got warm and so a great many of the pictures are yellow. The six new pictures are all fairly good and some are really lovely. Too bad they do not show the colors.

Friday, March 29   Toots' Patriotic Program! The day began by raining and I was almost ready for a phone call from her, saying the meeting was postponed, but the day improved as it grew older and the evening was lovely. Pat was coming in after Mr. Dresden and me, but aside from the fact that he was the only one to bring us, I wouldn't have gone two blocks with him. There was one bad mud-hole just inside of the city limits but we howled right through it.

The program was fine. It would naturally be, with Toots back of it. Mrs. Carmain and I missed some of it, because we made coffee at Pepper's, and this time coffee-making was a success, only sufficient cups were lacking. After lunch we played games and the crowd—one and all—were the jolliest you ever saw. Even Mr. Dresden got into the games and played.

I could write a dozen or more pages about Pat, but as none of it would be complimentary, I will refrain from expressing my opinions. He wants to take me to the show on Thursday, but I won't be here when he comes! I shall snub him properly, if he dares to come!

Saturday, March 30   Dad came up to Ladysmith but he went home on the scoot. Our last note to Thompson's is paid—Joy!

Toots and I followed him later, on the limited, and both Dad and Bob met us with Sophie. The terrible mud-hole grabbed us again and we all had to get out and push.

We talked until after twelve, but there is always so much to tell that I, for one, cannot wait until the morning. Even when Toots and I are apart for only one whole day, we have so much to tell each other that we could talk until midnight.

All clocks are to be turned ahead one hour and we will lose one hour of sleep to-night. I wonder how the Day-light Saving Plan will seem to us.

Sunday, March 31   Easter Sunday!! A rain threatened all morning while we burned brush in the south forty. The ground is still very wet, but the piles are dry and each one burned with a roar. I wish the fire had run just a little bit more than it did, but fire is a hard creature to order about. About noon a few showers came up and in nervous haste we began to pack, hoping the rain would wait until Bob had come back from Ladysmith. Several bad mud-holes made us gasp. We lost both chains while getting the car out of the yard, but the drive was lovely and after unpacking, Bob speeded off for home. He loves to drive and I am beginning to feel perfectly safe with his capable hands on the wheel.

Alas and alack, when we began preparing for supper, we discovered that our provisions had been forgotten at home, and the thoughts of all the homey things we would be without this week almost brought the tears to our eyes.

After supper, while we were sitting "in comfort" Audie dropped in suddenly with Eddie and Orville at her heels, and so we were invited out for a ride. Oh! It was fine to loll back on those lovely cushions. We went to Bruce and *warmed* ourselves with some ice-cream and then "motored" home again.

Eddie's news that Ernie and Roy came home this morning is most astonishing. I wonder whether I will see him. I hope so. They have allowed all Wisconsin boys to go home to vote.

"Are you girls going to the Dance?" Dear me, how we'd love to go but the usual obstacle comes up— "What will we wear?"

Eddie and Orville left us alone for a few minutes when we got back, and in the interim we did some feverish planning, and by the time they came up again, laden with "junk," we had everything settled to a pinpoint, just what we would wear.

Monday, April 1   Observe, Little Book, that this is All Fool's Day! Who is fooled?? 'Twas office day, and lucky for me, because I had three pair of shoes to buy. My mind wasn't on the dead, dry stuff of our office for many minutes at a time and as soon as Toots returned we began preparations for the dance. We bathed and powdered, curled our hair and doped our feet and dolled and fussed, almost as much as a girl going to her first party. Everything was fine, both of us looked lovely (for no one would say it, if I didn't). But—listen to the sad ending of my tale!

Nine o'clock came, but we knew the boys might be late—9:30 also came and our eyes began to take on a sleepy look. We lay down for ten winks and soon the clock's hands showed 10:00—10:15—10:20! Where is Eddie?—10:30 and our patience was gone. "If they come now they will find us in bed," and slowly and sadly we took off our gowns and furbelows, and before 11:00 we were asleep. If they *did* come after that we never heard them. April Fool!!

Wednesday, April 3   We were almost certain that Eddie would come up last night and "explain," but again we looked in vain. Wednesday noon someone came scurrying down the hall and Eddie stood at the door when I opened it.

"I'll come up and tell you all about it" and he skipped down again for a few minutes. He is so hoarse that he croaks when he talks. The story—well, it is like some of our thrillers. Eddie and the three Dicus boys had gone to Chippewa and Eau Claire on Monday, and about five o'clock had headed home, by way of Chetek—, Strickland, and thusly. After being lost a dozen times, more or less, they finally landed across some ruts near Strickland, and with a heated car, they couldn't get out. At 1:30 they gave up and curled up to sleep in the back seat. At 5:30, some fellows helped them out and at 6:00 they were home. "Yes, indeed, Eddie—Some trip!!" Many hours we might have waited for the boys.

Eddie leaves for Canada to-morrow morning and Ernie and Roy go to-night. Just before he left I gave him instructions. "Tell Ernie to come up before he goes. We'd like to say good-bye to him, *at least*."

Truly I had great news to tell Toots when she came home and we both were nervous as witches as the evening drew on toward limited time and no one came. Then a soft knock _____

_____

_____.

It cannot be written, little book—words cannot tell how you feel. Nothing seemed natural and nothing we said seemed to be what we wanted to say. He was here only about five minutes, but I lived an age those few minutes, and never, as long as I live, will I forget one look, or one word.

As the door closed after him the very earth seemed to collapse from under me—I wanted to scream, to run after him and call him back, but I couldn't do either and for several minutes Toots and I shed the real tears that we had kept back while he was here. Oh—Ernie, Ernie, we are very foolish and you will never know how we feel. I watched for the limited and all too soon, that one-eyed monster, that relentless dragon came and went and Ernie was on his way to Camp Perry again.

We waited for a little while hoping that Eddie might come up, but 10:30 came and no Eddie, so we went to bed, but I could not go to sleep. My thoughts followed the limited a long, long way.

Eleven o'clock came and suddenly the hall door opened and two people came to our door. They have gone to bed, I heard Orville say. How I wanted to jump up and say, "Yes, but not to sleep," but I lay as motionless as Bunny Cottontail. There was a whispered consultation in the hall, some paper rustled and I looked to see a note tossed over the transom. It came under the door instead—then a little laugh and the boys tiptoed away. The instant the hall door closed after them, I was up like a shot and had the note. I called Toots three times but the dream spirits held her fast and she did not waken. There were "xxxxxx" at the end of the note, three for each.

Thursday, April 4 I was awake early this morning and when I heard the 4:35 come in, something told me that No. 7 was also late and a wild idea seized me. "Toots, let's hurry and dress and go over to the depot to say good-bye to the boys." Toots was out of bed and dressing almost before the words were out of my mouth. Clothes went on in a frantic haste and scarcely two minutes later we heard the train whistle. "Never say 'die'"—there's plenty of time, and grabbing our coats, we rushed down the stairs—shoes half-laced, caps on askew, and no more clothes on than would make us lawfully presentable in the early morning light.

We couldn't see them anywhere and at last I got on the train and luckily caught Eddie's eye and in a minute both boys were on the platform beside us. Another farewell, but there was no sadness noticeable *this* time. We returned some of the kisses Eddie had left for us, six was more than we could keep, of course. Then the train began to move and they were gone. Likewise, we—in a wild run back to shelter. Yes, verily we are possessed of the very imps to do such an outlandish and nervy act. It is done, however, and I am not sorry.

In order to make a day, I went to Conrath on the local, visited the French school and then the Conrath School in the afternoon and waited *hours* for a slow train back to Ladysmith. I came back at nearly eight o'clock, hungry, tired, and sleepy, foot sore and I know not what else. Oh, yes, we shall *sleep* tonight!

Saturday, April 6   Yesterday's wind blew up a drizzling rain. Audie came up and after office hours we went shopping for hats. Toots and Audie each bought theirs, but I have not found one to suit my fancy. I do not feel like fitting on hats to-day, this rain makes me restless. That, and one sentence of Audie's has set my brain in a whirl—"Ernie and Grace W. were together almost every minute of the time he was home." Oh, I am wild with jealousy. And then he dared to come up here and bid us a fond farewell. I want to wound his feelings as much as mine have been hurt. And I am one who imagined she had no jealousy in her make-up.

Sunday, April 7   Sunday was intensely cold and our rooms were excellent refrigerators. Mrs. A. invited us into her rooms for the morning and we absorbed *some* heat.

Audie phoned to "Spec" Dicus to come up after her, but we at least were glad when he finally left the rooms. He is a "boob" right, and belongs to a class to which we have consigned Pat. He talks too much and knows not whereof he talks, unless it is horses and I am not so intensely interested in that quadruped that I care to discuss the merits of this, that and the other horse with Spec. If he knew one-tenth of the things we said about him, he would never speak to us again.

Monday, April 8   In my school visiting Monday I drove by Woodbury's house and my anger pounded in my heart. In my vivid imagination I could almost see the Buick's tracks in and out of the driveway.

Good news awaited me when I got home again. The boys are permitted to go home to work on the farms and will receive credit in their school work. The boys are happy as larks. I know that Dad will be pleased and

needless to say, Toots and I are happy, too. We will have a little more peace and quiet now.

Thursday, April 11   Roy C. was in town to-day, and after a little maneuvering with our cars he managed to get within speaking distance and he agreed to go after Toots with me. After my long and rough ride in Sophie, the Overland went so smoothly, it was a real treat.

We made our boxes for Laura LaBerge's social to-night. Mine is a fairly good imitation of a shrapnel shell, and Toots' is a Zeppelin. They are different, at least, from the detestable "coffin" boxes.

Friday, April 12   I made one of my much postponed visits this morning, postponed because much dreaded. I was prepared for very bad roads the last few miles and I actually parked the car about a mile from the school and walked the rest of the way. The roads were bad, but not impassable, and if I had tried, I know I could have managed to get through. But neither Sophie nor I suffered from my walk, and though I worried a little about letting the car stand for several hours out of my sight, she was safe and sound when I got back.

After a trip back to Ladysmith for dinner, I went down after Audie and then started out to get Toots. We had just passed the old Grieshammer place, when *BANG!* only about a thousand times louder, and I really saw sparks fly from the hind wheel. Yes, a blow-out, and a real one, too!! It scared me so, I hardly knew how to stop the car, my nerves were all to pieces. We both got out and saw the gaping hole in the tire, and when we investigated our tool kit, we didn't have a thing to fix it with. Another car came up behind us and they advised us to go limping back with a flat tire, as carefully as we could, and they would go out after "the teacher." I felt as though everyone was eying our flat tire, almost as though I were going down the streets with a big hole in my stocking. The tire was past mending when we reached the garage and we were without means of getting out to the Social this evening. But my luck was with me again and just as we were leaving the garage, I saw Mr. H. and he was willing to let us use his car and even furnished a driver. Isn't he nice?

Well, the dance was nice as dances go. Archie was all ready to be mad at us, but I spoke first and he couldn't snub me then, and he actually danced several times with each of us, and, as usual, he got Toots' basket. I made a crush on a most despicable "boob" out there. Yes, isn't it a shame, the people who fall in love with you are almost always people you hate. Like Pat, for example. This fellow, Mr. Burke, runs the pool hall in Lemington, and though he was a fairly good dancer, I couldn't stand him at all. Waugh, he sickened me!

We had put fully a half cup of corn starch in our shoes, to relieve our smarting feet, and mine behaved pretty well. But, I didn't waste many minutes getting my shoes off, and they hurt so then that I could hardly sleep. Such feet!

Saturday, April 13 Bob went home last night and came back on the scoot with one of the new tires I got for Christmas, and by noon the car was O.K. and immediately after dinner the kids went home.

As usual, when I am alone Saturday evenings, I write to Ernie and so it was to-night. My jealousy is wearing away, or rather, I am reasoning myself into a sane frame of mind. I can be a friend, at least, though a Platonic friendship is said to be an impossibility (almost). At any rate, I shall write to him just as often, or much, as I want to, and no one is going to stop me.

Sunday, April 14 Sophie received a general wash-up this morning, inside and outside, with almost the entire family at her. By noon, she was a spick and span, glistening beauty, so we had to take her out for a little spin.

After church, Dad and I took the minister to Sheldon and then I gave Dad his second lesson in running Sophie. The first one was without much result, because I was hardly able to run her myself then. Dad did very well though, and another lesson or so and he will be able to run it almost alone. I hope that Mother, too, will be able to run the car, even if it is only a little. It is a knowledge worth having.

Our ride up to Ladysmith was just lovely, Bob drove and we girls sang nearly all the way. The evening was perfectly grand. This is the boys' last week of school and I suppose they want to make the most of it.

Louise with a well-scrubbed Sophie in the yard at Sheldon.

Thursday, April 18   We celebrated the boys' home-going with a candy-pull and "among those present" were Alice and Mabel H., Eunice and Elizabeth Ryall, Lizzie G., Audie, Toots, Bob and Lee, and myself. We kept the wires hot all around with our telephoning, but everything came out jolly. Bob gathered up our company in the flivver, even Mabel and Alice. The candy was lovely, and it was more fun than you can imagine, to stir and beat your own candy and watch it cream. The boys couldn't get theirs to stiffen until one of us girls took the dish for a few minutes. Olives helped us to surround the candy and we even had enough delicious fudge to treat Mrs. A and Bee and Donald.

When it came time to convey our guests homeward, we piled six grown-ups into Sophie. We had considerable trouble (and then some) to get her warmed up and only after the third attempt did she really navigate. There was a most unusual clanking and clattering under the car, but though we all heard it, no one said anything. Just beyond the Vance Miller school the radiator began to boil furiously, and we stopped because we didn't know what else to do. We didn't have a single pail or can or even a tin cup with us, and in sheer desperation Eunice and I went up to J. Miller's and borrowed a milk pail. When we got back to the car, the radiator had stopped boiling. Who would have imagined that it would freeze up in the short time the car had been standing at the curb?

Well, nothing very serious had happened, and since Sophie could still run, we started once more. The clanking seemed worse than ever, and finally Toots broke out, "I simply can't stand this any longer. Stop and let me get out and look." One look was sufficient. Our muffler was dangling by one bracket, banging back and forth against the rear axle. We couldn't pull it off so we had to let it swing, but since we now knew what the noise was, it didn't seem nearly so bad. With our load lightened after we had dropped our "excess baggage"

we speeded for home, hoping the muffler would hang on until we reached the garage, but when we clambered out and looked—behold—it was gone, and no one knew where. Next morning I sent the boys back over our trail and near Ryall's they found the poor battered up muffler. It cost me two Thrifty Stamps, however, but I consider it money well spent.

Friday, April 19   See how Patriotic I am, Little Book!! I took my whole "family" out to Mae Carter's supper. It was a new experience for the boys but we certainly had a dandy luncheon. It was served cafeteria style, and in the crowd it was a slow promenade to pick up a tray full. We couldn't find a place to sit down, so we all went out to the car and had supper by ourselves. It was a first-rate supper, even the boys admitted that.

Saturday, April 20   I felt sure that there would be a dance at Sheldon tonight, and I "dolled" and dressed to fit the occasion. But when I reached Sheldon, all was dark and I was properly stung. 'Twas better so, perhaps.

Sunday, April 21   Dad's birthday, though to tell the truth, I do not know how old he is.

Bob and I worked on Sophie all morning, oiled and greased every bolt and bar that was greasable, cleaned spark plugs and drained out the oil. She ought to run without any gas at all, now.

We gave her a tryout, to Tate's, and Mother arranged to have Bessie come to finish out our school. I suppose she will eventually board with us, though I would rather she wouldn't.

Yes, the flivver is *some* car!!

Monday, April 22   We begged a whole gallon of maple syrup for our first candy pull and we decided that what was left was enough to make candy for Ernie and Eddie. Some fudge helped swell the amount. With all our anxious watching and testing and beating it just wasn't quite as good as it should have been, but we were too tired to boil it over again.

Tuesday, April 23   We cut the candy this morning and hoped it would harden enough during the day so that we could pack and send it that night. We had a great time packing it and found that we had enough left to send Vicy a box. I hope Ernie finds some of the love I've stowed away among the pieces of fudge.

Friday, April 26   My plans were considerably upset this morning. I had promised to attend a picnic and program at Magna Johnson's school in the afternoon. In the morning I was going to call on Mrs. Loper, but kind Providence made me stop at the Court House just before I left town. Mr. Householder told me that the program had been canceled because of an epidemic, and we were not to go. For a little while I was completely at sea, but I saw Dr. Stephenson, and when I learned that he was going north of Crane to make a call, I asked to go along and, of course, he said yes. I was mighty glad because I had dreaded that long lonely trip to Grace Woodbury's school. Eddie and Roy Fults were usually too busy to go with me, and I had postponed it several times. The visit was shorter than it should have been, but it was long enough for me to be sweet and civil to my rival, although I am quite sure she doesn't know it. The ride was just fine and I'm glad I was alone. Dr. S. is a puzzle to me.

We rambled down to a Social at Maple Center in the evening—Toots and I, Mr. and Mrs. Rice and B. Mack. It was a tedious program, and when it came time to sell baskets, our dear little canoes that we had spent such time and work upon went for next to nothing, mine to a "Boob" and the kids' to Lester Bliffert, who wouldn't eat with them. Yes, really, it was a most disastrous evening, and Toots was mad enough to cry. We have all vowed, "Never again!"

Saturday, April 27   The others all went home with Sophie and as usual when I'm alone, I use the time to write letters. I sent Ernie a long one. Then I went home on the limited.

Monday, April 29   We came up last night in cold and rain, with very muddy roads—a nasty day. Received a letter from E. and as usual, my spirits have gone sky high.

Tuesday, April 30   We motored down to see Audie this evening and all stopped at Hanson's. We had a jolly evening, but if I had known how they feel toward me, because of Eddie leaving, I don't know whether I would have gone. It hurts dreadfully when you are so misunderstood. Mabel and Alice went down with us and we were just the right size for the flivver.

Wednesday, May 1   We carried out our promise of coming home for supper, and made it, too. Our beloved deer head had arrived and Toots and I went into raptures of joy over it—it's just beautiful, words can't describe it.

Bessie is so queer, I can't understand her. She keeps to her room almost entirely and is so distant and reserved. I wonder whether she feels she is too good for us or whether we do not want her. It isn't pleasant for Mother at all.

Thursday, May 2   I have had enough Polish to last me a long, long time. I took Mr. and Mrs. Rice to a meeting at the Polish school near Conrath. It was a double program, first English and then Polish, divided about one to three. At first it was interesting to listen to them talking, but it finally made my head hum and nearly set my nerves of edge. The priest's sister sat beside me and told me the substance of what the speakers said, or I really believe I couldn't have endured it for those three hours. The difference in the attention of the audience toward the English and Polish parts of the program was really very marked. Few grown-ups there understood enough English to know what Mr. Rice or others talked about, but when the Polish program began and their children recited a little "piece" or sang a song, it was wonderful to see the change in expression. It was more fun watching the faces in the audience than listening to the program.

The real purpose of this meeting was to raise money to help the Polish soldiers and to arouse the people to help work for a new Polish nation.

Friday, May 3   No one is half a fool, they say, either all fool or no fool, so we are surely all fools! To help out Mrs. Pepper, who was sick, we promised to go to Bill Mutch's surprise party, although after the party of last year we vowed we'd never go again. But we went, had a good time, considering all things, and tried to take an early departure. We stayed at Pepper's that night and managed to get up in time to reach Ladysmith in fairly good season.

Saturday, May 4   Toots went home alone with Sophie, as part of our most complicated arrangements for this evening. Sheldon has a Red Cross Dance and we are to play, and Audie likewise has her Red Cross Social. As Lawrence said, Bob and Sophie will have to be the solution, and he was correct, too. Toots went home in the morning with Sophie and just before supper, Bob came up with a lovely lunch, still warm, that Mother had packed for us. Then, in due season, we started with Bob and Mr. Dresden, accompanied by Mr. Anderson (State Inspector), down to Audie's school, and hurried home to dress for the dance. All our plans worked beautifully, and shortly after twelve Bob and Audie buzzed into Sheldon. The crowd danced until almost four a.m., and Sophie carried home a very tired and worn out bunch, six grown-up people. We were not angry this time—the Sheldon folks were all nice to us and we had a really nice time, thank you.

Sunday, May 5   Eleven o'clock found us drowsily crawling out of bed, a very sleepy family, hardly caring whether we had dinner or not. Mother had a dandy dinner almost ready for us, however.

Monday, May 6   After yesterday's intense heat and humidity, it had to rain. But even so, I finally met Sarah Icke, for whom I've watched every day for almost two weeks. I knew she was in town, but did not know where she roomed or boarded, though with a little effort I might have found out. It was a joyful meeting, you may be sure, and we promised to see each other again on Tuesday. Perhaps if it hadn't rained we might not have seen each other.

I have finally sent the letter to Owen's for my "forty" of land, the one west of Dad's. Now I will soon be a "landed man" and likewise, I will have to begin to save to pay for it.

Tuesday, May 7   It rained nearly all day, but toward evening the sky cleared and Toots and I decided to go for a joy ride with Sarah and Threse. We went toward Bruce, all four chattering away—Toots and Threse making plans for their Red Cross Dance, and Sarah and I recalling past experiences. It was splendid to hear again about our old classmates. They have all scattered, but Sarah has the addresses of a great many of them, and I shall have all that I can get, you may be sure, Little Book. And before many weeks are gone, some of them are going to receive a long letter from a long lost classmate. Won't they be surprised! Oh me! yes!!

Thursday, May 9   No letters ever make me quite so happy as those that come from Ernie, and the one that came to-day was the longest one he has ever written to me. I find myself thinking about him so much and so often, and I wonder much, how often he thinks of me. Distance seems to lend a kind of glorified charm to him, and he is growing to be a soldier-boy hero, perched on a pedestal with an adoring "me" gazing at him from a distance. Perhaps he doesn't even *see* me!

Friday, May 10 By merely signing my name to two pieces of paper I became the proud possessor of a parcel of land. It is likewise a pledge that I will begin to save more money. I told G.M.H. about it, and he only said, "Where is the man to go with it?" But this land deal is only an investment from my point of view, although no one can foretell the future enough to say— "I never will do this or never will live here." But I really never expect to live upon my "forty," unless when I "retire from business" with money enough to live as I wish for the rest of my life(?)

Sunday, May 12 Dad and Bob, Billy and I took a tramp through the woods to-day, across the creek, through my forty and through the one that Vicy wants to get. We found the "Witness Tree" and also some of the old blaze marks and were quite correct at the end of a half mile of pacing through the woods. At least Dad was, I only tagged along behind. Land looks much the same anywhere you go, though "my forty" is just a bit better to my eyes than any of the land around it. That is only as it should be, however.

Monday, May 13 This is Dad's second attempt to get his second citizenship papers, and again they were refused him because of the war. It is discouraging!! Mr. Hanson also tried to get his, but because too long a time has elapsed since his first application, he was also rejected. It doesn't seem at all right, with his two sons fighting for Uncle Sam!

I made one flying trip out into the country, stopped at three schools, and was back a little after four. Dad

came in shortly after and we left for home, picking up Audie on the way. Her school is out and she is home for good.

Tuesday, May 14 The second day of eighth grade examinations! I wonder how many poor eighth grade pupils have any nerves left. I stopped for a little visit at Maple Center, and a very large class is writing there.

Wednesday, May 15 A dreadful mix-up about the exams has happened at Maple Center. Katherine Hanson was gone on Monday, and Eunice Ryall substituted for her. Now Mr. Rice won't accept the papers written on Monday, and wants the children to write them over again. Eunice and Katherine came up to our

Louise and Audie on a trail in Louise's "forty" of land.

rooms in the evening and we had a regular pow-wow. I knew it was useless for them to go to Mr. Rice and try to get him to take back what he had said. But I am sorry for the children from the very bottom of my heart. They have had a most unfortunate year, and if any class in this county deserve to get through, they surely do. I have just simply made up my mind to *get* them through somehow. Just wait until I find Mr. Rice in a favorable mood and I'll manage it. See if I don't!!

Saturday, May 18   The mountain of exam papers has melted rapidly under my red pencil. I went through them like a whirlwind; no two weeks of reading and rereading every paper handed in, just to change each and every standing. I have come to the point where I thoroughly hate this method of conducting exams, and I hope with all my heart that next year will see a different system. It cannot be a success, where the teacher conducts the examination for her own pupils—marks the papers herself, knowing just what the children are capable of, and what they haven't had. Here's sincerely hoping for a change next year. I know it can be done.

Sunday, May 19   Toots and I came home last night and I am really glad I was home. The most destructive storm ever known struck about the center of the county about three o'clock this morning. We didn't discover until Sunday night how bad it really had been, but the wind at home seemed strong enough to take the roof off. It was dreadful, but didn't last very many minutes. In the evening we stopped at Leighty's for a few minutes on our way back to Ladysmith, and when Toots came back to the car she said, "If you want to see something you have never seen before, or may never see again, just drive down that road for half a mile and then turn north." "What is it?" I asked, "a house blown down?" "Yes," she answered, "Bliffert's house blew down last night, killing Mrs. Bliffert and injuring Mr. Bliffert and Lester." It was such sudden and dreadful

news that I didn't quite realize what it really meant. On the way over there, she told me a few more details, and I had in mind a house lying on its side, neatly tipped over, like a box. As we turned the corner, we looked for the house, but nothing could be seen, until we were almost beside it. Then the wreckage gave us a little idea of the intensity of the storm. Nothing but a tornado could have caused such complete ruin! The house was completely flattened and hardly an article of furniture remained that was not crushed and broken. Other cars were there, too, and we were pointed out the two places the house had struck before it went over. It had plowed up a deep furrow each time and then had been tipped over on its side and crushed flat. Every tree was twisted and torn as though a giant had taken each one separately as we would a twig. Mr. Bliffert had been thrown against a tree, but Mrs. Bliffert had been buried under two partitions and the stove and had lived less than nine hours. Lester had been blown clear of the wreckage, and had found himself out in the field several rods from the house when it was all over. The sight of the nails and broken glass made me sick. To think that in the dreadful rain and hail, lightning and wind, among those nails and glass, Lester had dug out his father and had tried to get his mother out, was almost too much for me. We turned away and finished our trip to Ladysmith, but we both had the creeps all evening. The sight of the house fairly haunted me.

Tuesday, May 21   About five o'clock this afternoon another dreadful storm came up. Toots had gone out to school with Sophie and I was worried for fear that she had started for home and would be frightened and not know what to do. It really looked much worse than it was and everyone who could left the Court-House because, as Mr. Speich said, "I'd rather have a house fall on me than this brick building." I didn't think I was any safer in our rooms than in the office, so I stayed. By six the storm was nearly over, and it hadn't been so dreadful after all. After the tornado on Sunday, everyone is afraid of storms, and no wonder, either. We found out later that this same storm had been dreadful in southern Wisconsin, with another tornado and had almost wiped out the little village of Lone Rock. A number of people were killed and scores were injured. Truly, something seems to have happened to Mother Nature—Wisconsin was so rarely visited by a tornado that it was quite a thing of wonder. But this spring we have had two in three days!!

Thursday, May 23 This is the second night we have spent decorating Pepper's barn. Last night Threse and Sarah came out with us and we tacked up spruce boughs every place we could. The barn is so large, though, that all the greens we put up show only a very little. Toots has two large Red Cross banners (sheets, really), one at each end of the barn, and they help to give the proper atmosphere. The air is full of plans and expectancy, it seems fairly charged with electricity.

We tried to improve the floor by putting cornmeal on it and dancing like wild. Then we swept both floors and put wax on them and danced again. When we left the floor was fairly smooth except for humps and cracks that we couldn't possibly wear off.

Friday, May 24 Audie came up on the scoot and all during the day we tried to get everything done and out of the way, so that only the things we couldn't do would be left when Toots came home. We expected her to come home at five o'clock, but it was nearly six when the car stopped before the stairway. We were just ready to phone and see why she was so late. Then followed the usual scramble of packing our boxes, dressing and "dolling up," though we weren't overdoing that. Threse went out first with Toots and the ice-cream, and at 8:30 I made my first trip out with the musicians. Roy and Jack Belbeck were in town but were having considerable tire trouble. I came back once for Mae Carter and

on our second trip out the sky looked quite threatening. The storm clouds seemed to part, one going north and one south, so we put aside our fears and made ready to enjoy ourselves, and to see that everyone else had a good time.

The floor was good, considering what it was, and the crowd was democratic and really jolly. The yard was full of cars, even Pat Wilson's limousine was there. As the evening passed, a storm seemed to be gathering and the lightning grew steadily worse. The baskets were sold in record time and many people ate and left immediately. Some had long trips ahead of them and the storm of a week ago was still fresh in everyone's memory. About two o'clock the storm broke in grand fury, though we felt quite safe in the big barn. The rain made such a noise on the roof, that we hardly heard the thunder. The musicians' nerves gave out and they said they couldn't play in the storm, but it seemed so much worse to sit and listen and watch for the lightning, that Toots and I played for a while. I was so nervous and shaking that I hardly remember what I played, and I can hardly understand how anyone could dance to our music! I know my face was white and it seemed almost too stiff to smile.

The "raging elements" finally calmed down and we had almost an hour of dancing again. It was almost three when everyone made preparations to leave. Threse left ahead of me and I was just out at the car with Mr. Pepper, cranking to see if she would "buzz." The wind was rising and the lightning seemed quite healthy again. He came to my side and said suddenly— "I won't let you leave with that storm coming up." I looked at the clouds for a moment and said, "I don't believe it is much more than a shower." We both watched it for a minute and realized then that it was a genuine storm. "I'll put your car down in the basement," he said suddenly, and I went back to the barn. In a minute he came to the door and told us all to run to the house. It was a panic-stricken crowd that ran through the rain and mud and wind, nearly falling, into the house. Several of the men lost their hats, but we were all safe in the house before the deluge came down. Then for almost an hour we sat on the floor, since all the chairs were in the barn, trying to be comfortable. The wind blew terrifically and there was considerable hail, but the house and barn were still standing when the worst was over.

After the storm clouds went over, the moon shone clear and bright in the west. It was wonderfully bright, almost supernatural, almost like a sunrise in the west! Archie and I stood by the door watching it, and deciding whether or not to put the chains on the cars. We decided not to and then started for the barn basement to get the cars out. They were literally covered with chaff and hay-seed. It was quite thrilling to back out of the narrow doorway, but I came through a-sailing. Then Archie went to help a stranded car and I loaded up and left for "home, sweet home." Just around the corner below Carmain's I came upon Threse with a stalled car. In all that dreadful wind and rain, she had been stuck on the road, and now the car refused to start. I got around her and then backed up sufficiently so that they could fasten a rope to her car and then tried to tow her car to start it. But it was so wet and soaked that it only popped and sputtered, and I finally gave up and promised to come back for her load. I led the procession into town, everyone wet, cold and spattered with mud, a sorry spectacle. It was almost daylight when I went back for Threse and her car. And again, I tried to tow the empty car, but it was simply impossible to do it. After towing for a dozen rods or more we both saw that we could never get to Ladysmith over such muddy, water-covered roads. So we ditched the car and I drove back to Ladysmith.

In town we came upon Threse's brother and picked up him and his suitcase, and as an act of kindness, I started to take them home. But just one block from Deiderich's an open sewer suddenly yawned right in front of the car. Before I could stop, one wheel was over it

and the other was down in it, with the car just rocking on two wheels. It was the worst accident this eventful night, and I nearly broke down and cried. I didn't see how we would ever get the car out again. But Charles was a very handy man, and with a shovel and a few boards, a good push, the car was back on terra firma again. They walked the rest of the way and I turned around and took Sophie to the garage and dazedly found my way to the rooms!!

Lo and Behold!! Here in the hallway I found Toots and Audie nearly undressed, locked out. Poor kids, they had waited over half an hour for me and looked more dead than alive after this adventurous night. Our faces looked almost gray and our eyes were heavy and bloodshot—we hardly knew ourselves.

It was just six o'clock when we got in and for about two hours we lay down and tried to sleep, but it was impossible to really rest. Every time I closed my eyes I saw the car jumping over the sewer or plowing through the mud and water.

Saturday, May 25   Toots had to teach to-day so at eight we were up again. Our four windows had been open all during the storms and we found all our papers scattered everywhere and everything within reach of the windows was soaking wet. The floors were lakes of water, and I truly wonder how much leaked through down into the store.

I didn't feel one bit like working, so I simply played "hooky" from the office.

Thirty-four men from Rusk County left with the afternoon train, though I only knew two of them, Jake Speich and Dave Vasseur, I felt that I had to see them go. It was one of the saddest crowds I have ever seen or hope to see. Most of the people were crying and no one could look one bit happy. Poor Boys—I wonder when you will see your hometown again.

We left for home as soon as we had the dance money surrendered—$70.50. Pretty good, don't you think, Little Book? We wanted to make so much more, but we will be satisfied with this. The roads were covered with water in places, but we splashed right through, and were home at last, a very tired, very fagged bunch. Mother, too, had a storm story to tell us—Bessie and her father and mother had bunked with them all night, and all of them had been caught in the first storm of the evening, though they weren't entirely drenched. And still, with all this rain, I really believe we will have another storm to-night. Will they ever cease?!

Sunday, May 26   My wish last night was all in vain— another bad storm passed over us during the night, with hail and terrific rain. Truly it seems like the beginning of the flood—I have never seen the rivers as high as they are now.

Bob and Toots took me back to Ladysmith Sunday night and I do not envy them their trip home again. A long stretch of water over the road is really quite a scary sight, especially when you cannot see the bottom.

Monday, May 27   Such a lonesome day!! This week will seem ages long without Toots. Law came up for a little while in the evening. Same old tease!! I nearly cried I was so mad at him.

Tuesday, May 28   I spent the night with Sarah Icke, just to really renew old acquaintances. We first went up to the Class Night Exercises at the High School. I wore my new suit for the first time, only the weather looked so threatening that I put my rain coat over it, and so no one saw its beauty. Sarah and I talked until long after twelve, it would be our one night together and we both wanted to talk so much. I saw all her pictures and read some of the last letters that the girls in our old crowd wrote to her, Genevieve, Edith and Elizabeth. It carried me back years and years to hear of them, and I wish now that I had made a little effort to

keep up enough correspondence to know where they were. Edith is married, and is living out west. Gene is in a Hospital at Rochester and will soon be through with her course. Betty is teaching in the west. I have all their addresses and I surely will write to them before an age goes by.

The rain came down steadily all night. Rain, rain, rain! Nearly every day! What will become of all the crops?!

Wednesday, May 29   Oh, Joy! Toots came up this morning, in order to attend to her alumni work. I am so happy that I will have company for a day. Ora Deerwester has enlisted in the naval service and leaves for Milwaukee to-night. He came into the office for a little visit this afternoon while we were working on the letters. He seems so down-hearted that we have both decided to "see him off" to-night.

I lost a purse, to-day, Little Book, with about four dollars in it. My absent-mindedness has cost me dearly, this time. I can't even remember where I put it down, but it must have been in the Rusk County Bank. It's gone, I suppose, so there's no need to fret and worry about it. I miss the money, though.

Ruth helped us all afternoon and had supper with us at King's. Such beefsteak! We walked partway home with her and had a ride back to town with Archie. He has promised to call me up sometime for a date. Think of it! Almost an hour before limited time, so we decided to pay a visit or two, and down we trotted to Mrs. Thompson, saw Tom, Mr. and Mrs. Robelia, and then started off for the depot. On the way up we met Alice and Mabel and took them along with us. Ora and Eddie were such good friends to them that it seemed only right that they should go, too. We formed part of the big crowd that went from the High School to the depot. Three Senior boys are going to-night, they have just graduated, and now they are going. The crowd was so large at the depot that it was impossible to get through it and we couldn't find Ora anywhere. We fought our way down the platform and then back again, and then we found him. The train was coming and there was only time for a "Good-bye—and Good luck—and please send us your address," and he was gone. Poor boy! he was so excited that he hardly knew what he said.

I was so crushed and pushed that I couldn't breathe, and it was so stifling hot, I thought I would smother. Mercy! such a crowd!! After the train left, we walked for a while and let our nerves calm down, so we took Mabel and Alice home and sat on the porch for nearly an hour. Mabel told us all about the tornado and the tragedy at Bliffert's. This is the first time I have heard the whole story. M-m-m-m- It makes me shudder to think of the awfulness of it all!!!

It began to fog up so Toots and I went home and packed up our goods—the curtains and the scarfs, until almost eleven o'clock. We believe in putting in a whole day, you see.

The eleven-seven came in and a little later I heard heavy footsteps coming down the hall. They came right to our kitchen door, it opened and someone with a gray coat—and there I stood, with very little on—Heavens! I was ready to drop in a heap, when Tis came 'round the door————!!! There was just one joyful shriek and we were in each other's arms! "How *did* you get here?!" "Oh—Merton took me to Rice Lake, and so—here I am!" and then followed another joyful crush.

Sleep was out of the question, now! We almost emptied a box of candy that was to be sent to Tis and talked and talked and *talked* until almost three o'clock. I do wonder what the folks across the hall thought of us! The sleep we got didn't amount to anything and they probably were kept awake by our talking. It was nearly three o'clock when we unanimously agreed that we must snatch a few hours of sleep.

Thursday, May 30   Memorial Day—Ladysmith had planned a very imposing parade for the afternoon, but

the day shed tears continually, so those who marched were nearly drowned.

In the morning we went after Mabel Hanson and then the four of us walked up to Maple Hill so that Toots might give Mr. Weston the school register and get her check. But he was not at home so that part of her mission (getting her check) was not fulfilled. Mabel is a dear girl and I don't see why people think she is so proud and "stuck-up."

We just got home before a heavy shower came up and from then on it rained almost constantly until suppertime. The girls went home on the scoot and left poor me very much alone. I was dreadfully lonesome, so much so that I could not stand to be in the rooms any longer. So I *dressed up*, in Tis' new hat, my new suit and shoes, and Toots' gloves. The "entente ensemble" was very effective, judging by the effect I had on most people I met. I must have made quite an appearance. I saw Law at the hotel window and almost half-wished that he would come after me, but instead Roy came and walked *four* blocks with me and bought me an ice-cream. He might have stayed longer if I had encouraged him, but I didn't, so again I was alone. I sat at the window a long time, watching the people below, but sleepiness got the best of me finally and I crawled away to bed and peaceful sleep. Not entirely peaceful, because there was a storm during the night, not so very dreadful, though.

Friday, May 31   A letter from Ernie made the whole day pleasanter and when Tis came up on the local, all was fair again. Her visit home was very short, but if only the weather had been more favorable, we could have taken her back on Sunday with the car. Instead we had a terrific down-pour just about suppertime—the rain just came down in torrents! I don't suppose we can use the car at all for a few days.

I spent money for a new dress to-day—a green viole. I am very fond of green this year and I wonder what next I can find that is green.

Summer 1918

Louise and Toots on their cousin's Harley-Davidson motor-
cycle at their grandparents' farm near Neillsville.

Saturday, June 1 This should have been moving day for us. But I looked for Dad to come up on the scoot, and when no one came I was completely lost. I didn't know what to do and so I didn't do anything, and when Toots and Bob came up with Sophie about five o'clock, we packed up all we could carry and headed home, via Sophie.

Of course I knew a great deal of rain *had* fallen, and I knew that the creeks and rivers would be high, but I had not imagined nearly enough, and to ride for several rods through a creek over-flowing its banks on both sides was a new and not entirely pleasant experience for me or any of us. The streams were still rising and it was hard to tell what they would do before the water went down again. There were sure to be wash-outs and we were rather afraid to drive through a stretch of muddy water. Nothing happened, however, and we were finally home, bag and baggage or rather, junk and junkage!

Sophie behaved badly on the way home—she had no speed whatever, and missed constantly, so after supper we three, Bob, Toots and I, plus Audie, all turned mechanics. We experimented first with the coils, then the sparkplugs, and when all of these seemed O.K. and in good running order, we hardly knew where else to look. Then Bob suggested that we take off the timer and clean it. No sooner said, than all agreed. But taking it off was no joke, and again and again we had to read what the "Book" said, until suddenly, *IT FELL OFF*!! Just like that! Of course it was dirty, very dirty in fact, and so we cleaned and rubbed it until it must have been as clean as new. Then came the task of putting it back on again, compared to which, getting it off was a mere trifle. We screwed and looked and almost got our heads under the radiator, but twice the timer *fell* off, when we

were sure it was on. Finally it stayed where it was put, and it must have been in the right place.

Then Bob cranked the engine, and while Toots and Audie took refuge behind a stump, we let her buzz for a minute. A big cloud of black smoke came out of the exhaust, and we had one dreadful moment when we almost believed "something" was wrong. But nothing happened, and the engine buzzed so smoothly that we all five climbed in for a joy ride—and it was a real *joy*, too, because Sophie was O.K. and *we had done it all ourselves!* We were black and greasy from working around the engine, but there never was a more hilarious bunch that whizzed down the road. When we came back Bob took Dad and Mother for a ten-minute spin. Joy, joy, Sophie is O.K.!!!

Sunday, June 2 Early this morning Grandma awakened us and gave us a great surprise. We knew she was coming soon, but did not know the exact date. And here she came without letting us know and so she had to walk out from Sheldon, carrying a heavy suitcase. It really was too bad.

Dad and Bob went to Ladysmith this morning for some more of our goods, and when noon came and they didn't return, we were almost sure they had had some trouble along the road. Sure enough, when they finally came, they said they had spent nearly an hour digging the hind wheels out of the mud near John Pember's. Dad had to do the pushing, of course, and he was pretty well spattered up with mud.

Mother and Grandmother and I were going to make another trip in the afternoon, but now I was scared to death of the mud-hole. And since it was a new stunt for me, I had to get stuck. But the wheels didn't sink very deep, and with Mother and Grandma pushing, and full speed ahead, we got out. I felt proud enough then but I didn't have to do the work.

I had a little chat with Joey and also swiped a picture of him. Not that I care a snap for him, but he has always been a friend, at least.

On the way home, I vowed to get through the mud without a stop, and so I just howled through it. The mud had dried just a little and I knew a little better where to go and so everything went beautifully and we were through. My heart was going pit-a-pat, and I know my eyes were big, but I made a "go" of it.

The trunk was the only thing left now to be moved, except our furniture, which will stay for a while, I suppose.

Monday, June 3   I went to Ladysmith alone this morning, the first of my driving trips. When I came to the two mud holes, I just held my breath, gritted my teeth

and dashed through, covered with mud and glory. It wasn't at all bad.

It rained nearly all day, so I changed my plans of going home and went home with Carrie. Frank Parks came over for a while and it really was laughable to listen to him. He is so purely funny without knowing it, that I could laugh steadily at him.

Tuesday, June 4   A happy day with beautiful sunshine, almost anyone could sing!! This morning's paper says that six or more American ships were torpedoed off the Atlantic coast, almost in New York harbor. It almost makes my heart choke me! What if some of those were transport ships with our boys on them! To me that seems the very worst of all, to be killed before they even reach France and have a chance to do something.

Archie phoned about five o'clock, and said he'd come and take me for a ride. I stayed with Threse and

The Wegner women working on Sophie, following instructions in the book. Louise is kneeling by the front wheel, Audie is reading the book, Toots is under the car and Tis is crouching by the side.

at eight he came. Though I have known him for nearly two years, I never felt as though I was very well acquainted with him. But I admit that I really like his company. He comes the nearest of anyone I know to being a pal and he certainly is jolly company. I like the sparkle in his eyes. The girls will tease me, I know, but I don't care a snap—I really enjoyed the ride.

Wednesday, June 5 Just a year ago to-day all the boys registered and to-day all those who have reached twenty-one since last June 5 registered. The total at the Court House was over a hundred. Some seem mere boys, but serious times are ahead of some of them, I think.

I had a card from Ora D. to-day and was really glad to get it. He is going through the regular routine of entrance that all sailors must endure. The "shots" must be painful for some.

Thursday, June 6 A letter from Ernie came to-day, and I cannot help but notice how they are changing. This one is so different from the first one he wrote that I can hardly believe that the same person wrote them all. I sometimes wonder, whether, if I knew him personally, I would like him as much as I do from our letter acquaintance. I know I like him, but whether face to face he would measure up to my ideal of him is something I wonder about.

I went home this evening. I simply had to go because I knew how the folks would worry about me. I believe they thought I was dead and buried in some river, and Toots was going to Ladysmith in the morning to find out whether I was dead or alive. As though I couldn't take care of myself—quite well indeed!!

Friday, June 7 Alumni Reception, so the kids came up with me. I played hookey from the office in the afternoon to go up and help the girls decorate. Getting a large flag was our greatest difficulty, but after chasing all over town and asking nearly everyone we could find, we finally got the High School flag from Mr. Rohr. The decorations were red, white and blue, and though they were very simple, they were truly effective.

We really had no place to go for supper and so Laura and Ruth invited us to go. The girls weren't crazy about the idea, but we all went. Archie hardly spoke to any of us, and never said a word to Audie.

The program at the reception was rather a new stunt, each class was represented by one member, the selection to be their own choice. So the program was varied and new to all of us and really good, I thought. Most of the numbers were songs. Toots and Audie sang the little "Button Song." It was effective and really quite appropriate to these times.

We went home with Ruth and Laura and I know I was glad I went. I had plenty of smiles from Archie, at least.

Saturday, June 8 The girls went home with Sophie in the morning and I spent a long day and a much longer evening in Ladysmith. I skipped out from the office for several hours of the afternoon and walked around with Ruthie. There was a Woodman Dance at Ladysmith that night and I did so much want to go. I know Archie wanted to ask me but he was going with Ruth and Laura, and two girls are enough for one fellow. And so all my longing was in vain and I went to the limited, after spending nearly all evening at the library.

I had rather an interesting conversation with Marchie Dresden. She is a girl all full of "pep" and for a stunt, has suggested that we hike out to some pretty place and camp out for a night. I think it would be a perfect lark, but Mother will surely object. Perhaps the fall would be better for the camping part of it—no mosquitoes then and not so much rain and dampness as right now. I won't forget our plans even if Mother does object to them now.

Sunday, June 9 A day of rest!! (Not much.) Here is a list of the things we did to-day.

Planted potatoes in the morning and to see the rows you would think they were at least a half a mile long. Then Toots and I were possessed with the idea of cleaning out the barn, and we worked at that until our backs were tired and I had acquired a blister.

Church in the afternoon and we girls went, like dutiful children. I was the victim when one was asked to play for the hymns though I am sure now that they never sang what I played. At least that was the effect produced. Awful!!

And then to make a day of it we came home and cleaned the car. Unless you had seen how really dirty Sophie was you wouldn't think it much of a task. But the mud of ages seemed caked upon her sides and it took the elbow grease of the whole family for almost an hour to put a nice polish on her again. But the result was really worth all the efforts, and she looked as nearly like a new car as any Ford I ever saw. The whole family admired her and were proud of her again.

Monday, June 10 A beautiful day! I often wonder if all people are as susceptible to the weather as I am. A beautiful day always makes me happy, just as a cloudy, rainy day always makes me blue. Troubles seem to fade before sunshine, they have no place in it and the real troubles seem so much less on a beautiful day. I can hardly say that I have any real troubles however, so my thoughts can't reach both sides of the question.

Tuesday, June 11 Another beautiful day, but warmer than yesterday! Archie phoned again, but all my Ladysmith friends seemed to be out of town, so Archie insisted that I come out there. I didn't want to and yet I did, and since my heart does sometimes rule my

The Wegner women cook over an open fire on a camping trip in 1918.

head, I went. We went up the Big Falls road to the farm itself. On the way up we saw two deer, and I am proud to say that I saw the first one. The second one Archie saw long before I did. Oh, but they are beautiful, so graceful. And the strangest thing about them is the fact that they seem able to change their color to fit their surroundings.

Coming back, we had the lights on and just as we turned one corner, we nearly ran into a young fawn. It was so startled and blinded by the light, it didn't know which way to run, and bounded this way and that, whirled and started right for the car, turned again and then ran into the brush. Archie stopped the car or he would actually have run over it. I wanted to jump out and catch it in my arms, it seemed so close. I have never seen anything like it, and hardly expect to see the sight again. It was laughable to see it skidding in the dust and trying to get out of the lights. We saw two more deer, both good shots, making five deer in all. I never saw so many in that short a time and to me the ride was a wonderful experience.

Now we have planned to go hunting Thursday night and Archie says I must do the shooting. I am excited already!

Wednesday, June 12   In marked contrast to other days this was a very busy one. Mr. Dresden and Mr. Doyle each brought in some extra work for me. I earned fifty cents from one piece of work and that made it seem worth while.

But no letter came from Ernie and I am blue and also jealous. I know it's foolish but I can hardly help it. I look for certain letters on certain days and if they do not come, I am all upset.

This is Mother's birthday, so, of course, I went home. The girls have made a real birthday cake with real frosting.

Bob went after the mail after I came home and brought back the bluest letter from Uncle Max, or rather, it made us feel so blue. He is still in bed and there doesn't seem to be any prospect of his getting up for a while. I cannot get him off my mind.

Thursday, June 13   After office hours, I went over to Dresden's to talk with Mr. D. and Marie about our proposed picnic on Saturday, and there Ruth and Laura found me, and carried me off home with them, in my car, however.

Then after supper Archie made serious preparations for hunting, even whetting his knife. We drove up slowly, thinking another car was ahead of us, and wishing to give them ample time to get back. We drove to the very end of the road and couldn't see a car anywhere so we turned around and started on the home trip. I had the gun, loaded but "on safety," and though I wasn't shaking a bit, I didn't have the least confidence in my ability to hit anything. No eyes gleamed anywhere, until suddenly near a corner a deer leaped out into the road, stood a moment, and was gone. I had the gun up to my shoulder in an instant, but forgot about the safety and by the time that was off, the deer was out of the lights, though I believed I shot just as it jumped. Of course, I didn't kill it. Archie was very nice about it and said he was glad I didn't kill it, because it was a good-sized doe.

The best hunting-grounds were behind us, though twice more, eyes gleamed. Once I was all ready to shoot, but we couldn't quite see whether it was a deer or not, and Archie kept saying, "Don't shoot! Don't shoot!" I'd have shot the instant he said, "Shoot!" but the deer, or whatever it was, kept out of sight. The other eyes were just a gleam over a hilltop and that was all.

Oh!! It was wonderful! I never came so close to getting one and perhaps I never will again. But it was a grand experience and Archie is pleasant company.

Friday, June 14   The Training School Juniors gave a party to the departing Seniors to-night and with their invitation came one also for Toots and Audie. It meant my going down after them, but I went, so that they, too, might have a good time. It was almost a "hen-party" but they are quite the fashion these days. We had a short program, with Eunice Ryall as umpire and a fine one she made. Then came a light lunch and then games and dancing. Toots learned a new walk and now she'll have to teach us the fancy twists and turns of it.

We took Eunice and Miss Hawes home first, or rather, Eunice and the dear Lord took us. Her knowledge of driving is tremendously small, and the car is speeded up considerably. Across the tin bridge is rather a sharp sandy turn and Eunice hit it at a "Barney Oldfield" pace. I felt the car slew in the sand, the horrid sick feeling of being thrown, which I will never forget. Something, perhaps her speed, saved us from going over, but we came so near to it that Toots can be forgiven for the scream she gave. The park road was new and rough, but Eunice drove like fury, from this ditch to that and only my foot on the brake stopped Sophie from going right into another car in the yard. I was trembling so, that I could hardly drive back steadily and imagined a dozen things wrong on the car. None of us talked much on the way home, our nerves were still so tense, but sleep came in spite of the excitement, and besides, I had a trip to make back to Ladysmith before nine, at least. Early rising for me!

Saturday, June 15   You will say, when you finish this day's account, that it is another red-letter day—but wait! let me tell you all about it in proper order.

It was our picnic day, you know, and Mr. House-holder had finally said he would come. At three I left the office, filled the tank with gas, and then filled the car at Dresden's with my first load. We found the picnic grounds safely at Shaw's Dam and then I went back for the second load. With all our eats, both loads were real loads.

It was necessary to park the car at the road-side, and though it was quite near us, I decided to take off the new spare tire and carry it to our picnic spot. It's a clumsy thing to carry, so Mr. Dresden took it, finally, and as we reached the crowd he tossed it down upon the ground. Somehow, some way, it bounded a little and began to roll right for the river and in it went, kersplash! circling, around and around, while we all stood and looked on, eyes like saucers and perfectly speechless, except for one long Oh!!

For almost a minute we saw it slowly sinking, while Catherine pulled off her shoes and stockings to go after it. But the bank was steep and muddy and she slipped

Louise with Sophie's tire after it was recovered from the river.

once and sat down rather abruptly. By that time the tire was out of sight. All we could say was, "Did you ever see anything like that?"

At first they brought a long pike pole from the mill, but Mr. Dresden's most strenuous throws into the water brought nothing back but some soft mud. Then he went after one of the mill men, and he waded in as far as he could, but nothing caught the pole. We ate supper, meanwhile, a perfectly wonderful supper, a feast, rather, though all of our minds were more concerned with the tire than with anything else. The fellow became discouraged finally and went to supper, saying he *might* come back. My heart sank. Mr. Householder suggested getting one of the boys from Ladysmith who were fond of swimming, and I thought of Archie. That big tire certainly could not completely disappear in so short a time. It must be somewhere.

The boy came back again and after another attempt to wade, using the pike pole, he threw it aside and swam. Such luck! His knees struck the tire almost instantly and he held it up above the water. We all went wild for a minute, cheered and yelled like a pack of Indians! The relief was so great that we hardly had any sense of reason for a few minutes. "Good as new!" Mr. Householder pronounced the tire, and I was all happiness again.

We walked up to the bunk house, drank some water at the well, took a few pictures and as the mosquitoes began to be annoying, we packed the baskets and started for home. Mr. H. took nine people in his car, leaving me only five. It really was too much, but they all found room to hang on and we reached town in safety, so what need I say? I wouldn't try such a stunt, unless I had to.

To talk over an incident is usually more fun than the incident itself and for an hour or more, we laughed over the "Tire Escapade."

Then I left for home, but only got across the tracks when I met Archie, looking for me, and he persuaded me to turn back and go to a dance with him. He had Ralph Goldsmith's bug and to ride a block is an experience, to ride several miles is nearly torture. The bugs and gnats were so thick that I had to keep my eyes tightly closed. The crowd out at Pepper's was very small, but I had some nice dances. A storm was brewing somewhere and the lightning brought back memories of the other Barn Dance, so we left early.

Archie wouldn't hear about my going home alone at midnight, so I put the car in the garage and we went home together. It was a much pleasanter trip than I have taken over these roads for a long time.

I was afraid Mother would scold me for my escapades, but she was really lovely. The kids, however, made up for it and teased until I became angry. I suppose it's fun to tease and sometimes I think it's almost fun to be teased, but I wasn't in any mood for it.

Sunday, June 16 Sunday was a dreadfully hot day! The kind of day you prepare for a dreadful storm, and we really expected one.

Archie came after me at about nine o'clock and we had a long ride together, longer than I really expected or cared for. But I can say this about him, that he's really different from any boy I know, or perhaps I only know one type.

Monday, June 17 Monday was a sleep day for me, and after my trip home, later than usual, because of a repair job at the garage, I went to sleep and slept the sleep of many postponed nights.

Tuesday, June 18 My last ride with Archie. We went up to the new bridge north of Tony and for a stunt, climbed the steep hill on the other side in the car. It was quite the steepest hill I ever went up or want to go up. No car, but a tip-top one, could have done it. Coming down Archie put on both brakes and even then the car just slid down hill with plenty of speed. I wouldn't exactly care to try the hill again, unless I was sure of both the driver and the car.

Perhaps when I come back Archie may be gone, so he says, at least, and though I can't hardly realize that it might happen, still I suppose I ought to be prepared if he is going. We talked considerably about Ernie. Archie doesn't like them evidently. He told me some things about Roy Hanson that I can hardly believe, and yet I have no way of knowing that they aren't true. I truly believe that Archie would not tell me an untruth, not even if it would favor him by wounding someone else. It makes me think a whole lot, sometimes!

Wednesday, June 19   My last day at the office!! I made out my final report and checked and balanced every column. I know it is correct. I said good-bye to some but since I was coming back on Saturday for a final wind-up, I didn't see everyone. I wish Mr. Rice had been in the office to-day. It means that I must come back on Saturday, though there really is nothing to see him about.

Hooray! No office work until August! I wonder how much Mr. Rice will be able to do on the tabulation sheets and how many times he will almost swear in looking for things I have packed away.

Thursday, June 20   I was mason-tender and what-not to-day. I really helped a little, packing stones and pebbles into the soft concrete. What fun!

I sewed for a little while, but the call of the outdoors was too strong and so I stayed in the new basement nearly all day. The new house is actually materializing!

Friday, June 21   I packed my trunk to-day. Wonder how many things I will discover that I have forgotten, when I reach Stevens Point. The thought of Summer School gives me no joy. I'd much rather stay home.

Friday afternoon is Red Cross afternoon at Sheldon, and we five went down to sew. Pajama suits were that day's work and we all sewed busily, and then, to do a still better, we took four nearly half-finished suits home with us. Marie came to us after we were nearly ready to leave and we joy-rided about Sheldon for nearly half an hour.

Mother was filling out those wretched Registration papers for "Alien Females" and it was such a red-tape question affair that she finally took them home with her to finish without them without Mr. C. Hebard's very *gracious* assistance. Grr-r-r! But I dislike him!

Saturday, June 22   My trunk had to go to-day, in order to reach Stevens Point when I did. Mother locked it with a key and then, somehow, the key wouldn't unlock it again. We tried a knife and a screw-driver and both failed to open it. Time was so short, however, that we couldn't experiment very much, so we took the trunk to Sheldon and I trusted to luck to be able to open it at Stevens Point. Considerable worry went with the trunk—What if I couldn't open it on Monday?

Immediately after dinner Mother, Billy and I went to Ladysmith. There were a score or more of things to attend to and I disposed of them, one after another, as fast as I could. We were at the depot when Tis came. Dear Girl, home at last! And I go to-morrow!

There was no letter from Ernie, though I was so sure of getting one. This is the first week that he hasn't sent at least one letter. I wonder why he doesn't write. Perhaps he knows about my newest affair, but why he should care *one iota* is more than I can see.

I saw Archie for one minute at the garage and incidentally Mother had her first glimpse of him. I said good-bye at least and I'll not soon forget his smile and sparkling brown eyes.

Sunday, June 23   A long day and also a very sad one. We four girls dressed up and took a number of pictures, just to fill a film that Mother had for her "Registration Pictures."

At nine we four went down to Sheldon and sat in the car at the depot, talking until we saw the reflection of the head-light of the limited. It always has the same effect upon me, the brilliant, blinding glare of the head-light, like some fire-eating dragon. It always seems alive.

Mr. Gohlke was also on the train and so, until we reached Gilman, I had company. From then on until Marshfield I became more and more sleepy, my head nodded again and again and part of the time I was hardly awake. "Marshfield!!" Oh, then! no more sleepiness for me. I scanned the faces on the platform and saw Vena and Hub and had a royal welcome from them and a lovely ride on the paved streets. They are no comparison to Rusk County roads.

Monday, June 24 I visited with Max and Eda all morning. Max was his jolly old self and really surprised me by his good appearance. He doesn't look one bit sick and he gets up and walks around each day, though not very much or very long. There doesn't seem to be any doubt about his getting well, just a matter of time and care. I'll be able to send a very encouraging letter to Mother and Dad. Aunt Eda seemed very distant, almost as though she didn't want me. Perhaps I misjudge her, I hope so.

At two o'clock I was at the depot, waiting for the train. Yes, Marshfield is really homelike, though nearly every face is a strange one, very few that I knew.

At Stevens Point everything went smoothly. I went immediately to the Normal and registered and then went to the Director of my department and waited hours, *Hours,* I tell you, for my turn. Four o'clock came and went, five, and then six o'clock. Hunger nearly ate me up and I left at last without making out a study slip and went to the Dormitory. I was scared green to go in, but I did, no one ate me, and a very obliging maid showed me to my room, and then took me to the dining room. I'm at the Matron's table and the dignity of her presence quite overawes me. If this meal is a sample of future meals, I fear I am going to starve. There isn't enough for one of my capacity, and I can hardly change my whole way of living.

I saw Betty Solter as we came up from supper and we had a little quiet reunion in the living room. She is the only soul I know among this crowd of girls and I feel very, very lonesome right now.

My trunk! That was the thing of next greatest concern, because I doubted very much my ability to open it. But my wonderful luck came to my rescue, and after one attempt, the screw-driver turned the lock and it was open. Such a load of worry slipped from my shoulders, tons and tons of worry! "My heart is light, as the winds that blow!" I unpacked my belongings, wrote several letters and went to bed and straight to dreamland.

Wednesday, June 26 Yesterday was a very busy day, but early as possible I made out my study slip, gathered up my books and had two classes. To-day work began in real earnest and there will be no joking about it. One thing has made me very happy and that is the announcement that we are to have only five weeks instead of six, by having classes on Saturday. It makes me genuinely happy, because I'll have a few days at home and still be able to begin work August first. I had to share my good news with someone, so I wrote more letters.

I'm lonesome, Oh, so lonesome, and I want letters so badly that I would almost hire someone to write to me.

Thursday, June 27 A letter came to-day, but instead of making me happy, it plunged me into the depths of misery. It was from Archie—my first—and the one sentence that hummed over and over again in my heart was—"Oh, Lou! I'm *drafted!!*" I never saw anyone so proud and so hurt at being taken by the draft. He has tried so often to enlist, that he almost lost enthusiasm, and now —!

My heart was aching so, that I couldn't write a decent letter. It cried out heart ache in every word, but it was as I felt and I sent it. I came to the verge of tears a dozen times that afternoon, but each time I fought them back.

I was in the mood for confidence and when Betty came to take me for a walk, I told her as much of my trouble as I could. But, how much I'd rather be walking with Archie himself.

Friday, June 28   No letters! School work is beginning to crowd dreadfully. My mental depression of yesterday is acting like a load that I cannot shake off.

I enjoyed the thrill of being locked out with Betty, but Miss Wilson came and opened the door for us and nothing dreadful happened. Me locked out! Who would imagine I could be so wicked.

Saturday, June 29   No Letters! The phrase is growing monotonous. But truly the feeling of lonesomeness is growing more and more and I am all eyes for letters. Since the session has been shortened a week, this is our first Saturday school and in every way it is like any other day. Everyone is remarking about the "long week." To me it seems like ages. I feel as though I had been here a month or more. If only I had some letters time would go so much faster. I found another friend to-day, Jessie LeRoux, and we had a nice talk and walk that evening. It is like meeting home-folks to talk with someone from our county.

Sunday, June 30   I awoke to find it raining heavily and steadily. Nothing could have been worse for my mental state. I had some work to occupy my thoughts but how time did drag! I wasn't tired enough to sleep and still didn't feel like doing anything. A stranger in a crowd—I can sympathize with a lonesome person. The deepest, loneliest woods couldn't make me feel as lonesome and homesick as this crowd of girls who were all strangers

to me and did not seem to care to know me. I don't remember that I said three whole sentences to anyone the whole day. Yes, I'm truly homesick, lonesome and lonely.

Monday, July 1   *And no letters to-day!* I am nearly desperate. Has everyone forgotten me or is it only to me that time drags so slowly and each day seems like a week and the weeks like years? I've threatened to go home to-night if no letters come, and if another day goes by without letters in my pigeon-hole, I'll be on No. 17 when it leaves Stevens Point Wednesday morning. I wonder if our soldier boys are as crazy to get mail as I am.

Tuesday, July 2   Mail at last! And this morning I saw Jessie Sergeant at the Normal. My little cup of joy is nearly running over. One letter was from Mother, one from Toots and, last but not least, one was from Archie. He is much more cheerful and really seems glad he's going. All my homesickness vanished with the sight of mail. Everything is busy at home, and I'm afraid I'm almost a stranger when I come home for a brief stay.

But right now I'm truly happy again.

Wednesday, July 3   A letter came from Ruthie and I answered at once. Just a business letter in a way, but it was a letter from a friend and that's a whole lot.

Mr. Spindler requested the students in his department to present their credentials and so I took that opportunity of asking about the value of my standings. Just think!! They will accept every one of passing standing. He told me to write at Madison this fall and then write to him for more information this fall. He says I can finish Normal in about half a year plus another summer school. The advice was so good I feel twice as good as yesterday, if such a thing could be possible. I'll have my State Certificate before "Miss Tate" even though I fail at Madison, which I hope won't happen.

Thursday, July 4   The Fourth! Nothing here reminded me of the fact, however. No cannon, no crackers, no flags, no bands, no people, nothing to inspire one. I couldn't arouse any more than just a faint spark of patriotism. It rained nearly all day and the main idea of everyone was to kill time.

Jessie had supper with me, a picnic supper, out on the porch, and on the way home with her, she told me that Loren Trotter was coming to spend Sunday with her. A wild idea seized me to ask Archie to come also, the boldest idea I've ever had, I know, but I was pretty sure he wanted to come, and was only waiting to be asked. I scribbled just a few lines and walked to the Post Office in a steady rain to mail it. We are speculating much whether and when the boys will come. Archie will have time to answer, so I'll know whether to look for him. Jessie and I are making great plans to escape the matron's eyes for one night. Archie says I'm S-M-A-R-T, so I'll have ample opportunity to demonstrate my ability. I wonder if I can live until Sunday!

Saturday, July 6   Of course, a letter came from the dear boy, "I'll see you Sunday." I think he said it six times at least, so I really believe he will come.

Jessie and I have planned a picnic dinner and supper down at the river, and with the movies, it ought to almost fill the day. We are going to pack our own lunches and Jessie is coming to stay with me Saturday night and I will stay with her Sunday night, thus giving me the privilege of staying out as late as I choose.

We've done everything we could think of to prepare for the day. I bought a middy, for picnic's sake, it's so much more comfortable than a silk waist. We earnestly hoped and prayed for good weather, but during the

The Normal School in Stevens Point where Louise attended summer school in 1918.

night I was quite sure I heard it raining and my heart sank and I wanted very much to cry. I couldn't help it, however, and finally I went to sleep.

Sunday, July 7 We didn't quite get up at day-break, but not much later. When the breakfast gong rang, we were ready, all dressed and dolled up. I am sure we were both equally nervous and excited, and I know I couldn't keep my mind on anything except the clock and Archie. From 8:30 on, I waited for a phone call, but none came, and at 9:30, Jessie persuaded me to walk down Main and perhaps we might meet the boys. Mental telepathy must have made us decide to go, because at the corner of the Normal grounds we met them, all smiles. I was just too happy to talk. We went to the Dorm first and then to fix our lunch at Jessie's boarding place and shortly after eleven we were on our way to the river.

I couldn't tell you all we said and talked about. I didn't care about Jessie and Loren, and so we left them as soon as we could gracefully. There was so much to say during that short day and most of it was only for us, so we naturally parted.

The war and Archie's going were on our minds, of course, and we talked about that almost constantly. After supper, we ran away from Jessie, did it deliberately, too, because neither of us were comfortable in their presence and Archie said he actually despised Loren. We crossed the railroad bridge and after sitting by the side of the old dam for a while we went uptown, had an ice-cream and then went to the movies. It was so warm there I nearly smothered and we left early and walked up to the Normal. And then we really talked.

I wanted to be real brave and keep smiling to the very last, but when Archie began to talk about being in France, the dangers of being a machine-gunner, and that it might be a very long time before we'd see each other again, I couldn't keep the tears back and I had a real crying spell. It scared Archie a little and he said I was not to feel one bit sorry for him, because he was

Loren Trotter and Archie in Stevens Point visit Jessie Sergeant and Louise before the men leave for the service.

glad and happy that he was going. He can say it, all he wants to, but I know his heart aches as much as mine and I do not want to see him go. It won't keep him here, however, so I dried my tears and laughed. Archie's only very human after all, but I know him better after this day than I ever did before. In some ways I like him less and in some ways a whole lot more. He's been the nicest to me of any lover I ever had, and I'll never be anything less than a good friend at least.

At 12:30 we were at the depot, looking for Jessie and Loren. She didn't come; but Loren finally came in. Oh, I do so hate a public good-bye, it is so hard to say what you want to. Archie didn't say anything, but I could feel him tremble and I felt too numb and dead to say much. Just "Good-bye," a squeeze of his hand and I turned away. I couldn't look again.

Perhaps I may never see him again and that dreadful thought sends a chill right through my heart. I will never let that idea come near me again and the only ones I'll let my heart hold will be about his return when the war is over.

Monday, July 8   There never was anyone quite so sleepy, dead-to-the-world, and heartsick as I, unless perhaps it was Jessie. I lived over every word of yesterday and again and again my mind would wander away from Spin's dictation and think of something Archie had said. Time and again I almost wrote his name, instead of the psychological names in the lesson.

Miss Rowe only remarked that they had missed me Sunday, and I only smiled for an answer. She might have said more if she had known more but I didn't care to enlighten her. I slept all afternoon and the nap greatly improved my brain power, but took some valuable time from my studying.

"He who dances must pay the piper!"

Wednesday, July 10   In all I received three letters today, quite splendid. I had one letter from home, a very short one from Vicy and a very real love letter from Archie. I had written and sent one to him in the morning, but when this one came, I had to answer it at once, and Archie had two letters in one day from me. That's going some, I say.

Hazel C. and I went for a long walk, incidentally, of course, to mail our letters.

I haven't felt very well for two days and it makes the work seem more of a drag than ever before.

Thursday, July 11   Perhaps a brief little list would schedule all of the events of this day. They are a queer jumble, but no one item is very much more important than another. Here they are:

1. Took two pictures of the Normal.

2. Had a card from Sarah. She says she may come to see me here. Hope she does.

3. All changed places at tables. Hazel C. sits beside me. I like my table much more than Miss Rowe's. It's mean to say it, but 'tis true.

4. Last but never least, I wrote letters. Not a day goes by but what I write at least one and many days I've sent three. There are very few days when I get three, however, and many days when I do not find any in my pigeonhole.

Friday, July 12   Another good-bye letter came from Archie this morning. He doesn't say so very much, but I can easily see that the very ground seems to be knocked out from under his feet. Boys who haven't quite his spirit would actually go all to pieces, I believe.

I have conscientiously tried to analyze my feeling for Archie to-night. I like to be with him and I really like him but I cannot feel that I love him. A still, small voice within me says I am pretending that I care for him, and I almost believe the voice. But in answer to that, Miss Stearns said in Gen. Ed. the other day, "The least we can do for our boys is to show our affection for them in every way possible," and I am not ashamed that I feel a genuine liking for Archie. I know he likes me, in fact, I believe he likes me more than I want him to, but I don't see how I could have stopped him. Friendships always begin so easily and I have known that Archie cared for me for a long time. A dozen little words and actions made me feel it, even before I could put the thought into words.

I shall not neglect writing to him and if he never comes back, a thought which brings a lump into my throat and a dreadful chill over my heart, I shall never regret our friendship. He's the best pal I ever had, and when I think of Archie, I shall think only of him and forget Ernie completely.

Saturday, July 13 Two finals to-day! They gave me a pretty good scare of brain-fog. I went up right after dinner and found my papers already marked—95 in History of Education and 93 in General Methods. I am happy and feel that the studying I've done is well worth its effort.

No mail to-day, but I am not one bit lonesome or unhappy. Even the thought of Archie going does not make my heart ache. I cannot help him or keep him, so I am going to smile like a true American.

Jessie is going home to-night in order to see Loren once more before he goes but I have no desire to be in Ladysmith. I haven't money enough to go, and I know it would mean a scolding from Mother, so I wouldn't go even if I did want to. But I really do not want to. Good-byes are hard to say anywhere and hardest of all in public. I couldn't do it again.

Sunday, July 14 A long, long day as usual. I called on some of the girls, and am making a real effort to get acquainted with some before I go. It seems a shame that we are just becoming acquainted and then the session comes to a close. I read until I could read no more and wrote letters until I hated the sight of the pen. I have written one to Archie but haven't mailed it, and each

day I'm going to write one and seal it immediately and when he sends me his address, he'll receive such an amount of mail that it will take a day to read it all.

Monday, July 15 Two letters came this morning from two people who might really quarrel if they met face to face—one from Archie and one from Ernie. Archie's was written Saturday I suppose and was a rather brave letter. He will go through Stevens Point Monday night, but I cannot manage to be there to see the train go through.

The letter from Ernie was the first in three weeks and after the almost assured resolution that he was

Louise along the Wisconsin River in Stevens Point during Archie's visit, July 7, 1918.

never going to write again, it came as a perfect shock. It was quite a sincere apology for not writing and I suppose I can believe him. The whole letter centered about his sentence of his shore leave hours and it seems to say quite clearly that he would like to come to see me. I've been arguing with myself ever since I received the letter whether I'll ask him to come or not. There's no question about my wishing to see him. The main and only difficulty is in managing the late hours at the Dorm. It's almost impossible. I might fib a little and tell Miss Rowe that I had gone to Marshfield, but it's hardly proper. No, I don't believe I'll even ask him to come. Perhaps, however, he doesn't want to.

Tuesday, July 16 A short letter from Archie came, the last one he will send me from Ladysmith. "Only a few hours and I'll leave here." It wasn't one bit happy and it makes me feel very blue. I know he looked for me at the depot and I disappointed him, though really not because I wanted to.

My decision of yesterday has undergone a change and I believe I will ask Ernie to come and spend the last Sunday with me. Then he will leave on one train and I will leave on the next, and there will be no late hours to manage. I'll have shaken the Dorm dust from my feet and be my free, very independent self again. Yes, I think I'll write him.

Wednesday, July 17 The constant wear and tear on nerves and vitality is showing its effect on all the girls. I believe we are the deadest bunch that ever attended summer school. The work load is very heavy and each day the weather seems just a bit hotter and more uncomfortable. I feel more fagged and tired each day and the most comforting fact is the knowledge that we have only one more week of it. Thank Heavens, I say!!

Thursday, July 18 If anything I am more tired to-night than last night. I wonder if self-pity adds to our weariness. I really believe it does. Let's try a mind cure! Presto Change-o! I am not tired at all. (But all the same I *am*.)

Had a dandy letter from Toots, and also some of the pictures we took before I left, generally good, except one of me which I wanted most of all. I am more or less of a hoodoo, or else am very hypercritical. Both perhaps.

Friday, July 19 An eventful day, I must say, and so much good news that a great deal of my tiredness has vanished. Mail time is the bright spot of the whole day and I felt it more to-day than any other almost. One letter came from Archie, a short little note written at Columbus, Ohio. 3000 men arrived at the camp during the night he says, but he will only remain there temporarily and I should not answer until he writes again. Everyone is new and strange, of course, but he says he really likes it so I'm glad. I answered his letter, but I didn't send it. His pile of mail is steadily growing and by the time I get his address, it will be a *real* letter.

A joyful letter came from Mr. Rice informing me that I had a raise in my salary. It isn't necessary to say that I'm happy about that, in fact, it is already due me, and if I hadn't been given a little raise, I believe I would have refused the position. But now everything is jolly and that extra ten dollars per month will look pretty good to me.

Jessie came back after dinner and brought the pictures we took on that never-to-be-forgotten Sunday. I spoiled several pictures, but most of them were very good. I look funny on them, which is only natural, but the one I took of Archie is just fine. I'll send them to him in another "dormant" letter.

My hesitation of the last few days as to whether I will ask Ernie to come to Stevens Point has at last moved to one side and I decided I *would* ask him, and to clinch that decision I immediately wrote the letter. It was a difficult letter to write, and after it was written

I had half a mind to tear it up. I wonder, I really wonder what he thinks of me. I'd give a whole lot to know what's in his heart.

Saturday, July 20   I mailed the fateful letter. "The die is cast." "What's done is done." Truly I act as though I had done some awful crime that I'd be hanged for if someone caught me.

Monday, July 22   A card came from Vicy to-day. "I leave for camp on the 22nd." It was mailed on the 18th, but hadn't reached me until the very day itself. I knew, of course, that Vicy would be going soon, and Archie told me that Toots said he would leave in a few days, but all the same the news was a shock to me. I couldn't quite gather up my thoughts, and settle them on my school work. I wonder how Mother feels and whether Vicy wrote and prepared her a little. I do wish he had come home for a week when he knew he was going. I haven't seen him since Christmas time. But wishing is useless, so I'll try to make the best of it. I hope he writes soon and tells us where he is. Dear Soldier Boy!

Wednesday, July 24   We are nearing the end of summer school, only a few more days and this strenuous session will be over.

Toots sent my long-looked-for-money to-day. I had been living on one cent for almost a week. Even my stamps were gone and I was beginning to seriously contemplate robbing a bank. Now I feel fairly rich again, except when the fact looms up before me that my indebtedness is steadily growing and growing. I'll never reach that happy time when my purse will always have some money in it, even on the day before pay-day.

Thursday, July 25   The answer to my fateful letter came this noon. I was almost too excited to open it. "I can't make connections at Chicago," and so he isn't coming. I don't hardly believe his excuse and yet I won't doubt his word until I have reason to. His proposition of coming to Milwaukee is out of order entirely, first and foremost because I haven't money enough, and secondly, because I'd be scared to death to come to such a big city and not have anyone to meet me.

Though his letter is a disappointment, yet I am not sorry and there is just a little feeling of relief in my heart that he didn't come. Perhaps it is an unjust thought, but right now Archie is uppermost in my mind. Am I very wicked, I wonder?

Friday, July 26   I know now where Archie is. He has sent me his address and a long letter and emphasizes the fact that he is looking and waiting most anxiously for mail. He shall have it, too. There are six letters waiting to be sent to him, they will make quite a package of messages.

Last night and the night before I sat up very, very late, writing on my last resumes and my two theses, and it seems as though the general nervousness and tension has almost worn me out. This afternoon, only a little matter about returning a physics book when I wanted it to review, brought on a nervous spasm that actually frightened me. I broke down completely and my heart seemed to be in a mad race to get away from itself. It beat so fast and hard that I was soon all worn out, I had no strength to do anything. The girls brought my supper up to me and everyone was so sympathetic, I couldn't be sick very long. About nine o'clock Jessie phoned and asked me to come down to Burr's. I didn't feel like making the extra exertion to dress and walk over there, but it was so unpleasant being alone that I gathered my faltering strength and dressed up sufficiently to call on Jessie. We talked for almost an hour and when I went home at ten o'clock I felt very much better and my heart had stopped its wild racing. I hope I do not have another such experience.

Saturday, July 27   One last physics final to-day! I have packed my trunk and have everything ready to leave on the noon train. There is one constant chorus of "Good-bye," "Good luck to you," "Don't forget to write," etc. I don't see how Miss Rowe can keep her composure through all this excitement. I believe I would be ready to fly and snap at everyone who talked to me.

I mailed Archie's package of letters, and then continued my rather slow walk to the depot. I am still weak from yesterday's heart spasm. The train was very late and very crowded and I was hot and tired when we finally reached Marshfield. There was scarcely time to go up to Aunt Eda's, so I went directly to the Omaha Depot, stopping just a moment at the garage to shake hands with Max and Otto. I also saw Gustav Poppe, he's working for Max now, and Hub has likewise left the veneer factory for the garage.

I saw no familiar faces in Marshfield; it is a strange town to me in reality. I have always called it "Home Town" and have spoken of it fondly, but that feeling has undergone a very decided change to-day. Ladysmith is "Home Town" now, and comes first in my mind. It's there that I know the people and they know me and it's also there that my work and perhaps my future lies.

I had a glad welcoming at Neillsville, at least. Theo, Ella, Virginia and Aunt Cal met me. It was really quite a delegation and I was immensely honored. I enjoy visiting relatives where you are made a great deal of, and that is very true at Neillsville. Aunt Cal and Grandma are really going out west this fall. Aunt Cal says she is never coming back again, but Grandma will only stay a year, I think.

I wanted very much to see Rudolph and Lydia, but there was hardly time to go out there to see them. But fortunately, just as Aunt Cal and I were on our way to Aunt Emma's I saw a Ford go by and in it I was sure I saw Rudolph, and a little later, uptown we found Lydia. I had a talk with them even if I did not go to the country. I saw more people that I knew in Neillsville than I did in Marshfield.

Monday, July 29   Aunt Cal is coming home with me for a week's visit, and at 1:30 we were on our way to Marshfield. I was so anxious to get home that I could hardly think of anything else. I saw Mrs. Heisler in the garden and had a really nice chat with her. I told all about our farm and the wonderful new house, and about Dad and Mother and Vicy and about us kids. It was better than a letter to talk to her and I hope it was as pleasant to her as it was to me.

Hub took us out for a ride after supper and during that time I saw more of the country surrounding Marshfield than I did in all the fourteen years we lived there. Not that I missed very much, but I had my first real view of the Asylum from the road. It is more like some old castle than an Institution, with its walls almost covered with beautiful ivy.

Tuesday, July 30   We had a little sleep and at 2:00 we were down at the depot again, this time really homeward bound. It was an unusually cold night for July, came dangerously near the freezing point, I am sure. Toots and Bob met me, but to punish me for not coming a day sooner, they parked the car near Dietze's and forced me to walk those two blocks, bent nearly double under the weight of Vicy's music and instruments. I was almost angry, but I know I had made them come down on Monday all for nothing. Peace was quickly restored and we were on our way home.

They have given me a very strange and not entirely pleasant task for to-day. I am to be jitney for a funeral at Ladysmith and I do not like the prospect. I was tired and one extra trip up to Niepow's corner did not improve my mental state. At 12:00 I started off again, to find that my passengers had been waiting almost an hour for me. Poor management!! At Ladysmith, I did find time to see Mr. Rice and a few of my old pals, Mabel, Irma and Alice Johnson. This little bit of visiting was done as a side issue but I am glad I ran away from the funeral for that length of time. The ride out to the cemetery was one of the worst I ever had. We followed the hearse—a very foolish arrangement—and had to go in low nearly the whole way. The car ahead of me was working poorly and when it happened that we had to stop on an up-hill slope, they had to back down, in order to get a new start. At one place it was quite exciting for a minute, when they started to back right into me. I nearly lost my head for an instant, and came nearly going backward and forward the same instant. Several times I killed the engine and I'm sure the men in the car considered me a wretchedly poor driver, as I very probably am. The whole trip will be a charity affair, I suppose, but since it was partly a business trip for me, I do not feel mean about it.

There was one letter from Archie waiting for me, and one came to-day. He hasn't received my letters, and his one great comment is on the terrible heat. He hates the company he is with, Russian and Polish, and I think he is quite lonesome and homesick. All I can do is to write letters and I have let almost half a week slip by without sending one. My love for him can't be very sincere, or I would surely write more often. I'm sorry I've neglected him, however.

Wednesday, July 31 In sheer desperation, as Mother would say, we girls decided to pick enough berries to-day to fill the car, or more exactly all the pails the car would hold. It was my first berrying day of the season and naturally I wanted to make a good showing. I did, too, and picked my fair share of the forty quarts we brought home. We made it a day of confidences also, and I am glad that no one else heard the things we confided to each other. Soldier boys and lovers seem to be uppermost in our minds and there will surely be four weddings as soon as the war is over, if our words are to be taken seriously. Queer that we should all have the same romantic ideas, but it must be in the atmosphere.

There was another letter from Archie to-day, a very blue, unhappy letter. He must have been in a very ugly mood when he wrote it. No mail has reached him as yet, and I *do* so wish he would get some soon. I know he would feel so much better if he had some letters, even though his arms are very sore from the shots. I felt so sorry for him that I almost wanted to weep, but it wouldn't help him any and the girls would laugh, so I refrained from showing my feelings.

Saturday, August 3 Moving Day! Mother doesn't wholly approve of our going back to our rooms over Fritz's but I cannot find any others that would seem so homelike to me, and very few rooms are provided with heat and light as these are. I am going back again even if Mother does object a little. I want to be independent.

The War news is so splendid this afternoon that I could shout with joy. People everywhere were smiling and talking about it. The dear Yankee boys in France are certainly hammering away at the Huns and more and more it seems that the possibility of our boys being home for Christmas might really come true. Why can't the prayer of almost the whole world be answered!

Two letters came to-day, the two that so often come on the same day. Both letters made me very happy. Archie's sang joy from every page, he has my letters at last and I am so very, very glad. It was the first, the very *first* mail he received since he left home almost three weeks ago. Ernie's was in answer to my refusal to come to Milwaukee, an apology for asking me and a promise that he would come to Madison while I was there. Of course this letter couldn't help but make me a little bit happier than I was before. Archie can't quite push Ernie from my thoughts, though I could not say which one I like the most and I hope I will not have to decide that for a long time, if ever.

Toots and I invested in a beauty of a service flag for Vicy, a big one and we are *so* proud of it, almost as proud as we are of the dear boy himself. His belongings came this afternoon and it was almost like opening a treasure chest to open the two suitcases. He doesn't know what idolizing sisters he has, I am sure.

Laura had a long talk with us at Ladysmith and it seems almost sisterly to be with her. She imagines a whole lot more about Archie and me than there is really grounds for, and it is very difficult for me to say anything without making matters much more complicated. I am going out to LaBerge's some night next week at Laura's invitation. Freddie is home and I have had one glimpse of him but that is all, I could never like him as well as I like his big brother.

Sunday, August 4   A hotter day than this I cannot remember. It was actually suffocating. We had a last little load of hay to haul in and Dad decided to do it even if it was Sunday, and so, as usually happens at such times, we were all in our haying togs, curl-papers and such, when the minister came. There was nothing to do but make the best of it, but to dress in the heat of up-stairs was nearly enough to wilt us all, and I was nearly boiled done when I was sufficiently dressed to come down.

I don't like to go to church. There isn't anything about it that appeals to my spiritual nature, and it is only because I ought to go that I do. The kids are preparing several songs for Mission Festival, which will be held in two weeks but I am glad that I will not be there. Wicked thought! I suppose I ought to be ashamed of it.

Monday, August 5   Here goes for a write-up of my first week at the office, a long, rather lonesome week, with an unusual ending, at least. Everyone seemed glad to see me again and there was a general welcoming at the Court House and elsewhere. (Such ink! I am nearly wild with blotting up the drops.) Ruthie called on me

in the afternoon and we had a nice little chat, almost under O. E.'s nose.

Monday night I set to work with all my stored-up energy, to make our rooms fit for living in. They have been used for the painters for a store-room and rest-room and are as dirty as rooms can get. I didn't know where to begin or what to do first, but hot water seemed the first requisite, so I filled the tea-kettle and every pail and pan and made ready for a grand scrubbing. The oil-stove gave me a dreadful fright, and for a minute I thought it was going to blow up or burn up. The flames almost touched the ceiling and roared like a furnace and in sheer desperation, I poured water on them and put them out, though perhaps it was the wrong way to do it. The room was dark with smoke, but the flames were out at least, and after a time I stopped trembling and lighted them again.

I worked until after ten, dressed in as little as possible, for it was almost too warm for such strenuous scrubbing and sweeping and washing as I went through. But at the end of three or more hours, I had the rooms fairly clean and after a bath, I curled up on the couch and slept the sleep of the just, part of the time only, because the noises of the street were new to me and I could not shut them out.

Tuesday was another day of greetings. Ruthie called me up by phone and I have promised to go out there Wednesday night.

Threse met me on the street and captured me for supper. It was quite a reunion to talk with her. As far as writing is concerned, she is a piker, but I can readily forgive her. She has had a very interesting summer and has worn unionalls for part of the time. Brave girl!

Our two days of glorious weather turned into an all day rain and it never ceased for a minute from about four o'clock in the afternoon until late next morning. Archie has written nearly every day and since Monday I have sent him a letter each day. He needs letters and I wish he would not have to wait so long until they reach him. I have been neglectful in writing to him but not because I didn't want to write. His letter this morning had one sentence in it that hurt me very much. Perhaps I deserved it but it hurt all the same.

Freddie came to get me from the Court House but Mercy! how I dislike him. I can hardly talk to him and as far as being in the mood to enjoy his teasing—Nix! I will quarrel with him first. The whole family must have prepared a list of catch questions and I hardly knew how to answer them. I don't doubt in the least that I answered some all contrary, and I know I twisted up some of Archie's stories.

Ruth and Laura and I went to an ice-cream social and enjoyed some real "war-time ice-cream," quite sugarless. I met Genevieve Weekly who evidently is a very dear chum of the girls. I also met the Austins and enjoyed some jazz music and dancing on their lovely porch. I was too tired to really enjoy dancing and was quite ready to go home when Freddie came after me.

Laura tried hard to corner me that night and did her best to coax me to say what Archie was to me. "Is there anything serious between you two?" and when, of course, I told her, "No, of course not. We're only very good friends," she just said, "I'm sorry, I hoped you were more than that." But she imagines more than she ought to, I fear, and in the family's eyes it is all settled. It makes me smile and I wonder what Archie will think and say when I tell him what they have said.

Freddie and Laura took me back to Ladysmith Thursday morning. Freddie is a perfect idler about home, and from what I have seen he doesn't do one tiny bit of work. I wonder whether Archie would be like that. I know he loved the farm more than the others did and it would have been his in the future, and will still be his when the "dear boy comes home."

There was no letter from him this morning and the one sentence in his last letter hurts more than ever. I wonder whether he is trying to punish me for not writing oftener. I hope he feels inclined to write again when he gets my Ladysmith letters.

Carrie shared my supper with me and we had an enjoyable time of it. She is a nice little girl, but I would like her better if I knew less about her. She does some very unconventional things and Archie has said some things about her that are not very nice. Fellows are her only topic of conversation, and she has a new one every once in a while. L. Bliffert is gone again, though I believe she really liked him. It usually happens that the girls who capture another's fellow lose him again just as quickly and easily as they got him. Am I as bad as they are? Not usually, I hope.

Friday and again no letter. I hope he isn't sick with the dreadful heat. I worry just a little, but it can't help him any if he is sick, but I *do* wish he would write.

No letter from Ernie and unless one comes to-morrow, I won't know what he intends to do for our proposed Madison meeting.

Saturday and no letters. I am more than a little discouraged. I cannot live without letters and if ever I would be forced to live a month, or even less, without one letter, I really don't believe I would be entirely sane at the end of that time. It might help to know that letters were on the way to me but if I couldn't get them, I don't believe I could stand it.

A great surprise came this morning when Laura phoned and said Archie was coming home on Sunday. He had telegraphed just that much and no more. It has put me in a state of mild excitement, but not as much as it might be. I *do* want to see him but I can't hardly ask Laura to tell him that, and I am going to leave Sunday night and if he comes as an escort for the body of the soldier who died at Camp Hancock and is to be buried on Sunday, I don't suppose he will possibly find time to come down to see me. I hate to make a public display by going up to see him. What ought I do?! He may go back that same night and then we'll at least see each other on the way to Fond du Lac.

The girls had half promised to come after me on Saturday, but no one came and I felt a little bit blue. Laura and Ruth talked with me awhile in the evening and I judge by things only half said that some family quarrel has taken place at home. Laura wouldn't tell me anything, nor did I ask very much but it must be rather serious by what little she has said.

I have told her all I dare to tell Archie but perhaps she won't say it, or may say it in a different way from what I would. Yes, I am upset and unsettled. I wish I knew what I ought to do and also what would be proper to do. I know that I want to see him, but perhaps he is still a little angry at me and doesn't want to come. I can only wait and see.

The kids met me at Sheldon with a perfect jubilee of joy. "The cellar is *all* done! No more cement! No more gravel! Oh, Lou!" I'm glad with them that it is done, but they can realize it more because they have worked *so* hard at it. As far as the house is concerned, I am the "lazy man" of the family, not that I am less interested than the rest are, but I am not at home as much as the kids. I wish I could work in two places at the same time and then I would feel a whole lot better about the house. But all the wishing in the world wouldn't make that come true, so I must do all I can, when I can.

Sunday, August 11   I can't remember when I have spent a longer, more lonesome day than this Sunday. To celebrate the completion of the cellar, the whole family celebrated. The girls went for a picnic with Brown's. Dad, Mother and Billie went up to Aunt Eda's

Archie and his sister Ruth prepare for a trip during his short stay at home in 1918. Archie had been the military escort for the body of Ralph Roehrborn from Camp Hancock, Georgia. Roehrborn was a victim of the influenza epidemic.

and Bob went bee-tree hunting and poor little me didn't do anything but wish myself somewhere else. There was a grand rush and scramble when Clarence Brown and a friend of his came sooner than the girls expected, and I helped, as a big sister should, fill sandwiches and frost cake, until I was nearly as excited as they were. I wanted very much to go with them, but it wouldn't have been very wise to go just when I should be packing for my trip, and what was much more truthful, I really

Fred and Archie LaBerge in August 1918. Fred was on leave from the Air Force.

looked for Archie to come down. In fact, I looked for him so hard that I couldn't keep my eyes off the road and I was actually drawn out to the gate again and again. Several cars went by and set my heart a-fluttering but Archie did not come. I tried to talk down the ache in my heart, he was very tired and very busy and very glad to be home and I was soon in a "don't-care-much-anyway" mood. I wonder if that is self-control or heartlessness, or both. But the hurt was there all the time, though it was covered pretty deep with reasoning and excuses.

Freddie was on the limited when I got on, and told me that Archie would leave again on Tuesday. He didn't say much more about him, except that he was dead tired and talked less with the family than he would have liked to. The funeral took away the greater part of the day. He, too, tried to find out a whole lot about us and insinuated much more than he ought to. I don't like him any more than I did before. He is so self-important and spoiled, and he has such a big-head, that I was really glad when he excused himself and went into the smoker. He was very good to me, even though I couldn't appreciate his kindness.

Connections at Fond du Lac were very close, so close they were actually thrilling, but with some running and puffing and considerable excitement we finally got on the right train. We had gained almost six hours and it was well worth the effort.

Monday, August 12   I was so sleepy and so tired when we got to Madison that I could hardly keep my eyes open. I took a taxi and went straight to the Capitol Hotel, the only "homey" place I know in Madison. I slept for several hours, but my room being on the east side, it became so warm that I was actually suffering when I woke up. Heat always makes me think of Archie, and always will make me think of him.

I found a cool place in the lounging room and wrote several letters, one to Archie, one to Ernie, one to

Mother and one to Irma N. They were all hurry-up, rush-order letters, but I felt so much better after writing them.

The convention met at 2:00 and my first questions about the exams gave me the worst heart ache I ever felt. They do not begin until Tuesday, and here I could have spent one whole day at Ladysmith and seen Archie. It makes me nearly wild to think of it all and I vow I will never let him know, because it would hurt him more than it hurts me. If he never comes back, it will not matter and if he does, we can laugh at it as a joke!

I had the most staggering surprise this evening. Just as I left the dining room, someone behind me said, "Why, Louise!" and when I whirled around I saw Amy Cox behind me. I never was so completely surprised in all my life. Louis is going to leave for Washington to-morrow and she is spending the last days here with him. She said something about Lawrence driving his car home to-morrow, but Louis himself came up just then and I talked with both for a few minutes before they went in to supper. There will be one more wedding "when the war is over and the boys come back."

Tuesday, August 13   If yesterday was hot, to-day was hotter. It was simply dreadful and to sit in the Senate Chamber and write while the sun was beating down upon the roof and the air was simply stifling was almost as much as I could do. I thought of the boys in Camp again and again and that thought did more to brace me up than anything else could have done. I discovered that several of my Normal Credits will be accepted, Physics and Algebra both, and I am so very relieved that I feel almost giddy.

I met Miss Jordan and Miss Donaldson and now I won't be a lonely little lamb anymore. Just at supper time a terrific storm came up, a real, old-fashioned kind, with the rain coming down in sheets and the lightning doing zig-zag stunts across the sky. The relief from the terrible heat of the last two days was simply wonderful, however, and I know I will be able to sleep to-night.

The heart-ache of yesterday has all vanished and I feel almost happy again. It doesn't pay to mope and mourn about the past and even though it hurts still, I am not going to think of it again. I want Archie to enjoy himself while he is home, to have the very best time he possibly can, and if I am not there to help him have the good time, I really hope somebody will be there. I hope he misses me a little bit but not so much that it makes him unhappy.

Wednesday, August 14   Letters came to-day, but none from Ernie, as I expected. There was one from Vicy and a little note from Irma. This is my first from Vic and I am mighty glad to get it. His letter seems rather conflicting, in one place he says "when I get your letters" as though he hadn't had one from us yet, and at the close he says "if you send a box," just as though in answer to my question of what he would like. At any rate he wants some soap, tooth-picks and a jack-knife. Of course, he shall have them, just as soon as I can get them for him.

I suppose Archie is on his way or else is leaving to-night. I wish a lot of wishes but they can't be answered, so there is no need of wishing, absolutely none.

The convention is good but I see only snatches of it between my exams and from what I hear others say I see only the poorest parts. I really do not seem to be able to concentrate my thoughts on anything serious. I am almost ashamed of myself, but I can't seem to do otherwise.

Thursday, August 15   This is my last day of writing and the tension has made me very tired. No mail came and I could not help but feel a little lonely and just a little bit blue. It seems to require a definite effort of will to keep myself cheerful and as soon as I relax and let myself go a little, I am unhappy and cannot help but see things in rather a moody way.

Miss Jordan was not feeling well to-day and decided to go home to-night. I do not care very much, for although she has been company for me, I cannot really like her. She is a nice old maid but sometimes I do not like the things she says nor the way in which she says them. I went down to the depot with her, to pass the evening and I feel quite sorry for myself now. I am really lonely.

Finale To My Second Book:

Another book filled, My Diary, another part of my life completed, and Oh! how much you differ from your predecessor. How little I dreamed what all would be recorded in you! The last Book ended so happily and you, Little Book, end with such suspense and longing as I never imagined I could feel. My sincerest, most earnest prayer is that though the Third Little Book begins in clouds and unhappiness, it may close with all my prayers answered! *Amen!*

My Diary, Third Book, Beginning August 15, 1918

Friday, August 16 At Madison: This begins where my Book II stopped and my very thoughts are carried from that day over to this.

A slow, steady rain fell and the fact that no mail came this noon made me really blue. The Convention adjourned at about 11:30, and the very best part of the whole week came at the very end. By special request, the matter of charging expenses for the use of our own car was discussed, and the result was all that I could wish it to be. I am allowed mileage, ten cents per mile, and that is going to help some toward paying for the wear and tear upon the car itself. Yes, I am glad that I stayed for Friday.

Why doesn't Ernie write? If I don't hear from him to-morrow I am going home Sunday noon. I can easily make connections that way and still get home by Monday morning, for I simply must be there in time for work then. Yes, I'll almost hate Ernie if he doesn't write and doesn't come.

I went down to the office at about five o'clock and there was a letter from him, forwarded from Sheldon. He says he's coming if he possibly can and I am to meet him. Everything seems to be coming out so nicely that my heart is light again. The long day is soon ended and to-morrow will pass quickly while I am with Miss Crow. I listened for the ten o'clock train and imagined twenty-four hours hence. I could almost see him and hear him, and I could hardly sleep for thinking what all I would tell him and ask him.

Saturday, August 17 A cold, damp, cloudy day as only days near the lake can be. I killed time all morning. I wrote a letter to Archie and then tried to put him out of my mind completely.

At noon I went down for dinner, and incidentally to get any mail there might be. Yes, there was a letter from Ernie and as I read it my heart went down, down, until I really had to go after it and bring it back by main force. There was a very strong probability of his not coming and he even said that I was not to meet him. I hoped against hope all day, unwilling to let one disappointing thought creep into my mind.

At 1:45 I left for Evansville and at 2:30 I was with Miss Crow. In the short while we were together it was impossible to think of all we wanted to say and ask and many things were left unsaid. But we talked busily while we were able to and at least we saw each other. Seeing beats letters by many miles. She asked about all her Ladysmith people and of some I could give a fairly accurate account, but some were almost strangers to me. I've promised to write and she says that sometime she will come back for a visit. I sincerely hope she does.

The train left Evansville at 8:30 and at 9:20 I was again in Madison, so nervous that I was almost "seein' things." I took a car over to the Milwaukee depot and though I felt like a lost sheep, yet I really enjoyed the feeling of being absolutely independent and care-free. I had a little while to wait for the train and when it pulled in I waited with all the patience I could gather. A sailor was the first one to step off, but it was not Ernie. I watched and waited until everyone was off and he was not there. I felt quite blue and very, very sorry, and just a bit angry, but all the suspense of waiting is over and the thought of seeing him that I have had with me every minute has collapsed. If I hadn't been at the depot I would have hoped until morning that he had come, but now I know there is no further hope and I can sleep.

Sunday, August 18 I will not be spiteful and even though there is a big hurt in my heart, I won't let it make me peeved, so I have written a long letter to the dear Boy, trying to be as cheerful as I could.

Then at 1:00 I was on my way to Merillan, with a great weight removed from my heart after I had paid my hotel bill. I was sure it would not be a cent less than $10.50 and knew I would have barely enough to reach Ladysmith, but I was charged only $7.80 and the shock was so great that I didn't say a word, just paid my bill and decided I'd have a good dinner before I left Madison. I had two good magazines and I settled down for a good reading, because I knew it would be nearly six o'clock when we came to Merillan.

Just before Elroy came in sight, the train stopped very suddenly and we stood there for a long time. Finally, curiosity got the better of some people and they went out to investigate. The engine was off the track and it seemed impossible to get it back on again. Two engines came down from Elroy but all the bumping and backing only made matters worse and the engine was soon hopelessly off. I wanted very much to get off and go up to see the engine but I could only go alone and that wasn't pleasant, so I did all my gazing from the window. The coaches were finally backed down to the next station below and

we were brought back on the other track. Two hours had been lost here, but so far as I was concerned, it might have been four.

As we came into Elroy, someone came down the aisle toward me and there was Vivian Ure beside me. We were both so glad to see each other and have someone to talk to, and our own topic was our Soldier Boys. She had been down to Camp Grant to see Paul Bartell, and only saw him for a short while before he left for France. I was as sympathetic as I could be, but my spirits were rather low and I couldn't spare much lightheartedness.

At Merillan we had a long wait and we sat near the edge of the little dam and just talked our very hearts out. I am sure it did us both good and was a thousand times better than a lonely wait with only our very own thoughts for company.

The train came at last and soon we were in Neillsville and then Marshfield. The town looked familiar but not home-like—only Ladysmith could do that. I slept very little after I left Marshfield and was very tired and very sleepy when my home town came in sight at 4:35. I tried to sleep out my tiredness from then until 8:00 and I succeeded fairly well.

There were several letters waiting for me in the post office. One was from Archie, written in Ladysmith. He stayed until Wednesday—and I had to be gone during that time!! My heart aches so, I could weep all day. I know he found several letters waiting for him when he got back to camp and though I know I felt very badly about not seeing him, I know he feels worse. The long lonely evening passed at last—my thoughts were wretched company and I was soon in bed and asleep

Tuesday, August 21 There was another letter from Archie this morning, and if the letter I had yesterday was unhappy, this one was miserable. He found seven letters from me waiting for him, and though none of them were blue letters the effect on him was far from what I wanted it to be. I couldn't help but cry when I wrote to him this evening, though it doesn't seem to me that he deserves it. My kind heart is quite running away with me, I fear.

I went down to Thompson's this evening and Tom surely talked enough about Archie. He must have kept the town in a continual fit of laughter with his stories of camp doings. My Hero!

Wednesday, August 21 A more cheery letter came from Hancock this morning and I feel happier than I have since I came home. One also came from Toots, a very nice letter, describing their trip on Sunday, the day I left for Madison. I am going to keep it as a typical letter describing a "thriller."

I met Betty Ryall and had a nice walk and talk with her. I've been invited down there for some night next week and I did not wait long to accept the very kind invitation. The evening was lonesome and long and I'd have given anything for someone to talk to. Lacking that, I reread some of my letters, and got almost as much comfort out of that as though I were talking to a real person. "'Tis not good for man to be alone."

Thursday, August 22 This morning I heard Mr. Householder say in the hallway, "There's a troop-train going west in about ten minutes." Mr. Rice wasn't at the office as yet and when, a few minutes later, I heard the train coming over the bridge, I couldn't stay away a minute longer, and calling Alice, we both ran all the way over to the crossing. We saw the whole train go by and the fact that everyone on it was a stranger to me didn't make a particle of difference to me. They were all soldier boys wearing Uncle Sam's uniform and they were not just ordinary fellows. They threw cards and slips of paper from the windows, and when the train was half way out of sight, we picked them up and had a good laugh with the watchman at the crossing. We have decided to write to some of these boys, and the whole Court House is quite interested in our "new soldier boys." I wonder what they are like and whether they are Negroes or whites, and whether they laugh as much over our letters as we did over the cards of addresses.

My new sweater is growing rapidly and I am intensely interested in it. They are so popular, just at present—everyone is wearing a middy sweater or knitting one.

Friday, August 23 A very excited letter came from A.V. this morning, a wild letter, in fact. Fifteen men have been picked from the 4th Co., to go across soon, and he is among the fifteen. Just like the dear old

Archie LaBerge at Camp Hancock, Georgia, 1918.

hot-head—I can't help but admire his spirit. Somehow the letter sent a chill all through me, but all the same, I am very proud of him.

I also had a letter from Vicy, a nice happy letter, and I answered his letter and Archie's letter and wrote one to Mr. Joseph Brenner, who was on the troop train that passed through here yesterday. Three soldier letters in one day, that's going some for a staid lady as I am *supposed* to be. This is the last lonely day of this week for to-morrow the girls are coming up after me.

Saturday, August 24   Archie called his letter this morning a "good-bye letter," though he hasn't gone, and the order to be ready at ten minutes notice is sometimes a long time at being fulfilled.

As I came around the corner at Fritz's I saw 69569 [Sophie's license number] standing at the curb and I knew the kids were upstairs. I could hardly wait to see them after being away from them for two whole weeks. It was a joyful meeting and there was chattering and questioning and a good deal of teasing. I knew I would get it, but sometimes teasing goes all against me and I want to run away.

After three o'clock, Laura, Ruth and Genevieve joined us and we were a jolly crowd of school teachers. Grace W. talked with us for a while and we attracted nearly as much attention from the general public, as though we had been a band of gypsies or a carnival company. There was considerable sad leave-taking; Laura and Ruth go next Wednesday.

At four o'clock or soon after we were speeding for home and if we talked at Ladysmith, I don't know what you would call the noise we made at home. And most of it was about Archie—Archie said this, etc. It was nice to hear them talking about him, but when Mother emphasizes the fact that he is *so little*—I don't want to listen. It is the one cross of his life that he isn't taller, and I don't see what difference an inch or so in a person's height amounts to.

Laura gave me his picture, and though he looks very serious, I can see his jolly smile just back of the picture, and the twinkle in his eyes not quite there, but coming. He looks right at me, and seems to read my very thoughts.

Monday, August 26   We took several pictures yesterday, but no one was in the right mood for a snapshot-ing, and I am afraid the pictures will be failures. Mother hesitates to develop them in this warm weather, so I am going to have them done here at Ladysmith, and I can also get a first glimpse of them.

Monday morning was a grand scramble as usual, but rather more than usual, because it was after seven when we got up and I had to be at the office by nine at least. By getting the whole family into a state bordering on nervous prostration, we managed to get away with half my things or so, and at five minutes before nine, I was at the P.O., the mecca of all my hopes and fears. There was no letter and I felt considerably disappointed. At five o'clock, when I came from the office, I found one from Archie, still at Camp Hancock, and waiting rather impatiently for the orders to go.

I saw Laura for a last talk and have promised to see them at the depot Wednesday morning.

Tuesday, August 27   Again there were no letters in the morning, and at 5:00 I found two in my box—I can't see why they come at such unusual times. Little Book, letters seem to be all I can talk about, but they mean so much that it is not surprising, and I write as many or more than I receive.

The night was very stormy and I lay with my nerves as tense as steel wires, expecting every moment to hear a terrific crash of thunder. When I am alone during a storm, I work myself up into a perfect tempest of nerves and my imagination just runs away with me. I wanted to wake up in time to go over to the depot and see Ruth and Laura, but at 4:00 o'clock I awoke and though I tried hard, I couldn't keep awake until 5:20. When the train came in and left I was in dreamland, and only by chance woke up at 7:30, in time to get to the office. The girls were gone and I hadn't seen them. Too bad, but I couldn't manage it.

I went to a party last night, a party of girls, and not knowing very many people, I couldn't enjoy myself as I might have. It's rather mean to the hostess to say so, but I had a good time only on the surface. I really believe I have become so accustomed to being with the girls that I can't have a good time unless they are with me. That is really a sad state of affairs and I must make an effort to change. At least I met a number of nice people and added a few more names to my list of acquaintances.

Wednesday, August 28   Eunice Ryall phoned at noon and asked me to come home with her, and at 5:00 I found them looking for me. I was mighty glad to be somewhere besides in the rooms with only my thoughts for company. I will soon reach the point of talking to myself.

To say that I had a pleasant evening is only half expressing it. I had a royally pleasant evening—just a dandy time. The supper was delicious and after supper Eunice and I knit and Betty gave us some music on their Victrola, and when Eunice and I went to bed we talked for hours and hours. She told me some things about Ernie that I wish I didn't know. Especially since I had a letter from him to-day and somehow, I like to keep him the really nice boy that I have learned to

Building a house was truly a family project in 1918, with everyone working to get the job done.

know from our letters. The little thought often comes back—Would I like him as well if I really knew him better? He's not young, I know, and he knows people as well as I do, and very likely he has had a lot of experience in this little old world, but still I'd like to keep him the nice boy I think he is. I am going to forget what Eunice said.

Thursday, August 29 I wrote five letters this evening, a record breaker, even for me. It took me practically all evening to write them and I was tired out when I finished the last one. All were long letters, too. Alice had an answer to her Camp Funston letter, a very nice letter, perfectly proper, it seems, and I don't blame her for wanting to answer it. Wonder whether my new soldier will answer—I don't much care whether he does or not.

Saturday, August 31 I had a pleasant surprise this morning when Toots and Vena walked into the office. Hub had brought them all up in the Chevrolet, and at noon we had a regular picnic lunch, with neither dishes nor chairs enough to go around, but plenty of eats for all. Immediately after dinner, they left for Girard's and told me I was not to come home that evening. I was blue, to say the least, but when at 5:30 they came back, after considerable tire trouble, they had relented and said I could come home that evening. It was splendid riding in the big car, the flivver couldn't compare with it, but just after we turned Gibb's corner—*B A N G!!* went the rear tire on my side. When we got it off, we saw that it was simply blown to pieces, it actually blew the casing off from the rim. We had to patch an old inner tube, and while we were doing it Dr. O'Connor came along, but

The Wegner homestead in 1918, with the barn completed and the new house going up. Note that many stumps remain to be cleared from the fields.

seeing that we had a "man" along, he didn't stop. I always imagined that a demountable rim was much easier to handle than a Ford tire, but this one certainly was not. With all of us pushing and punching and kicking we finally worried it on again, but we were so afraid that it might blow out again that all the joy went out of our "joy ride." Toots drove the greater part of the way home and Hub watched the tire, though how he could have prevented a blow-out is more than I can imagine.

We were home at eight and of the whole bunch, I alone was supper-less. I made up for it, by lunching from everything eatable around the house.

They tell me that Sophie is absolutely out of commission, as I might imagine Max or Vicy to say when they really examined her. Her wheels are as bad as my worst dreams pictured her and Max says how we ever managed to run her as long as we did is more than he can see.

Fall 1918

LADYSMITH, WIS.   NOV. 11, '18 -

Part of the crowd waving flags in a show of patriotism on "Peace Day."

Fall 1918

Sunday, September 1 Max made Bob take off the front wheels on Sophie and when he saw them, he wouldn't let us use her, not even to go back to Ladysmith with. So Hub took us back in the Chevrolet, Bob beside him. And now, Little Book, comes a sad, *sad part,* how really sad I did not realize until afterwards! Going through Gibbs' a Ford truck came towards us, down the hill, a sailor driving it, and as we whizzed by, one glance told us—it was Ernie! The surprise was so great, we could hardly believe it. Only an instant and he was gone in a cloud of dust. I wanted to stop him, but as Toots said, he looked as though he knew where he was going, so we only slowed down, and though he did the same, he didn't stop. I thought of him every blessed minute of the afternoon. I wanted to see him so much and yet I didn't suppose I would. Oh! If only I could have stopped him!

We had to do something, or I know I would have gone wild with pure unrest, so we moved! It was only next door, down the hall, and our possessions were very few, but we must have walked several miles with a few things in our hands each time. It took us so long to begin and the biggest trouble came in deciding where we would place the furniture. We were both dead tired by evening and a little after eight we decided to go to bed and then—!! As a long time ago, someone came softly to our old rooms and knocked, and no one had to tell me who it was. I was nearly undressed, but Toots hastily put on a waist and went out to talk to him while I dressed. It's a shame, a perfect shame! But he is going back again to-night and I only saw him for a few minutes. It wasn't as bad as the parting in the spring, but I did hate to see him go! Oh, Ernie, you will never know all I think of you! After he had gone, a sudden wild thought came; to dress and go down to Stevens Point with him and come back on the morning train! The thought was almost too much for our excited nerves, and only the money (or *lack* of it) kept us home. I was really in earnest about going, though perhaps I might have been very sorry for it. But we stayed and my heart longed and wished for things it had no business wishing and soon the limited came and took him away. But he says he is going to ask for a furlough, "and then—"and he did not finish the sentence. I really must reason myself into a sane and sensible state of mind again, or I really shall not be able to keep my mind on serious things.

The first night in our new "house" was a wild night and it was long after twelve before we closed our eyes. Mrs. Jordan has promised to call us at six or I know we would never wake up in time.

Monday, September 2 I couldn't help but feel a little sad and disappointed all day. Being Labor Day, there was little to do and I spent the greater part of the day writing letters. I wrote to Ernie and told him about our foolish ideas. I don't suppose he will say anything about it in his next letter, he very seldom does, but perhaps he may think a moment about it.

I met Mrs. LaBerge at the P.O. this afternoon and had a long talk with her. She treats me almost as one of the family, and though I don't exactly resent the attitude, I do not enjoy the feeling. Why do people jump to conclusions? Mr. Spindler says we all do, however!

Tuesday, September 3 This morning's letter from Archie began "Good-Bye, Camp Hancock," and in it he says, "I am going in a few minutes now. Oh, I am so happy to be leaving! Don't know where I go, yet, but the next letter that I write will be from a different camp. I think we go to Boston, but am not sure."

The news doesn't upset me very much because I have been expecting it every day and I know Archie is glad to go.

Toots and I had a real homey supper with Alice J. and the dill pickles were the best of all to me. I like her more every time I am with her.

Wednesday, September 4   No letters at all to-day, and I feel almost lost, something the way a ship would feel without a rudder. Jessie came up and said good-bye, before leaving for Withee. She came up again after supper and Toots and I went to the depot with her. Br-r-r!! but the nights are cold!

Thursday, September 5   No letters again, though I hardly look for any so soon.

My standings came from Madison to-day and I feel rather disappointed, because I have failed in American History. The letter contained only the statement of standings, nothing more, and unless I hear from Madison soon, I am going to write and ask what I may do, in order to get my Certificate. I *will* get it, one way or another.

Mrs. Beveridge had supper with us and we girls took her over to the depot. Fifteen "Select Men" went away to-night and the crowd was something terrible. Also the train was an hour late, which made it all the worse. There was no visible sadness in the farewells—somehow these boys seem to feel that they will not see any actual service. They are all special service men, and will never be real soldiers, but they go all the same, and it may be a long, long time before they come back.

Just as we left the depot, Law and Roy asked us to ride with them and it was a ride to say the least. Law can be so desperately mean, that no words could ever express my feelings toward him. I can never have any real respect for him again.

Friday, September 6   Vicy wrote me the dandiest letter to-day. I have read it to several people and they have laughed over it as much as I have. Here is the really funny part, Little Book:

In the afternoon the fun started, and I almost forgot my disappointment in being left. We were ordered to furnish ten armed guards for duty at a quarantined camp down the line a-ways and as most of the men were gone now, I was hastily forced into service and twenty minutes later, I was marching down the street, armed to the teeth and looking with contempt at the mere rookies. Mind you, I did not know how to do any of the manual of arms properly and all that I knew about guard mounting was a little that I had picked up at Camp Douglas. As luck would have it, I was not put on the first relief. There are three of them who take turns at two hour intervals and I had two hours to practice in, two hours that were never better spent and I mastered the rules so well that I never got bawled out once during the time I was on guard.

My first turn came from three to five in the afternoon and my post happened to be at the end of a row of tents occupied by Negroes who had just come into camp, and I marched up and down my post, with my bayonet fixed, my jaw stuck out and all the snap and expression of a regular. The Negroes eyed me from a distance.

Now let me tell you, there is something very nice about the way a bayonet looks when it is at the end of a rifle. The new ones are long and thin and look just as if they were made to cut meat. Also, mine was new and nice and bright. You must see one and size it up to realize how it looks to the *other* man and then just let a tough-looking, hard-boiled regular look at you from beneath it—well, 'nuff said.

The Negroes were playing ball, when a strong arm threw it so that it rolled a little *past* my post. I saw it out of the corner of my eye and I also saw that the Negroes were holding a council of war, keeping one eye on me. Finally, two of them slowly walked like frightened sheep toward where the ball lay. I watched them and you can bet they watched me. They came at last to the guard line and stopped to think it over once more. Right here I gave them a little invitation by turning my back and walking a few steps in the other direction, then turned quickly about. Both of them had crossed the line and, picking up the ball, started back rather hastily.

Right here I let out a yell, lowered my bayonet and with a regular diabolical expression on my face, I charged right at them (I had read how to do this an hour ago). I'll bet all their hopes of a happy life just went "kerflop" when they saw what was after them. They *"ran."* One of them fell and when he got up, and saw that I was gaining on him, I heard him gasp, "My Lawd!" and he *RAN!* He was so pale that he was almost yellow. Then when they got toward their tents, I quit the chase, mostly because I was laughing so hard, "to myself" that I did not want to give myself away.

They, however, did not forget about it and I am sure they still think I was in earnest, for they would not come anywhere near my post and in the night I heard one of them say, "Lawd, it am just like suicide to try to get past that guahd!"

Don't you think it is a splendid letter? And just like the dear Boy. He wouldn't hesitate a moment to try the same trick on us, and I know, if he did, I would just naturally drop dead of fright.

Saturday, September 7   Toots is having a very stormy time with her school-board, or rather, just one particular member. They have told her they "will let" her teach for $45.00 and I will drive her until she asks and gets $55.00, or I hope she quits. With her State aid, that will make $59.00 a month, and that is only one dollar less than the $60.00 she could get at home, though I do not want her to teach there.

Had a letter from A.V. to-day but no address, he's still on the way, bound for Camp Devens in Massachusetts, I think. One also came from Madison that clears up all doubts about my Certificate. When they receive letters sufficiently good from some of my friends, they'll send it to me and then it is *Mine*, to have and to hold!

Bob and Billie came up for us after we had almost given up looking for them. But we were home in time for supper, and then it was just like the first time I came home after Archie had been there, though this time it was "Ernie, Ernie" everywhere. Audie had to tell me again about the ride and the nice time she had with him. Regrets are useless and so I won't even think about it anymore, though I wish things had turned out altogether differently that day. No one feels the same toward Ernie as they do toward Archie and I can't see the reason.

We made pictures this evening but our luck was wretched. Either the paper or developer is very poor and I distrust the paper. We gave up in despair, finally, only half done, or even less, but we have some pictures of the house and the "carpenter crew" to send to Vicy and I have those to send to Miss Kurs, and one for A.V. of myself. All the rest can wait until we try our luck again.

Sunday, September 8   Just two words would describe to-day—"as usual." Sunday has a routine all its own, but it somehow always ends the same way —. We are on our way back to Ladysmith, usually well laden with junk. We found a note from Tis, just to tell us that we had had callers, that was all.

Monday, September 9   To you alone can I show, Little Book, that I had two letters and two cards from A.V. this morning, and not feel that you will raise your hands in horror and say, as all the others do, "Lou! I'm shocked!" I have decided not to mention A.V. to anyone in the family again, because both Toots and Audie act as though he were meaner than dirt. I can't understand their attitude, though I believe it is jealousy alone. I do not know what to do or say, but I know that I cannot and will not suddenly tell him to stop writing, because it would send him right down to the depths of recklessness (or are they heights?).

His new address is Co. B. 43rd M. G. Battalion, Camp Devens, Mass. He is only about thirty miles from

Boston and he says the camp is heaven compared to Hancock. I've sent my "diary letter" to him and it may be the first mail he gets in his new place.

September 9—and we had strawberries, fresh strawberries for supper. Mrs. Carmain gave Toots enough for both of us for supper, and to say they were delicious is only mentioning a fact. Perhaps Dad will see and believe that such things are possible, at least we will do enough talking about them, and hope that next spring will see our own bed of ever-bearing strawberries.

Tuesday, September 10 The first Fair day—a most unusual fair this year because it lacks the attention of other years. No one cares very much about it, no one wants to exhibit many things, no one has any interest or enthusiasm for it. In some counties, Fairs have been discontinued for this year, and perhaps it is a wise move. There are so many other more necessary outlets for your money that no one will spend liberally, and with all the nice boys gone, who is there left to spend money?

The weather, too, seems determined to make the fair a failure. It began raining late this afternoon, a cold, steady rain, and kept on all night. In spite of it Toots and I went home with Sophie, a foolish and useless trip, but worth it all the same. Somehow the foolish things often appeal very strongly to us.

Wednesday, September 11 We found the roads much worse this morning when we went back, but in spite of an all-night's steady rain, we came up without chains. In one place the wheels sank right down in the soft mud, and Toots had to get out and push. The roads were heavy and slippery all along except where they were graveled.

I didn't do one bit of real work to-day—didn't even go to the Fair Grounds. Toots and I were at the office all afternoon and wrote letters and in our diaries. It was much more pleasant than being out in the rain and hail, wet grass and mud. Br-r-r! I shivered at the very thought of it.

Archie is at last at Camp Devens, Mass., and judging from his letter it must be a lovely place. He just raves about it, and it's only natural when he compares it with Camp Hancock.

After some housework we settled down for a quiet evening alone, but interruptions came thick and fast. Mabel came up first and asked us to come up to Cass' Hall with her and Alice and Eddie. It didn't seem just right but we finally said yes, and no sooner was she gone than we were undressing and redressing. *Me* going to a dance at Cass' Hall! Think of it!! But in spite of the dust and lack of men, the fear of the "Forty-Niners" coming in and being tired out besides, we had a really good time and I am not sorry I went. The nature of the crowd was worth noting, and most of all its genuine toughness. For once in my life, I can really say that I have seen when dancing can be a positive sin. We enjoyed watching the bowery dancers and commenting upon the clothes of some of the "Ladysmith elite!" Striped socks and short skirts are the very latest, I note, and it is also very proper to dance with your hat on (if it is a new fall hat) and with your furs around your shoulders (if they are fox). Yes, we had a good time.

Thursday, September 12 This morning while I was knitting, half-expecting Tis, she came tripping in, just in time to help me prepare our little dinner. Then about two o'clock Miss Hawes came up, and although we had at first said we weren't going out to the Fair Grounds at all, we hastily changed our minds and putting on our half-best clothes we went out. We found Mrs. Girard and a lot of old friends. It was quite an ordinary fair day but we had more fun looking for old acquaintances than watching the races.

We indulged in the movies, for a wonder, quite an extravagance for these war times, but the pictures were really splendid.

Friday, September 13 Another beautiful day! The auto races attracted us this afternoon, and while Tis and I were standing at the fence, Toots suddenly joined us with a "Hello, kids! Aren't you surprised to see me?" Of course, we were. Mr. LeCount came up to talk to us while we were standing there, and I wished for a bayonet or something in my heel that I could use on him, while my back was turned toward him. I dislike him more every time I see him, and the feeling is growing into a real hatred.

And the races! Well, they were as good as wartime material could make them, but I surely wished for Law and a good car for him and I know he could have walked away from Ralph Goldsmith and his little green bug. Four flivvers—three of them built over—raced, and R. G. came in first easily and after some really exciting changing of places, Ernie Mitchell came in second. I hope that sometime I'll have a chance to race, and at the same time have the courage to take it.

Archie's letter to-day told about passing in review. "I wish you could have seen us when we passed. We were in a column of 4's until we got near the review stand when we swung into a Battalion front and crossed the field. Not six inches of bow in the line. It sure gave us a good send off. The only good thing I have to say for Hancock is they put out snappier soldiers than the eastern camps."

Saturday, September 14 On our way home this afternoon we dropped Audie at what we supposed would be her boarding place but wasn't. At Leighty's we stopped for our new dog, Prince, a lovely big collie. Getting him into the car wasn't so bad, and with a hitching strap around his neck we were quite sure he couldn't get away. But as soon as the car started, he became frightened at the noise and rattles and began to struggle and cry. It was almost impossible to hold him and I told the girls to let him go, but they hung on like grim death. I stopped the car and they quieted him with petting and loving words and when we started on again he was quite contented, didn't make one move to try to get away. I am sure he was only scared by the noise of the car. I tried to drive softly and quietly, but the car seemed to have an extra number of squeaks and rattles that day. If by any chance we'd have had a blow-out, it would have been good-bye dog, girls and all, but nothing happened and Prince had a royal welcome when we got home. But the poor boy was homesick and sat by the door, as sad as three rainy days. Rex looked at him with evil eyes and growled like fury. I wonder whether the two dogs will ever become friends. They must, or it will be constant war.

Sunday, September 15 Tis came home with us on Sat., so it was up to us to bring her back to Girard's on Sunday. We wanted to make a real picnic trip out of it, but Dad didn't care to go, or Bob either, and since we couldn't be gone all day with no one at home, it was perhaps well that someone *did* stay at home. It was a cold day for a picnic, but we bundled up in heavy coats and had both fur robes. My one worry was the left front wheel on Sophie. I knew it was in need of fixing and it felt loose up in the very steering wheel. I had absolutely no confidence in it, but mile after mile passed along without a breakdown and I felt quite safe. The Flambeau Hills were beautiful, every tree a different color and the reds and yellows and browns blended into one glorious whole, from a distance. We took the longest way there going, because I wanted Mother to see some country, new regions, and I think we did. I wish Dad could have been along. We had our lunch with us, but Mrs. Girard had been expecting us for dinner, and since we had missed that, she made an extra supper for us, and such a supper! Oh! my, Oh!

my. I ate until I could hold no more. If I had to live at Girard's for a year, I know I would gain a pound a day, until I could gain no more. I really believe that all of them eat too much, and I feel sure that life would be just as pleasant if they ate a little less.

We came home by way of Port Arthur, across the dam, and home on the old familiar road, just in time to save Dad and Bob the awful trouble of making supper. Bob had been out after a bee tree again, but had his usual luck, which means "no bees." We were in no mood for supper ourselves, so before it was very dark, we were piloting the poor lame Sophie on the way back to Ladysmith. This has been a "joy ride less" Sunday and the cars are very few that you pass on the road.

Monday, September 16   There were two letters from Archie and a dandy one from Vicy. This has surely been my mail day—five letters in one day. Vicy's letter was almost all description, about guard duty and it was splendid. A. V.'s letter had a very homesick vein all through it. My letters are on their way to him and are surely in his hands now.

Toots says it is because she was driving and Sophie just naturally balked because she was driving, but it would surely have happened with Mr. Fults himself. One wheel nearly came off. Toots had struck this day, had really quit until the school board agreed to make out her contract for the salary she asked, so she went out visiting with me. On the way home, I heard two very decided "clicks" in the bum wheel, but an inspection from the exterior showed nothing wrong, so we kept right on. Toots wanted to get some books from Maple Hill, so while I wrote a hasty little letter to A.V. she went out alone with Sophie, promising to be back by five o'clock and surely not later than 5:10. Five o'clock came, 5:10 and then 5:15 and something seemed to tell me that she had had trouble. I knew it so surely that I could think of nothing else, and my worry was growing at an alarming rate. I was nearly frantic.

Then Mrs. Anderson came with, "Someone wants to talk with you on the phone." It was Toots, of course, and I did not need her excited, "You can't guess what I've done to Sophie!" to tell me what had happened. The wheel wasn't off, but was badly chewed up, and since she wouldn't drive it home and neither would I, Ray Fults took a garage car and went out after Sophie. He wasn't afraid to bring it in. Poor Sophie!! Now they will *have* to fix the wheel. That is about the only comfort I have about the matter.

Tuesday, September 17   Such rain as we are having! Ladysmith was visited by a War Special to-day, a train of war relics and tokens. The train was very late and only stayed a little while, and it was my sad luck to miss it. I am truly sorry, because I am sure it was good. Machine guns and all manner of captured German guns, helmets and grenades, etc., pieces of that terrible barbed wire that they use for entanglements, all manner of bayonets, etc. A part of the Great Lakes Naval band furnished music and several speakers gave short speeches. It was reported that between two and three thousand people passed through the train, to see the exhibits. It is a beginning of the Fourth Liberty Loan drive, and is sent out from Chicago, I believe.

Wednesday, September 18   At the garage, Sophie was only temporarily fixed and I was just naturally provoked. Anything is good enough for me, it seems. I could almost weep. They will fix it to-morrow or I won't start out. I won't run her as she is now.

A genuine period of showers seems to be passing over us, one after another, sleet, hail and all.

A.V.'s letter this morning made me angry, but my anger didn't last long. He told me about his trip to N.Y., not *all* about it, but I can imagine what he didn't say. I can't understand lots of things and some parts of his letter I certainly do not understand. But I know that I would not like the Miss Hattie Landis who took him to N.Y., nor her car, nor her chauffeur, "who is very well trained."

Thursday, September 19 Sophie was fixed to-day. Thank Goodness! I was nearly desperate and on the very edge of tears. Now I hope she is as good as new with her new hub.

Br-r-r—r! Such cold days! My teeth chattered all day, and with the ceaseless showers and muddy roads, new grading and all that, life is just one sweet dream. I ran down to see Audie and had a little chat with her.

I have such a dreadful cold, that all I can say between each sentence is, "Oh, my head!" and "Oh! my nose!" Poor me!

Friday, September 20 This evening we had a real old time Joy Ride. Toots and I stopped for Miss Hawes and then went down after Audie and then over to Ryall's. We surprised them, of course, but we had a jolly evening. I laughed until I was on the verge of hysterics, and my cold gave me such a head-ache that I could hardly see. I know I looked like a patron of Tony, my eyes and nose especially, and everyone laughed about me so much that I finally went into a dark corner, where no one could see me. I felt just as bad as I looked, perhaps even worse, because I know how I felt and had only other people's words for my looks. Although the evening was cold, we had a nice ride. I, for one, could breathe in the open air better than in-doors.

Saturday, September 21 Tis and Audie came up to-day, and the family was all together for a day again. Only Toots and I went home, however, Audie went to Ryall's and Tis went back with Girards. Sophie had a torn fan-belt and Eddie F. discovered it just as I was ready to leave. While fixing this, he found a short-circuit on the timer, and had to fix that, too. He worked until after seven, overhauling Sophie, and was in a savage mood when he finished. I was so sorry for him going

without supper that I brought a bunch of grapes to feed him. But he was so ugly-looking that I didn't dare give them to him. Someday I'll tell him what he missed.

It was nearly nine o'clock when we got home. For almost five miles we drove with only the moon for light, but it was too risky for me, going as fast as I could, although I was sure I knew every foot of the road. I wonder how Lawrence had nerve to drive as fast as he did in the dark. His nerve is quite remarkable, also his speed.

Sunday, September 22 A red-letter day in very truth, and little did we dream it until it all happened. Bob and I went to Flambeau after apples this afternoon. The day was lovely and we left early, with the usual parting words, "We'll be back by five, not later than six o'clock," and Mother, from previous experience, added, "I'll give you until seven." Away we went, gay as larks.

We found apples at the second place we stopped, not just what we wanted, but good apples and we bought two bushels. On the way back, just after we left Flambeau, a black cat crossed our path, from left to right. All sorts of pictures flashed through my mind and I caught Bob's arm. "Never mind," he said, "it can't be anything worse than a blow-out and we have an extra tire and several extra tubes." The fear did not leave me, however, and I was ready for anything that fate might decree, but hardly ready for what really did happen. Just in front of the White's, on an up-hill, the car suddenly "spewed" down, popped a few times, ran on a few more feet and then stopped dead. My first thought was "No gas!" but the tank was over half full. We opened the hood and found the gas leaking from the carburetor, the elbow of the gas feed-pipe (or whatever it is called), and when Bob tried to tighten it, it broke off. I shall never forget the look of perfect terror that he turned upon me. "Lou, I've broken it!" The first thing we did was to shut off the gas, and then we racked our brains to figure out what to do to fix the pipe. We were only such a little distance from home, about five miles, or a little more, but it might as well have been five hundred, for the help we could get from there.

First we tried to wrap some tire patches and cloth around the pipe to try to hold it in position, but the gas leaked out so fast, it came in a perfect stream. We got the engine to spit once or twice, but it wouldn't move, though Bob pushed like a Trojan. It wouldn't work, so we shut off the gas again and tried to think of something else. "Let's try some soap," Bob suggested, so again I walked up to White's and bought a bar. We plastered soap on all sides, top and bottom, and wrapped strips from a handkerchief around and around, tight as we could, but when it was all done and we tried to get the engine to start, she flatly refused, and only a few feeble sputters could we get from her. I was ready to cry and Bob was blue as indigo. All our ideas of fixing it were gone, so I decided to phone Cox's and see if Lawrence or Roy were home. They had never yet

refused to help me out of a difficulty. Roy was home and said he'd come over and see what he could do. In a few minutes he was there, but even a good piece of rubber tubing failed to help matters any and as a last resort, he suggested that we tow the car over to the house, where they had tools, and also to wait for Lawrence. I was ready to agree to anything, so they towed Sophie. It was the first time I had been in a towed car for any distance and the feeling of being jerked and pulled was far from pleasant.

I gave up all charge of the car when they got there, and Art West first offered to solder the broken pipe. It sounded like a sensible idea, so he took the carburetor home, while we ate supper. I was so nervous and so unhappy that I could hardly swallow a mouthful. Lawrence had come home, with Clara and Harrison and Miss Kinzelin. I wanted most of all to get word to Mother and Toots, but Lawrence and Roy were both so hopeful that we would soon have the car in running

Bob Wegner and a friend try to get the car running again.

shape that I waited. At seven-thirty Art West came back, but when Lawrence put the pipe in again, he broke it right where it had been soldered. I didn't hear him swear, but I'm almost sure he did. Then he went to work and soldered it and that took him until eleven-thirty. Poor Mother and Toots! I could just see how they were watching for us. What wouldn't I have given for a telephone to get word to them! I was nearly sick. From eleven-thirty until nearly one, they worked to start the car, and even using another car to start it with wouldn't make Sophie purr. They finally got about two cylinders or less to working, but the noise she made was terrible. At one o'clock everyone gave up and Lawrence took us both home in his car.

I couldn't hardly believe his goodness, but he offered to wait until limited time and then took Toots and me to Sheldon. He was so good that it was hard to believe he was the same Lawrence I always knew. He hasn't any reason, of course, for being otherwise to me, but even so, I was sure I was dreaming.

Monday, September 23 Lawrence gave me careful instructions as to what parts I should bring home for Sophie. He offered to fix it up if I got the parts down to him. But when I told all my troubles at the garage, Mr. Fults sent me down with a mechanic, "Clifford," in other words, and with all the new parts we might use. It really was the best arrangement, after all. It was a success, too. We found only Amy at home, busy washing. At nine o'clock Clifford began to overhaul Sophie and just at eleven, he had her purring as smoothly as any pussy-cat ever did. He found a dozen or more things wrong with her, but nothing more than Lawrence had said.

He pronounced her cured and I went home with her, stopping only a minute there and then on to Ladysmith. It was just one o'clock when I reached the city and Sophie was still running smoothly. I put in one very full afternoon and went out to meet Toots, to tell her the news, and also to see how sleepy she was. We had had only one short hour of sleep, and both from lack of sleep and nervous excitement we were nearly dead.

I am afraid to ask to see my bill for this day. It is as bad, I'm sure, as I can imagine. Such luck as we have had with Sophie!!

Monday usually brings me two letters from A.V. and sure enough they were there this morning. Rather a tinge of homesickness in one of them, and more allusions to hunting than camp life. This is the first fall he has missed getting a deer, I am sure, but hunting the Hun is ever so much more thrilling.

Wednesday, September 25 There is an account of a sham battle in one of A.V.'s letters this morning that comes very close to what the real thing must be like. Here it is, Little Book:

This time the Light Artillery helped us out. We had to shoot over the Infantry and the Artillery fired over all of us. You can hear the shells shriek through the air just above you. I felt kind of foolish for a while but got over it when we got the signal for M.G. fire. I wish I could have been standing where I could have seen it all. It lasted just three hours and I was glad when it was over. Am nearly deaf yet from the awful noise. Seems to me you could have heard it there. We did not know there was any artillery along until they started to fire. We expected to start at day light but thought the M.G. would serve as artillery. Just as it began to turn light in the east, the Four-pounders opened up. I didn't know what was going on. Thought there really were Germans after us, until I saw the Major giving Artillery signals. Didn't dare take our eyes off him because we didn't know when he would signal us to fire. When it did come, we were all so nearly frozen that we could hardly move, but we must have done pretty well or he surely would have called us. He said if we all do as well in France, we won't have to be afraid of any German Army. The worst was retreat. The Infantry passed behind us, left us as a rear guard. We were supposed to hold the Huns back till the Infantry got back to safety. Then the Infantry fire over us and keep the enemy back until we get back to our proper positions. It isn't one bit funny to walk back toward all those guns cracking right in your face. It would take me a long time to get used to it. It was great in one way but it makes one realize what war really is. Rain doesn't stop anything like that. When the time comes, you are out, rain or shine. There were lots of people on the hills about four miles to one side of us. They stayed all through the rain to see and hear our noise.

The other letter was written Sunday, the day after the sham battle, and says the whole camp is quarantined with Spanish Influenza, over 2000 cases in the camp and 71 deaths in one night. A.V. says he has a dreadful cold and has nearly sneezed his head off. Unless I get a letter from him to-morrow, I will surely think he is sick, too. It almost frightens me to think of him being sick in that wretched place.

Friday, September 27   I have had a letter both yesterday and to-day from A.V., short letters and rather blue, but very welcome to me. I can only imagine in a vague way how terrible it must be in Camp Devens. A.V. has been acting as a nurse, though he must be nearly ready to drop, Poor Boy!!

Though A.V.'s letter was very welcome this morning, I had one from Ernie that made me almost wild with anger. He said, in fact, "I only expect to be your correspondent friend, I never expect to be anything more to you. I always like to get your letters, but if you don't care to write anymore, why—*"machst mihr nichts aus."* Why should he say anything so downright cruel to me? After some of his previous letters, it is like a dash of ice-water. I don't understand either his letter or him. I wish I had never written to him.

Miss Hawes came up in the evening and in my desire for sympathy I showed her the letter and also one of his other letters. She declares that someone is exerting pressure upon him and that he did not write it of his own desire. I doubt that very much, and yet it is such a sudden change from the tone of his other letters that something has happened somewhere along the line. At any rate, I have classed him among the people who weigh lightly what they say, and say more than they should. But I certainly shall answer his letter, and he will think less of me then than he does now. I won't answer right away while my anger is at its height, but I'll answer sometime and likewise say what I think of him. I'm as angry as I ever was at anyone, and yet I could almost laugh at him and his petty way of trying to hurt my feelings.

Toots left before supper to go to Girard's and practice with Tis for her Service Flag Dedication program, but Audie came up and saved me from spending a lonesome evening.

Saturday, September 28   This morning Audie and I were sitting in the office when Mr. Rice came in and like a thunderbolt from the clear sky came a new piece of news. Without any preliminaries, he began, "I suppose you heard that Gertrude [Toots] lost her school this morning." We could only stare in blank astonishment—Lost! Lost her school!! It was a mystery. "It burned down," continued the tactless man, "about five o'clock this morning."

We must have stared at him like petrified mummies. Words failed us, and all I could gasp was "Oh, for Heaven's sake!" Toots was gone and wouldn't be back until mid-afternoon, and my one thought was to keep the news from her until after the program or else break it gently to her. I'm sure it would drive me nearly wild to be told such news suddenly. My thoughts were all in a turmoil this morning. Yesterday's anger, this morning's shock, and to cap the climax, a letter from A.V. saying that he couldn't keep up anymore and had to give in—all these nearly drove me frantic. I couldn't think straight and by noon I was almost cranky.

Tis and Toots came up at about three and Audie told them the news. I can imagine how I would have felt, just all gone.

Just before six o'clock we went out with Girards to look at the "wreck and ruin." The chimney was still standing, like some grim, old sentinel, and the stove had settled down upon the mid partition of the foundation with the very poker still hanging on the jacket. The trees were all scorched and burned but the woodshed—as close as it was to the building—was untouched. The wind was almost nothing while it was afire, because no walls fell outside, but everything, absolutely everything that could burn, was gone. The window glass was melted into all manner of shapes and the beautiful library was only a heap of white ashes. The maps were only rolls of white ashes and the seat iron lay where they fell. Nothing is left but ashes and the first wind will take them away. Mr. Darling managed to get into the hall and grabbed an armful of old textbooks, the old worn flag and the *empty* sweeping compound can, but before he could get in again, the belfry fell and all hope of saving anything more was gone. "All our pretty pictures are gone," said little Clyde, "and even the little tin drum!"

We hardly waited for supper, just a little sandwich, and away we started for Thornapple No. 4 [for the program]. Tis left before we did, but we were there before she was to open the schoolhouse door. Mr. Dresden went down with us and his talk was the feature of the evening. There were eight stars on the Service Flag but only one that I knew, Art G. The girls sang "There's a Long, Long Trail" and sang well, too. I liked Mr. D's talk, he always seems able to hold the attention of his audience.

The program closed at nearly ten o'clock and a few minutes later we were on our way back to Ladysmith. At one spot, a skunk nearly drove us off the road, not the animal itself, but what pervades the atmosphere about him. I held my breath so long that I almost forgot to breathe again. It was eleven when we came into Ladysmith, and as soon as we could gather up our belongings, we left for home. Sophie was unusually balky. I was tired and very hungry and felt so cold and miserable that I couldn't help but feel blue. A.V.'s letter this morning worries me a whole lot. He is sick, too, with that dread disease and even says that he is afraid. I cannot help but think of him. His letter has been on the way for three days and to-night he may be very sick, and no one to really care for him. I shed some real tears on the way home—perhaps they are foolish tears, but to-night I feel more lonesome than I ever did before. *[Editor's note: the flu epidemic was more severe at Camp Devens than at any other military location in the U.S. Several thousand soldiers died in the fall of 1918. Thus, there certainly was cause for Louise's concern for Archie's health during this time.]*

Sunday, September 29   Toots and I came back to Ladysmith after supper and at the garage another staggering piece of news was told to us. Bob Sands accidentally shot and instantly killed himself this afternoon, while out hunting bees with a party of hunters. I can hardly believe it. The whole town is saddened by the news.

Monday, September 30   There was no letter from Archie and I know that he is really sick. I am truly worried, would even like to telegraph to him, but that might seem silly. Even the shortest letter would be a comfort and relieve my worries a thousand times.

Toots had no school to teach, and hence was offered a vacation for a week at least. We visited the Polish school on the way home, something new for Toots, and by leaving before closing time, we got home just as the silo was filled and the man ready to leave. I fell in love with the Baby Tractor he had, I'd like to run one like that myself. It's pop-popping can be heard several miles away and it sounds so energetic and business-like.

Tuesday, October 1 There were no letters again when I reached Ladysmith at five o'clock and it seemed that I could stand it no longer. After supper I went out to LaBerge's and found them not at all down-hearted, quite cheery in fact. Mrs. LaB. had received a letter from A.V. since my last one and though he says nothing about being sick, still I can read between the lines enough to know that he hasn't told everything. I stayed all night, quite as a member of the family, Little Book. They are all very nice to me. I even read some of A.V.'s letters home, not at all like those he writes to me.

I must have eaten something very unpleasant to my stomach, at least it objected very strenuously and refused to let me sleep one bit. I turned and tossed and twisted, but I could not coax sleep and I did not want to arouse the house. It really was a terrible night. It required all my self-possession to appear normal at the breakfast table, and eat enough for manner's sake.

The road to town was a torture and I stopped only long enough to get the mail—a letter from A.V. that is almost better than medicine. Up in the room at last. I could not sleep even there. It seemed almost as bad to lie and think as to get up and do something, so I aroused myself and wrote to Archie, just to tell him that I was so glad to know that he was well again. That seemed to make me feel better, so I went back to bed and slept about five hours.

I had to take Sophie over to the garage so I dressed at 5:30 and took the little lady to her supper and called for my mail. My State Certificate came to-day!! The much-desired and much worried-about piece of paper. It is nice to have it, and makes all the work seem worth while. The day ended beautifully, with A.V.'s letter and my Certificate, and I am already feeling a whole lot better just because of these. Tis, Mary and Agnes paid me a hurry-up visit and as soon as they left, I went to sleep again.

Friday, October 4 Institute! I went home last night to get Toots and then came up this morning with her and Audie. The roads were very bad and the trip took us so long that we were nearly an hour late. That was quite too bad but really could not be helped. Mr. Hyer and Mr. Neale of Stevens Point conducted the Institute and really made it the best one I can remember. Nearly everyone said the same thing. Mr. Neale really was the better man, so far as new ideas is concerned, and he captured the teachers quite by storm.

I sat with Grace W. during part of the afternoon and she wrote to me, "I've got a mad on you." Ernie, I find, has told her about that unfortunate trip long ago, but just what he told her I do not know, except that she said, "He made an awful lot of excuses." I told her she could have him, but she insists that she is mad. I couldn't quarrel with her after last week's letter from him and the pity of it is that I cannot tell her how little I think of him right now. I would try hard not to see him, if I were to meet him on the street. Grace makes me angrier than ever at him. If only he weren't so fond of excusing himself!

I must not forget the "Kaiser," for he did his best to make "a day of it." Mr. Hyer's talk this morning was on "The Poison of Prussianism," and though it says Prussia, it means the Kaiser. His own boy is at the front, and in the very thick of the fight, so one cannot help but feel that Mr. Hyer means every word he says and that some things he thinks and feels are too deep for words. The intenseness of his face and actions only show the same thing. When he finished, my nerves were as taut as steel wires and my heart was skipping beats from sheer hate. His lecture was cut short so that we might attend the movies—The Kaiser, the Beast of Berlin. The title is bad already and the pictures themselves were the most terrible I have ever seen. The plot was nothing new, only there were more scenes of Berlin and the Kaiser and his follies than usual. His eyes would make anyone's flesh creep, they are cruel as steel knives. The latter part of the picture showed the German advance through Belgium, with all the harrowing details as that dramatic art can supply. The end was quite as one would wish it and showed the Allies in Berlin and the Kaiser a prisoner. He was turned over to the Belgian people and his jailer was the giant blacksmith, whose family his troops had broken up. Even that punishment seems too good for him. It was a thrilling picture and nearly set us all crazy with excitement. I clenched my hands so hard that they hurt all night.

We slept poorly. I think each of us dreamed of the Kaiser. I heard Audie say in her sleep in a low tragic voice, "I shot him for his gold." I was in an aeroplane all night dropping bombs. Morning was an actual relief to our worn-out nerves. We really had too much Kaiser for one short evening—but Oh! how I do hate him now!! I can't find words strong enough to express my feelings, but I can understand how some of our soldiers must feel about the *huns*.

Monday, October 7   I was in the mood for a courageous act this evening, so I wrote an answer to Ernie's strange letter of two weeks ago. My anger was all cooled and blown away, but still I said just what I thought and I hope he reads it slowly enough to know what I mean. I didn't write an angry letter and signed myself, "As ever, Lou." I wonder very much whether he will answer. I hardly expect it, nor do I ever expect to see him again or talk to him. I wouldn't have missed writing this last letter for anything in this wide world. I want to have the last say, if there must be a last. Yes, I really wonder whether he will write to me again, I don't think so.

Tuesday, October 8   A sudden scare has swooped down upon Ladysmith to-day. We have all known about

Influenza and its rapid speed, but somehow no one expected to have any cases or deaths in Ladysmith. This afternoon the Board of Education suddenly ordered the schools to close indefinitely, and an order like that, coming from the clear sky, makes queer little shivers run up and down one's spine. Just as though the epidemic's dark wings are over our city, too.

Thursday, October 10   Over the phone this morning, Mr. Rice told me that he had received an order from the federal government ordering all schools, churches, theaters and public meetings to cease. The suddenness of it all took my breath away for a moment. He told me to take the message to as many schools as I could reach and to phone to as many as I could from Bruce. It meant an all-day's trip and I did not want to go alone. First I asked Irma, but she couldn't leave, then I went after Miss Hawes, but she wasn't feeling well, so in sheer desperation I went out to Toots' school. She closed immediately, and tossing her dinner basket into the back of the car, we started out on a modern Paul Revere Ride. "Run, run! the influenza is coming!!" It was fun to see the commotion we caused and the consternation we left behind us. Some schools were already closed, and some teachers had already heard about the epidemic, but to the greater number, it was a perfect surprise. We went up to Crane, then west to the new bridge and then down to Bruce. We soon had nineteen schools on our calling list. Near Atlanta a shower overtook us, and we hurriedly put up the top. From then on, it rained more or less all the rest of the day. We had dinner at Bruce—our second dinner—and from here I phoned north and south spreading the wild alarm. It was raining steadily now, but we left in the midst of it, going north to Abbey's and then back through Beldenville and down to Caley Lake. "For Mercy's sake!" "Oh, goodness!" and similar exclamations followed our short call. Nobody near Bruce expected anything like this. The contagion of excitement had spread to us, too, and it became almost a game to see how many schools we could reach.

Even the rain did not affect us, and we splashed through the mud and water. We found one school already closed, because the teacher was sick, and it took only a guess to name Influenza. From Caley Lake we took a short cut to Girard's, around Spruce Lake, a road I vowed once that I would never travel again, but with a few bumps and jolts we went over it alright. We stopped at Girard's for a few moments and then went up to Tis' school and gave her a great surprise, too. She wouldn't believe us for a moment, but there was no joking about the report, and so she, as all the others did, told her children about the epidemic and that there would be no school for at least two weeks.

We had supper at Girard's, a perfect feast, but the darkness was coming on, and with the steady rain, I was eager to start soon for Ladysmith, and before it was quite dark, we left. One shower after another overtook us. As we went by Rasmussen's, we thought of Ella Anderson, and after going on about a mile, we turned back, picked her up and after one or more stops, for the sake of her order, we began the trip to Ladysmith, a very thrilling trip over the worst roads I have traveled for a long time. Near Ladysmith they were the worst, but bad as they were, we plowed right through, mud flying in all directions.

Here, news waited for us: Pearl Williams died this morning, the first death from Influenza. It seems to send a chill right through you. The whole town seems to feel frightened, as though the dread disease were hiding, ready to grab the unwary. You cannot help but feel the panic that seems to have taken possession of everyone.

Friday, October 11   Audie was waiting for us when we came home from Bruce. Her school had closed early Thursday morning. Early on Friday morning the three girls went home, still spreading the alarm. In a great many places the news had not penetrated, but it was traveling fast.

Ladysmith is more panic-stricken than ever. According to reports, more deaths have occurred, but when we come to investigate, they are only false alarms. Even at that, there is a funny, scary feeling around your heart. We have joked heartlessly about Influenza, the Flu, rather, but it is no joking matter.

Saturday, October 12   I went home on the scoot, the first time for nearly a year, I believe. I had Archie's sweater with me and knit every moment I could. I knew that I must hurry to finish it, and every one of the past days when I could have knit on it and didn't seemed to haunt me. It is going to be a beauty of a sweater, soft and warm and a lovely brown color. I love it so!

During the evening a very strong wind came up— almost a gale and a strange kind of smoky haze hid the sun and made the whole sky seem spooky and unnatural. "The weather is going to change, and we may have snow before morning," Mother said. "It looks more like smoke to me," I told her. "There must be fires somewhere." The wind howled all night—so mournfully, too.

Sunday, October 13   There were only a few more rows of potatoes still in the ground and early this morning the whole family trooped down to the field and dug like wood-chucks. That part of it was almost fun—*was* fun, in fact, compared to the job of picking them up after dinner. Oh, my poor knees, and my back!! I was sure I could never bend down again. To make it worse, we had a perfect siege of giggles and by the time we were all done picking up potatoes, none of us had much more than enough strength to walk up to the house. And still I knit all evening. The sweater will soon be done!

Monday, October 14   Since all schools are closed, my work is very light, is practically nothing, so I took my knitting to the office and worked at it nearly all day.

Being Monday—there were two letters from Archie and he said again that if I wanted to get the sweater to him before he left I must *hurry*. And faith, but that is what I'm doing!

To-day I heard that Miss Hawes has been taken to the Hospital sick with the Flu. For one as frail as she is, it causes some worry. She was taken sick on Friday, the day after our great "Paul Revere Ride"—and I am so glad, so very glad that she did not come with me. What a terrible thing it would be if she had been sick from the trip! I am really worried about her, but I know she will have good care.

Tuesday, October 15 The sweater is almost done. I am nearly dizzy from knitting.

This morning the cause of the wind and smoke of last Saturday was explained. There have been terrible fires in Northern Minnesota, fires so awful that no words can describe them. More than thirty towns were said to be destroyed by the blaze. The Duluth and Superior papers are filled from cover to cover with thrilling stories of rescue and scenes that make one sick. The wind was so terrific that escape from the flames was impossible. Cars could not keep ahead of it. Scores of people perished by the roadside. Others sought safety in root cellars and even in wells and everyone was suffocated. In one cellar thirty-five bodies were found. The list of dead reaches almost 1,000. We can only shudder at this horror—it is almost beyond our power of imagination. It sounds almost like the end of the world. The fires are not out, only smoldering, and another fierce wind would bring a repetition of Sunday's horror. I have read so much in the papers that I am nearly wild. It is the most terrible thing I can think of—death by fire. At Cloquet and Moose Lake, two towns destroyed, the people took refuge in the lake and nearly froze to death while their heads were being scorched and burned. Here the death toll was not so great as in the country districts, but the desolation seems greater.

The engineer of the train that took hundreds of people through the fire was made blind by the heat and flames. He was a true hero.

Miss Hawes is worse to-day, they tell me. Everyone fears greatly for her recovery.

Law was in town to-day. I saw him just before supper and while I was in King's, he also came in and we had supper together. Irene Savord went by while we were eating and evidently saw us, because in less than two minutes someone called Law on the phone. He was very careful to answer her questions, but I knew who was talking to him. The Imp of Mischievousness aroused itself and when Law asked me to go for a ride, I did not refuse, as I would have a short time before. I wonder whether she saw us go. Anyway, I had a speedy though short ride and a nice chat with Law, "Just for old-times sake," as he said. He leaves for camp next Monday night, and though I cannot help but feel that he should have gone long ago, still I won't accuse him of it, I'll only think and not speak those thoughts.

Wednesday, October 16 The sweater was all done last night, but it was long after the P.O. window closed when I finished embroidering Archie's name on it. And so it was mailed this evening. I wonder how long it will be before he gets it, and I hope he isn't gone before it does reach him. I feel so happy about sending it to him.

A perfect "Castle-in-Spain" arose out of pure air to-day and my brain has been in a whirl ever since. Miss Hawes is very sick, as you know, Little Book, and when schools reopen, it is very evident that she will not be able to teach. Mr. Dresden wants me for the teacher of the Model Department—says he is going to have me. Of course I would love it, but I cannot even begin to feel that I am going to get it. Mr. Rice will never consent. It would mean no more cold trips for me—an easier job in one way, surely, but I doubt whether I will be so fortunate as to get it.

Thursday, October 17   Toots and I with Mr. and Mrs. Rice went to Strickland this afternoon. The day was cold and very rough and the trip was anything but pleasant. I wore all the coats and sweaters I had, but nothing could keep the wind from going almost through me. Toots came up with the car and at five o'clock was on her way home again. I wanted her to stay but nothing could keep her, and so she went. She traveled from one end of the County to the other that day.

Nothing happened to make my dream come true, or to shatter it either. Mr. Dresden said he would talk to Mr. Rice this morning, but if he did, I am none the wiser. I cannot help but hope that I will get the new position, but it is only a dream as yet and I must not let it take too secure a hold upon my mind. I can only hope. Next year, if I am not fortunate this time, I am going to ask for that work. I know I can do it.

Saturday, October 19   Such a foggy day! The evening seemed to come before it was noon. There never was any mid-day at all. It was early morning for a while and then twilight came. I haven't seen such a foggy day for a long time.

I went home via the limited and talked about all my thoughts. I simply had to do that before I could go to sleep, though none of the girls seemed to care much about listening. I can't understand them at times.

Sunday, October 20   Mr. Dresden had made me promise to go to see Mr. Arnold to-day, and without any coaxing Mother agreed to come along, perhaps more to avoid a repetition of my former trip to Flambeau than that she really cared to call on Arnolds. It was a glorious day, perfect Indian Summer, and so was the trip perfect. Mr. Arnold listened politely to all I had to say but said very little himself and neither gave me much encouragement nor yet dashed my hopes to the ground. All I can do is to wait and hope.

Monday, October 21   Lawrence left this evening for Jefferson Barracks, New Orleans, with seven other boys. I doubt much whether he will see any service— I am almost sure he won't. I don't think he wanted to go very much, but perhaps he does not show his feelings as much as I would. I did not go over to the depot to say good-bye, but my thoughts were there when the limited came and took him away.

Tuesday, October 22   "The Kaiser Has Abdicated"— So read the headlines of the papers to-day. It is too big a mouthful to swallow at one gulp and still it gives indications of what is coming. The end must be coming soon. G. M. Householder leaves to-night for Camp Meigs, Wash. D.C. He has worn his uniform all day and no man in the city has been so busy, winding up the loose ends of his business affairs, as he. Lieutenant Glenn M. Householder. It looks well on paper, doesn't it? And so does he look well in his uniform.

I have deserted the ranks of the teaching profession and have enlisted as a volunteer in the War Dep't Office, or in Mr. Munroe's office, as I should say. Mr. Carow calls me official flunky for the Local Board. My work is purely mechanical—just stamping envelopes and questionnaires. I used the same stamps over a thousand times and was almost an expert at it, when I finished. The work is so very new and different that it is fun, although it would soon prove quite monotonous after several weeks of it.

Wednesday, October 23   Nothing but questionnaires all day, stamping them, folding them, heading them and dating them, each one separately and individually, truly this work is red tape itself. But that is nothing to us and as cogs in this great war machine we must blindly follow instructions and still keep both eyes open and make no mistakes, for the public has eagle eyes.

An answer came this morning to my letter telling about the ride I had with Law, a week before he left.

I should have known better than to tell the dear old hot-head about it, but since I have, the usual thing has happened and A.V. is angry, very angry. It is only a repayment of his letter about Miss Hattie Landis (if that is her name), but I am sorry he is angry, even though I knew he would be. He didn't scold, at any rate, and as it happened, the sweater reached him the same time as the unfortunate letter did, and his letter is a queer mixture, telling me how well he likes the sweater and then how hurt he is at what I told him. I'm glad he likes the sweater, very glad and now I must tell him I'm sorry, too.

Thursday, October 24 A Day at the Court House! I wonder more every day how Mr. Munroe can stand it. My heart would have to be made of steel to withstand all the sad appeals, and hear all the fathers' and mothers' worries and stories and not yield to everyone and everything. "Familiarity breeds contempt," they say, and in a small way it applies right here. In this office, where so many heart-breaking stories come out, and worried people come in, we who see so much and come to see through some of the stories have little sympathy to waste. To them the making out of the questionnaire, or the receiving of a card to appear, is an event in a life time, but to us who mail out hundreds at the same time, the incident is too commonplace to remember.

Here comes an old lady who wants her son put into Class IV A, he hasn't asked any exemptions, but her faith in Mr. Munroe to do anything he wishes has brought her here. She is hardly able to speak English, and is so nervous she cannot sign her own name, can't remember how old she is, nor the ages of her children. She is really deserving and Mr. Monroe will fix everything. The next one is a whole family—Polish—and they also want deferred classification for their son, but this case is much different. The father is able to work and there are other sons at home. This family belongs to the great class of foreigners who only half-way understand the draft regulations and do not want their boy to go. Again and again someone comes in, asking Mr. Munroe's help in filling out his questionnaire, and all are directed to some of the lawyers. Sometimes one of the children accompany them as interpreters, again the mother comes with her son, and in nearly all of their faces is such worry as I cannot understand. Each afternoon twenty young men, more or less, are examined upstairs. The Dr. is a busy man then and by five we are all tired and worn out by the nervous strain.

Sunday, October 27 Rain! Rain!! All day a steady rain—cold, wet, and miserable. Early in the morning Dad began working at the furnace and by noon he and Bob had some of it put together. Immediately after dinner, all of us went out to see the "Octopus" develop. Such a time we had! Nothing seemed to fit—screws would not go in, pipes were crooked or too large or too small and Dad's patience was worn to a thin thread. But from bent and odd-shaped pieces of tin, the many-armed "Octopus" slowly grew and grew, the pipes fit somewhere, the screws had new holes punched for them, the jacket fit beautifully after it was on, and it was quite as real a furnace as the one in the picture. We finished by lamp-light and by supper time, the furnace was ready for fire. Our basement will be a beauty, large and roomy and I believe that somehow the furnace room will be a very popular spot in the new house. The girls have been putting on lath all week and with the exception of the ceilings, several rooms are nearly done. The house grows slowly but steadily and to me, who sees it only once a week, the progress seems more rapid than to those who see it every day. No home will ever mean as much to us as this one, except perhaps my own, if that should ever come to pass.

Monday, October 28 Yesterday's rain made such muddy roads that only a mile of driving convinced us that it was foolish to drive to Ladysmith, and at the second corner Bob turned back and we went to Sheldon instead. The roads were muddy here, too, but three miles is only a fraction of fifteen. Of course, the scoot had to be late and I missed the whole morning. Even being a half day late, I managed to finish the one hundred questionnaires and surprised Mr. Munroe when they were all done. The pictures we took at the Court House are done and are good, Alice says. We are going to print on Wednesday night and then I shall have some to send to A.V.

Wednesday, October 30   Yes, we printed pictures!! But Oh! Massy me! Either we are the slowest, most finicky people on earth or else we are perfect fools, or some-one else is. We used A. Rockstad's studio and apparatus and also his kind assistance. But in some strange fashion, we managed to spoil about three dozen pictures. What mattered it to him whether he had both hands in the developer and hypo, or how long he printed the pictures or how many he put into the developer at one time. I would much rather have been working in our own rooms and in my own way. I was thoroughly disgusted, to say the least, and their system of "salting down" the pictures in the hypo was the last straw. There wasn't one good picture in the whole set and I vow it is the last time I will do any printing of my pictures there. I met Rev. Rutland this evening and now I know him—having known him by sight for a long, long time. He is a pleasant person.

Thursday, October 31   The latest call on Wisconsin is for 16,000 men and Rusk County's quota is 82. That will take all the men who are left from the September Registration and a whole lot from the August 24th list. Many of these are only boys. With 82 more men gone, what will we have left ? This call is almost as large as the one last summer when Archie went.

[No entries in the diary for ten days.]

Monday, November 11   PEACE DAY!!
    As the limited left town this morning, the demon of sound let loose, and for several miles out of town the whistle blew and blew. One big thought flashed through my mind—"Good News!"—and that could be nothing less than peace. For several moments I lay listening, the wonderful fact just beginning to make an impression upon my mind. Then suddenly the fire whistle blew—Tooo-ooo-ooooo-oooo! My heart skipped a beat! Then Bang - Bang! went Sadie's fists against the wall—"Girls, Girls! Do you hear *that!*" "It *must* be good news," I called back through the separating wall. "It is, it is!! The war is over!" I hear bare feet pattering over the floor and Sadie was at the piano, playing seven different pieces at the same time. I couldn't lie still an instant longer, and I jumped out of bed and ran into Sadie's room, caught Irene around the waist, and executed a wild hop-waltz while Sadie pounded like fury on the poor submissive piano. Then back into our own room I skipped, shook Toots, and in another moment we, too, were hurrying into our clothes, hardly knowing how we dressed or what we put on. The noise in the street had already begun—shots were fired and other whistles began to blow and some of the bells added their noise. The fire whistle kept up a continual shriek, and to help we clattered some pans at the open window. Before we could swallow our hasty breakfast, a small procession had gathered on the streets, men and boys with horns and cow-bells, and beating upon pieces of tin. The crowd grew slowly but steadily. By five o'clock Sadie and Irene were "out for the day" and by 5:30 we were also out. With Mrs. Stephenson we were only five girls, but we did our best. The crowd had doubled itself several times by this time, and more were coming every minute. "To Hell with the Kaiser," headed the procession, and a real "Liberty Bell" in a push-cart came

behind. Everything capable of producing some kind of a sound was out. Guns and pistols, horns, cow-bells, whistles and tin pans, an old cornet and a tambourine, a zither, even the Greeks' player piano, drums, ever so many of them, pieces of tin, wash-tubs and boilers, and above all this combined noise, cheers and shrieks, yells and hurrahs, whistles and glad cries of every imaginable kind.

And over all of this, a hundred flags, large and small, were already waving. Up one street and down the other we marched, calling people from their breakfasts. We helped ourselves to every flag we came to. "Oh, I will not teach to-day"—Toots could think of nothing else. "Don't," I told her. "Go out and tell them this is a day of celebration." And to save her even that much, Mr. LeCount came into town, and his answer was, "If the others don't have school you can have the day off, too." And Mr. Rice said, "No school to-day—the town has gone wild!" Not quite yet, but it was improving every moment. I was hot and burning with excitement and no power on earth could have made me settle down to a quiet day at the Court House! Never, Never! On this day of all days in our lives!! Work!!! No!!! No!!

"Let's go down and get Audie," and no sooner said than done and we were on our way, rough roads and all, not caring what happened to us or the car! She already knew the wonderful news, and at Wakefield's we danced and screamed and laughed some more. Excitement was nearly getting the best of me! "And the boys will be home by Christmas time!! Oh Joy!" And we hugged each other and danced around some more! And then back to town—we must miss nothing of this most wonderful day! We couldn't make noise enough! At Hanson's we stopped for a moment and talked with Mabel. We were Indians with excitement by that time. All we lacked were the feathers! We screamed and yelled and tooted the horn at every farm house. People must have thought we were crazy, just wild, and their guess was nearly correct. Oh, Joy—Joy—Joy!!

The crowd in town was almost a mob by this time, but it never stayed together long enough to show its

A band and trucks as part of the spontaneous parade on "Peace Day," November 11, 1918.

size. Girls and women with service flags on their arms, children by the score, men and boys and nearly everyone who could walk or run! The band was split up into several parts—the Liberty Bell was still in the parade and the drays and trucks and cars loaded to the limit were out. Our dear Service Banner with its 255 stars was over the street! The noise was deafening for a while, but even on Peace Day, people must eat, and by ten and ten-thirty the greater part of the mob had dispersed. "The parade begins at one o'clock from the High School," and in order to be there on time we had a very early dinner and made one more trip to Maple Center for Bunting and Flags. We had tried hard to get these at Ladysmith but all stores were "Sold Out." The trip was worth it and we came back in style. Our crowd had grown and we soon had with us all the Real Ladysmith Girls. Threse joined us with a real fife and drum and a kodak. How I wish we had had ours up here! Again and again we wondered whether Mother and Dad had heard the whistles in the morning. All mills were closed now, everything was closed—even the saloons at Tony and Weyerhaeuser, we were told. It was almost a necessity on such a day. What must a large city be like on a day like this!! My imagination fails me! I would like to see it, but still not be a part of the crowd. And what must a military camp be like! We are wild, I know, but size adds fury to a crowd like this and when hundreds of thousands are celebrating together, the crowds must be beyond all control.

At the H. S. the people were gathering in crowds. Then down the street came a number of mill wagons, and instantly we knew what they were for. We dashed helter-skelter for the first one and clambered over its high sides, like so many sheep over a fence. With flags and horns, whistles and a little drum, and our own strong voices we made ourselves both heard and seen. The parade formed quickly—the band, then the State Guard led by Old Glory and all the Allied flags, the Red Cross women, the wagons, all the school children with flags, autos, and every truck in town. One car trailed the Kaiser in his coffin, appropriately labeled "KAISER GONE TO H—," cabbages were his flowers. At the tail end of the parade came a manure spreader dragging the Kaiser through the mud of the streets.—an appropriate finale! The colors were wonderful—no painter could have done justice to the scene!

Again and again we looked back as the procession wound along behind us. We cheered and shouted, we made up several yells of our own and almost wore out— "When you're up, you're up, you're up; when you're down, you're down, you're down; when you're up against the U. S. A. you're upside down!" I clanged my cow-bell against the side of the wagon until my hands ached and all my knuckles were skinned. We saw dozens of people taking pictures and we all decided to get some permanent reminders of the day. Up one street and down the other we went, through mud and all. At one place old Mr. Kirvan stood at his front door waving a flag. His lovely white hair helped to make a lovely picture and as we went by, we cheered him again and again. And through it all we sang and cheered and were absolutely as happy as we could be. I smiled at dozens of people that day that I had never known before—it was a great "get-acquainted" day. The great jolting wagons made us nearly as tired as walking, but we had the advantage of being able to *see*, and also of being seen. At length, all those who walked were tired out and very likely the horses were tired too, and right in town they very nearly "dumped" the whole load. That was something we had been afraid of all the time, though our teamster carefully assured us that the evil-looking door was chained and perfectly secure. Near the Manley Hotel they deposited all of us, and as it happened to be nearly train-time, the whole crowd trooped over to the depot, gave our yells with mighty vim, cheered and waved our flags and clanged the cow-bells. Then we had to inspect the pile of boxes and other debris which was to consume the last remains of the "Manure Spreader

Kaiser." He was already swinging in the window and several small urchins were whacking away at him with a long slat. I wonder whether they had put a long nail into it. I hope so. We found Mabel Hanson and being somewhat foot sore and weary of walking, we took the meek and somewhat submissive flivver from the garage, still adorned with its bunting and flags and with "Old Glory" floating above us, we drove around and around the streets, up and down. Every time we passed a Home Guarder, he saluted the flag, quite as though we were the real thing.

The crowd was melting away very rapidly, for even on Peace Day man must eat. I wonder how many women were sorry that they had to prepare meals that day. In many homes I am sure that very little real cooking was done, and most of the good people of Ladysmith ate cold and hastily prepared lunches. We were beginning to feel the effects of celebrating—Audie had a very sore throat and it was not until right now that we gave the dreaded Flu a single thought. The signs of "Don't Congregate" were the most unnoticed and least popular things about town. I tried in vain to get some lemons for the girls, but either they had gone the same way as the flags and horns during the morning, or the stores never had any at all. My search was all in vain.

Sadie came in while we were preparing a hasty supper and told us that the bunch was going to dress up as crazy as they could for the evening. There was very little at hand to furnish the "trimmings" but we used up every bit of bunting and tissue paper, covered our hats and put on all the flags we had. The colors were fittingly displayed wherever we went. We were ready for the evening's fun. Down on the street we met our bunch and we paraded, hopped rather, up and down the streets, in winding trails and back again. We captured Fatty Levin—made him be our band—and with him puffing away on "Over There" and "On Wisconsin" we danced

The dump wagons that Louise and her friends rode in the Peace Day parade.

around the two blocks. Suddenly the flare of the bon-fire near the Library caught our eyes, and like a flock of chickens we ran pell-mell down the street toward the lovely light. Fatty was outdone—I do not know what became of him. I am sure at least that he never had strength or breath enough to keep pace with us. Then came the band!! Hurrah!!

The band stationed itself at the corner, and like moths toward a candle the whole bunch followed the call of the inviting notes. Music was too much for our feet and tired as we really should have been, we hip-pity-hopped around and around the band. "On Wisconsin" and "Over There"—whose feet could resist those melodies? Indian file and then by twos, around and around we went. I caught Mona Butler for my part-ner for a few rounds. Then Mabel Hanson came and I caught her hand, but ours was the pace that kills and Mabel did not last very long. Suddenly Alice dashed out from the crowd and again around and around we went,

faster and faster. I was so warm I felt ready to melt, but nothing could have drawn me away from the magnetic attraction of the lights and music. We hushed our clang-ing cow-bells while the band played, but our flags and bunting made up for the loss of sound or noise—whichever you please. We sang and sang—hopped and hopped—around and around. What cared we for stiff knees and lame ankles the next day? We were living in the glorious present and no thought of the morrow clouded the joy of the evening! Flu and all its dangers was cast into the discard! But even this became monot-onous after a while, even though we had an appreciative audience on the street corners, spectators who seemed almost amazed at our actions and gazed stolidly at our antics. We sought new fields of excitement. "The Movies! Let's go through the Movies!" No sooner sug-gested than all were ready to go. Would Cou Martin permit such disturbance? "We'll mob him if he objects! We'll do it anyway!" Permission was speedily given—

The Home Guard prepares to march in the Peace Day parade.

the good man knew better than risk his life and property by saying no. We waited until the signal of intermission came and then, like a whirlwind, we dashed in, down one aisle and up the other, cow-bells clanging madly, every horn and whistle blowing furiously, and shouting at the tops of our voices. I saw dozens of people I knew. The carpet tripped some of us but no necks were broken. It was all too short and in less than a minute we were all out in the street again, looking for more that we "might devour."

The Home Guard was forming in a column near the band and we followed in behind them. "Now we'll burn the Kaiser." Like magic the crowd poured in about the funeral pyre. The brave Home Guard formed a cordon about "His One-time Satanic Majesty—Biel Hokes zollern." A barrel, or more, of coal oil was poured upon the pile of rubbish and in another instant the flames were leaping to the Heavens. "Ready! Aim! Fire!" Bang! Bang, Bang! and then several scattering shots, as the State Guard filled the now-burning Kaiser with volley after volley of shots. Oh! If it had only been the real, last, and lost-kaiser! The rope that hung him burned through and he fell into the flames. Such flames! They blazed up as high as the buildings. Here the crowd broke up and after some minutes more of parading we went toward the garage, found Eddie on the way there, and after comforting him about his order to stay home we went back to the rooms for the robe. Alice J. and Mabel H. came with us to take Audie home. We found Ernie in the office talking to Mr. and Mrs. Fults. Either he was very blue that night or else he was terribly shocked at our actions. He made me angry, anyway. Perhaps we all felt the same way, so again we sang "Mr. Zip-Zip-Zip," wilder than ever before and just because I knew he did not like the foolish song we sang it worse than usual. (He did not even smile. I cannot understand him at all. I almost hate him, and still, I think more of him than ever before!)

We all piled into the car, and with a driver so excited that she could hardly drive through town, we made one

An effigy of the Kaiser being dragged behind a manure spreader in the Peace Day parade.

Monday, Nov. 11   **Peace Day!!**

91

As the limited left town this morning, the demon of sound, let loose and for several miles out of town the whistle blew and blew. One big thot flashed thru my mind — "Good News!" — and that could be nothing else than peace. For several moments I lay listening, the wonderful fact just beginning to make an impression upon my mind. Then suddenly the fire whistle blew — — — My heart skipped a beat! Then Bang-Bang! went Sadie's fists against the wall — "Girls, Girls! Do you hear that!" "It *must* be good news," I called back thru the separating wall. "It is, it is!! The war is over!" I heard bare feet pattering over the floor and Sadie was at the piano, playing seven different pieces at the same time. I couldn't lie still an instant longer. and I jumped out of bed & ran into Sadie's room. caught Irene around the waist and executed a wild hop-waltz while Sadie pounded like fury on the poor, submissive piano. Then back into our own room I skipped, shook Dottie

Louise recorded the celebration on November 11, 1918, in unique fashion with alternating shades of red, blue, purple, green, and black ink.

92

in another moment we, too, were hurrying into our clothes, hardly knowing how we dressed or what we put on. The noise in the street had already begun — shots were fired and other whistles began to blow and some of the bells added their noise. The fire whistle kept up a continual shriek and to help, we clattered some pans at the open window. Before we could swallow our hasty breakfast, a small procession had gathered on the streets, men and boys with horns and cow-bells, and beating upon pieces of tin. The crowd grew slowly, but steadily. By five o'clock Sadie & Irene were "out for the day" and by 5:30, we were also out. With Mrs. Stephenson we were only five girls, but we did our best. The crowd had doubled itself several times by this time, and more were coming every minute. "To Hell with the Kaiser" headed the procession, and a real "Liberty Bell" in a push cart came behind. Every thing capable of producing some kind of a sound was out.

Guns & pistols, horns, cow-bells, whistles and tin-pans — an old cornet and a tambourine, gather, even the Greeks' player piano — drums, ever as many of them - pieces of tin, wash-tubs and boilers and stove all this combined noise, cheers and shouts, yells and hundreds whistles and cries of every imaginable kind.

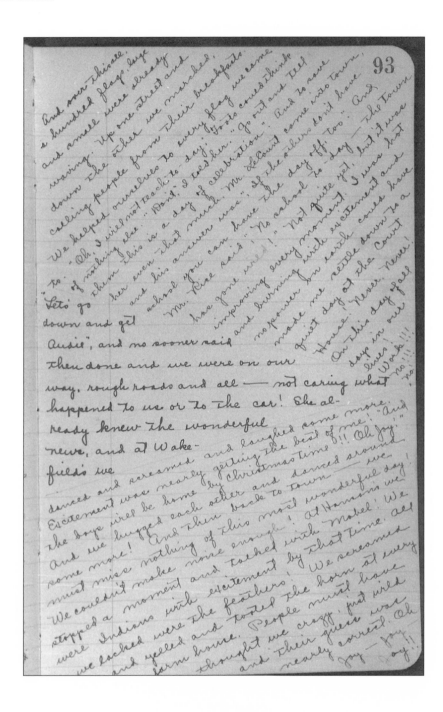

And over thistle,
a hundred flags. large
and small were already
waving. Up one street and
down the other we marched,
calling people from their breakfasts.
We helped ourselves to every flag we came
to.

"Oh, I will not teach to-day," I told her. "Won't, or nothing else." "Then this is a day of celebration." "Go out and tell
"Let's go her even "that much." Mr. DeLaunt come into town. And
down and get and his answer was, "No school to-day." the Town
Audie", and no sooner said school you can have the day off, too". And
then done and we were on our Mr. Rice said, "No school to-day!" "Not quite yet, but it was
way, rough roads and all — not caring what has gone well!" improving every moment. I was hot
happened to us or to the car! She al- and burning with excitement and
ready knew the wonderful no power on earth could settle down to a
news, and at Wake- made me quiet day at the Court
field's we House. "Never, never, never!
On this day shall fall
days in our
danced and screamed and laughed some more. lives! Work!!!
Excitement was nearly getting the best of me!" "And no!!!
the boys will be home by christmastime!! Oh Joy." no.
And we hugged each other and danced around — we
some more! And then back to town — we
must miss nothing of this most wonderful day!
We couldn't make noise enough! At Hanson's we
stopped a moment and talked with Mabel! We screamed
were Indians with excitement by that time. All
we lacked were the feathers! We
and yelled and tooted the horn at every
farm house. People must have
thought we crazy, but will
and their guess was
nearly correct. Oh
Joy - Joy
Joy!!

93

98

evening! Flu and all it's dangers was cast into this distance the next day? We were living in the glorious
— hopped and hopped — around and around —
sang while the band played, but our flags and bunting made up for the
some ankles the next day? but nothing could have drawn me away from the
ready to melt, but that did not last very long. Suddenly Alice dashed out from
I caught Mame Butler for my partner for a few rounds. — The Mabel Nannere
there. — whose feet could resist those melodies. Indian file and around the
that hips and Mabel did not last long Lij own was the floor and
two happy and around and around. — Around and around
around and around at the lights and music. "De Wisconsin out
scale! I saw over the barns the moon shone. The Lij the
rattle we had a very appreciative audience on the
long sing cow here while I felt ready to melt.

The Band started at the
[musical notes]
the call of the inviting notes.
Music was too much
for our feet and like
moths toward a candle,
The Band

ones here had a very appreciative audience on the
around and around the moon shone over the
window let me for still gone
"Wisconsin out there.
We hipped

more trip through town, Eddie and Clifford hanging onto the sides, cut corners everywhere, and then sped out into the country. We drove very slowly, stopped our excited chatter, and let our nerves calm down. We were all nearly on the verge of hysterics, in a state of excitement worse than anything I have before experienced. We motored slowly down to Wakefield's and no joy was quite as pleasant as the feel of the cool breeze on our feverish faces. It rested me as nothing else ever did before. No one was home at Wakefield's, so we took Audie up to Hanson's and left her with Mabel and then went slowly back to town.

After we left, the bunch went through the three coaches of the limited, just as we had raced through the movies, and then through all the hotels and restaurants. It was nearly 10:30 when Toots and I came back to town and had taken Alice home and the streets were already quieting down. By eleven there was no one to be seen. And no wonder, for only people made of iron and steel could have kept up the celebration past that time and those who went down to the dance at the Parish Hall were not those who had expended much energy during the day. I have never been as tired as I was to-night. I was beyond the point of being tired— too dead to feel anything. Sleep was wonderfully welcome, for to-morrow we will feel our celebration more than to-night.

Tuesday, November 12   "Morning after the night before, Gee whiz! But don't your feet feel sore!" The town was strangely quiet this morning, so different from the noise and excitement of yesterday. "How do you feel this morning?" was the greeting we all used this morning. And some of us were all feeling—Stiff knees and sore ankles, blistered feet and sore throats, chapped lips and bruised hands. The muscles about my ribs ached most of all, I cannot imagine from what cause. Toots wore off most of her stiffness in her long walk out to her school. Sadie's lips were black from blowing her little whistle so much and Irene could not put on her shoes. But in spite of all these after-effects, I wish we could celebrate for another day. I know I could never keep it up for a whole day, but I would try my best as long as flesh could stand it. Yesterday was the most wonderful day of my life and what if some people do think we girls were so very silly, I am glad I could act that way. We will never have another day like this, and my one great regret is that it all had to be done in one day.

But the world moves on, and now our main topic is, "When will the boys come home?" I gave vent to my feelings this morning, but I wrote four or five letters, all more or less excited accounts of yesterday's events. I feel so much better after writing them. What if they do seem stale when they reach their destinations!

Wednesday, November 13   "The Party." "Boric Acid for tired feet," Eddie said. How we did hate to go! Somehow Ernie's actions of Monday night made me feel that I wasn't wanted. Again and again we said, "Let's not go!" but still we kept right on dressing, and finally kept right on driving down to Hanson's. There were too many people for a jolly good time and too many poor dancers among the boys. But as usual, we girls had a good time, perhaps because we are as willing to dance with each other as with anyone else. From all appearances, Ernie was his usual self, but he seems much different to me. I cannot understand him at all. If he is angry, he has a queer way of showing it, and still I cannot see what he has to be angry about. Perhaps he is still shocked at our behavior of Monday night. I'm sorry for him if he is, but I am *not* sorry that I was so wild. I cannot feel right now that I know him very well, but I begin to think that I would not like him as much as I might.

Thursday, November 14   Just three hours sleep and then a strenuous day! I managed to keep my eyes open, but my thoughts were very woolly and fuzzed up. I went up into the Blue Hills, a very tough trip both ways and perhaps the nervous tensions of getting the car through the mud kept me awake.

Saturday, November 16 A steady rain all day and during a great part of the night! The great question of the day was, "Shall we go home or shall we stay?" We see-sawed back and forth, first yes then no, and finally decided to wait until Sunday morning and see what the weather promised. Continued rain would make us stay, but a fair day would see us on our way home. Saturday night was the dampest, coldest, most disagreeable evening I can imagine. The air seemed so filled with moisture that it came down without raining. Sunday morning the clouds gave promise of breaking and letting the sun peep through, and shortly after eight I had the car in trim for a trip through the mud and water. I had to *take* a chain, because one of ours had "walked" away from the car. However, I came out ahead on the deal and so I was satisfied. The graveled roads were good, and we made good time, but oh, me! clay was bad, but black loam was too awful for words. Nothing stopped us, however, we kept right on, through Conrath, up one hill and down the next, many times on low, but moving forward, ever forward. From Conrath eastward, they were worse than before and we agreed, at last, to leave the car at Stafford's and carry our stuff to Niepow's, if we could, and then have Bob take us back with the team.

The road ahead spelled terror to me, but when we had all our junk out of the car ready to carry it, we made up our minds to take the easiest path, and as Toots said, "We'll go as far as the wheels will turn," and so we piled the thirty pounds of nails, the suitcase, the robe and coats and other smaller items back into Sophie, backed into the road, and with a swift prayer for good luck, started on the last four-mile lap

of our journey. It was bad, but not as bad as it might have been. Evidently no car had been over it since the last time we had gone to Ladysmith. The ruts were deep but not bottomless and although we went nearly every foot of the whole distance on low, we kept right on traveling. Twice we stopped to let the engine cool, but it did not begin to boil very hard until we were almost home. Mother's first thought, when she saw us coming, was, "Have the girls been out in the car all night, stuck somewhere along the road?" We enlightened her within less than a minute and then proceeded to crowd as much talking and visiting into those few brief hours as we possibly could. Dinner was almost good enough to make the trip worthwhile. During that time, however, the clouds gathered thicker again and it began to rain again, and in a great hurry we began to gather up our coats and caps and start back on our perilous journey. It didn't seem nearly as bad as it did when we came down, but where several cars had gone, the ruts were deeper every minute. The graveled roads were a joy, just splendid. At the garage I had to exchange stories with the men, but they surely had the thrillers this time. With tire trouble and stripped gears, their tale was great against my tame story of "Mud and Water," but as they had gone through Tony twice, perhaps that may account in some measure for their misfortunes. I had no sympathy to waste on them, when I sensed the aroma of Tony.

The trip surely made me tired, dead tired, with nervousness and driving through such awful roads.

Monday, November 18 Ernie and Roy went back to Great Lakes to-night. Not even a good-bye this time. Queer, isn't it? But what do I really care? If he is angry, I would like to know why, but I am not going to worry about that. I found his U.S.N. 1917 ring after that one night he was here, and I have waited for him to come and get it, but now I suppose I'll have to send it to him. He is a puzzle, and I don't know if he is so very interesting, after all.

Tuesday, November 19   After scurrying about town, I managed to find some paper for our pictures and Toots and Alice and I printed almost four dozen. The difference between these and the ones we did at Rockstad's is too great to mention. These are excellent and I feel as though I could put these in my book with a sense of pride. We made a great many of the tiny ones Threse took on Peace Day and I shall send Archie some of them, even though they are very small. Alice made several pictures of herself and they were splendid, too. I am almost proud of our good luck, and with electric lights, the work is so quick and easy.

Thursday, November 21   Last night when I came back from a long trip to Amacoy and Soft Maple, the roads were beginning to freeze, and this morning everything was solid. I could weep at the weather! If the roads had only dried a little while before the change, they would have frozen in a travelable condition, but as they are now, in places, neither man nor beast can get over them. They are so rough, the ruts are so deep and so cut up. Such Luck!! I dread to go out visiting.

x x x x x x x x x x x x x
x x x x x x x x x x x x

Monday, January 13   Dear Little Book! Almost two months have slipped by! I feel as though we are almost strangers and as I look upon your pages, I realize how much has gone by since I wrote the events of my life. I must review some of it for you, but briefly for even as I write this past history, time is moving on and new events are ready to happen.

Our much-planned Thanksgiving in our "new house" did not materialize. Both Toots and Audie taught that day, or part of it at least. Mrs. Arnold had invited us to eat dinner with her, and although it was a snowy day and we were late, still we went. It was not at all like the day we had planned but it was very different and in every way pleasant. Mrs. Arnold is so kind and saw that we had a lovely time. We saw one of her beautiful sunsets on "her river" and I will long remember it.

The next week two new members were added to our family. Eunice and Elizabeth Ryall came to stay with us. We are a bit crowded, but it is much more pleasant, and the evenings are not so long and lonesome.

Isaac R. had such a longing for a dance that he persuaded Mrs. Davis to allow him to give a dance in the old store building at Maple Center and there we danced until the wee hours of the morning. We went out with Hanson's and had supper there and then walked over to Davis's. Boys were scarce and far between but that did not prevent us from having a good time. Eddie and Esther played, or rather Esther played and Eddie danced. I think everyone danced to their heart's content. Albon was there in all his glory, but I refused him point blank and Audie even told him that she had a "stomach ache." We spent the rest of the night at Ryall's, what little there remained. Eddie brought Sophie out for us and at night the whole crowd, Eddie, Esther and Alice Hanson, Eunice and Betty and Ike and we three girls all came back to Ladysmith in the two cars. Ike had all kinds of tire trouble, but that didn't seem to bother him much.

Monday was a stormy-looking day, and when I went out toward Bruce, a genuine shower came up, in fact it rained nearly all day, and froze as it rained. I was almost soaked before I reached Beldenville. I dried out some of the water from my hat and coat, and put up the top. At noon when I came back the car was encased in a coat of mail, glittering ice, and the roads were treacherously slippery. A rivet that held up one arm of the top broke off short and the last four miles I drove with one hand and held up the top with the other. It rained steadily and the windshield was encrusted with so much ice that I couldn't see through it, and when I put it down the rain came into my face so much that it blinded me. It was a terrible trip, and I was nearly drenched when I got back to Ladysmith. We must have been quite a sight when we came into town, ice all over and wet as drowned rats. I spent nearly all afternoon drying myself and getting warm again. I caught cold, of course, a bad one, too, but I went out again on Tuesday, and though I did not feel very well, nor much inclined to work, and sneezed and coughed, yet I worked all day. I even went out to get Toots. Next morning, I felt even more tired and went up to the office instead of taking another trip out into the country. At noon, Mr. Rice suggested that I had better stay at home for a few days and doctor up my cold, and against my will I had to go. At first the thought seemed pleasant enough.

For two days I played "Mother" to my family, and Thursday evening Eunice and I went out after Toots. Next morning I stayed in bed, and for two weeks I was a victim of a mild case of influenza. I couldn't really say just when I had it, and I almost doubt it myself, but the after-effects were those of the flu, so I guess that is what I had.

Thursday, January 23   Another long interval of neglect! Little Book, I beg your pardon! To resume at the point I left off —— ——

Those were long and lonesome days that I spent in bed. I was alone when the girls were at school. On Sat. I tried to make myself believe I wasn't sick and so I dressed and lounged around, but I couldn't drive away that dull, tired ache that held me. Sunday I didn't even pretend to be well. Toots went skating during the afternoon and I summoned enough energy while she was gone to write two letters. Both were cleverly camouflaged and were brave attempts to be cheerful, when I was feeling anything but that.

Monday was another long day and I didn't even care about eating. Tuesday things began bright and early. Only a little while after Toots had gone to school, Dr. Bugher came most unceremoniously into the room and said we were temporarily quarantined. It seemed such a perfect joke and yet we were so furious about it, that in sheer nervous excitement, I was suddenly all well again. Just before noon Dr. Lundmark came in and after the briefest kind of examination said I didn't have the flu, and hardly was he gone than Dr. Ross came in and went out again when he heard what Dr. Lundmark had said. Of course, the girls went to school that afternoon and we enjoyed a good laugh. I got up during the afternoon and called on Irene, but the halls were cold and I was chilled and was really sick for a while. Eunice and Betty were frightened and went for Dr. again, but by the time he came, I was warm and felt better. All in all, it was a most eventful day, five calls from three different doctors, plus a visit from Audie and Ike and some others. I was so tired and weak that night, that I couldn't sleep. Eunice went home with Ike, and Betty and I were alone.

Wednesday and Thursday I recuperated from Tuesday's excitement and on Friday I was up again. Tis came up before we expected, just dropped down from the clear sky. We were all together for supper, and then Eddie and Ike came up. We made enough noise for a dozen, I am sure.

Saturday I gathered up every ounce of energy I possessed, for truly I had need of it that day.

[This rather cryptic sentence is the last entry in Louise's journal/diary!]

Epilogue

The twelve children born to Louise and Archie. Back row: Catherine, Lorraine, Betty, Donald, Robert, John and Francis. Front row, Gene, Phyllis, Bonnie, James and Philip. Photo 1941

Epilogue

With a somewhat abrupt last entry, Louise's journal-writing ends on January 23, 1919. It is unclear what she refers to in these final words, though given the subsequent events in Louise's life, this mysterious reference could pertain to them all. Perhaps after her most recent horrific trip she intended to resign her position, for she had applied for a position in the county Normal School earlier. Or, perhaps she knew that Archie was to be mustered out of the Army on February 1, and she was uncertain of what their future would be. She did continue as county supervising teacher, however, and because of the influenza epidemic in Rusk County, she was called upon to substitute for sick teachers.

Shortly after the end of this journal, Louise's life began to undergo tremendous changes, many of which were of a more private nature. It is possible that as her relationship with Archie LaBerge grew and her career path changed, Louise felt it inappropriate to write of these events. Her journals have a consistently public tone to them, almost as though they were intentionally written for others, and not as an intimate personal record. In a sense, it is doubly unfortunate that her first "Little Book" has been lost, for in its initial pages we might have gained some insight into her intended audience.

On July 4, 1919, O. E. Rice died of a heart attack while visiting relatives in Ishpeming, Michigan. This event probably sparked a change for Louise, as, according to her youngest brother, Bill, she then applied for the position of county superintendent of schools. She

The graduating class of the Rusk County Normal School in 1920. Louise is third from the left in the second row, next to B. Mack Dresden.

felt that her five years' experience as a teacher and four years as supervising teacher qualified her for the position. She believed that she had a thorough knowledge of the rural school system in Rusk County. On July 18, however, the selection committee found it "more appropriate" to appoint Robert H. Burns as the new county superintendent. He had taught for about two years at the Rusk County Normal, was active in local politics, and had run against Rice for election to the position the previous fall. He held the office of county superintendent for one year and was then elected to the State Assembly in 1920 and continued on in state politics.

Although she was disappointed not to get the position of county superintendent, Louise continued in education in Rusk County. A notice in the Ladysmith *News Budget* on August 29, 1919, indicates that

Louise's wish of a year earlier was finally coming true. Under "Training School Notes," Professor B. Mack Dresden announced, "Miss Mary G. Shorna will be assistant and Miss Louise Wegner will be in charge of the Model School. Miss Wegner needs no introduction to the people of this County, as she has been the Supervising Teacher for the last five years." And on October 3, 1919, "Training School Notes" reported that "Miss Louise Wegner, for many years the Supervising Teacher of this County, resigned her position to accept a position in the County Normal School. She has charge of the Practice School, and directs the work of all the student-teachers. Her wide experience in the schools of the County has served to prepare her well for the intensive duties of her new position." The travels with Sophie were coming to an end.

Audie, Louise, Tis, and Toots on a lake outing in 1919.

After Archie returned from the Army in February of 1919, he courted Louise for about eighteen months. The courtship is recorded only in photographs—Archie and the Wegner women at picnics and canoeing outings, or Archie, his sister Ruth, and Louise on hunting trips. Apparently against the wishes of her mother, who seemed to feel that no man was good enough for her daughters, Louise and Archie began making plans to marry. In anticipation of the upcoming event, Louise resigned her position as director of the Model School after completing the summer session in August 1920. On September 22, 1920, Louise and Archie took the limited to Duluth, Minnesota, and were married in a simple ceremony. Her retirement from teaching was short-lived, however, for upon their return, she was asked to serve as a temporary principal of the State Graded School at Sheldon for the fall term. The widespread shortage of teachers in Wisconsin in 1920 made it difficult to fill the position, so Louise agreed to accept the job for one semester. The newlyweds lived in Sheldon near her school, and the Ladysmith *News Budget* reported that on October 15, Archie shot a large black bear that was raiding a local apiary. By Christmas of that year, Louise was pregnant with their first child, and though Rusk County had allowed her to continue teaching as a married woman—a most unusual allowance—custom demanded that she give up teaching. The Ladysmith *News Budget* reported in the Sheldon *News* on February 25, 1921, that "Mrs. LaBerge visited her former students in the upper room of our school last Thursday, and engaged them all in a candy-pull after school hours. A sweet remembrance."

Toots and Archie canoe on the Flambeau River in 1919.

Recently one of her former students recalled Louise's influence. Magdalene Sandbote Serley Becker was in ninth grade in the fall of 1920, Louise's last year of teaching. As she told Betty Silvernale, Louise's daughter, in April 1998:

"When I started high school in Sheldon I was very, very shy. I don't know why I was because I was the oldest of eight children in my family. I didn't know what to expect, and I didn't know what was expected of me. But I had an algebra teacher who took care of that. She taught algebra, but she taught much more than that. She was so kind. She must have read my mind when I was so nervous. She would come put her arm around my shoulder and say, 'That's all right, that's all right.' I expected to hate algebra, but I loved it, and that was all her fault. She certainly made a lasting impression. I wonder how many other children she saved? Anyway, she was the best teacher you could find anywhere. She knew when you felt down, and she knew how to lift you up. And she had such a kind, comforting voice. When she saw that you were having trouble she would come over and stand by your desk and say, 'Why don't you try it this way,' or 'Don't you want to do that?' She had such a nice way of pointing things out to you without telling you, 'Oh, that's wrong.' I don't remember any other teachers in the school, or any other classes I took. I think that is a compliment to her, because, after all these years, no one else stands out in my mind. This picture of her, taken in 1920, is just the way I remember her when she taught me. Oh, one other thing I remember about her—the way she played that violin! She could make that violin talk!! She played for dances and concerts. She also loved to sing and she had a beautiful voice."

Though the written accounts of Louise's experiences end abruptly, Louise did supply a summary of sorts in January 1969 in a letter to her daughter Betty in which she described her years traveling Rusk County. The summary was written initially for a school project in which students and teachers interviewed some of the pioneers of Rusk County. Years later, it became part of a history of Rusk County assembled by the Rusk County Historical Society. At the time the summary was written, no one in the family really knew of the existence of Louise's journals; it wasn't until after Louise's death that her daughter Phyllis mentioned two little journals that had ended up in her possession after the estate was settled. After writing briefly about a few of the events she had described in her journals fifty years earlier, Louise closed her letter with the following words:

If you are reading these pages, expecting to find some thrilling adventures, you are going to be sadly disappointed. Mine was a job to do, and there were no kidnappings, no hold-ups, I was never even very lost. If I had to name one feared adversary, it would be the ugly dogs that were to be found in almost every farm yard. The work, in fact, was all quite ordinary, sometimes even a little dull. What stands out in my mind, even now after all these years, was the great friendliness of the many people I had to deal with, their sincere desire to be helpful and cooperate toward improving their schools and securing the best possible education for their children.

Rusk County in 1915 had 125 rural school teachers, in other words, 125 one-room country schools. Some were very small, and even then, were being closed because of their small enrollment. One school in the Blue Hills area had only four pupils, and another near Flambeau had only eight pupils, from two families, and one of the mothers was the teacher. At the other extreme, some schools had from 53 to 60 pupils, all eight grades. In these larger schools, girls of the eighth grade often taught a primary class in reading or spelling to help the teacher. Double seats were very common, and they were far from being the adjustable kind.

To get around the county twice in a school year meant considerable traveling. The first year I walked from school to school. The second year I used a horse and buggy (a cutter in the winter) and the last two years, I was the proud owner of a Model T Ford. And the roads? They were a story all by themselves, 50 years ago. Gravel roads were a luxury, there were no black-top roads. The spring break-up was a time of no travel. Some schools had a mud-vacation, and then I only traveled where it was possible to go.

There was no Highway 8, it was old 14 from Ladysmith to Tony and farther East, nor was there any 8 to the West. Many roads were little better than trails, narrow and rutty. Did you ever travel over a Corduroy Road ? The road builder placed logs crosswise on the road, over some low spot or swamp and then he put enough dirt on the logs to make it possible to drive over them. There are still remnants of corduroy on some town roads.

A typical one-room country school was a blocky-type building—a narrow entry in front serving as a cloakroom. A large jacketed stove was in the farther corner of the room. Many teachers were their own janitors. The lucky ones had an older pupil who lived near-by, who came to school early, and made the fire. Or a near-by farmer came each morning to make a fire during the winter months. But many teachers hurried to school each day, made a fire and hoped the room would warm up sufficiently before the children came. It was not an uncommon event to have frosted ears or cheeks or toes. This first aid was also part of the teacher's many responsibilities. Sweeping the room was also a chore, often done by one or two of the older girls. But in many homes these elder daughters had work to do and then it devolved upon the teacher to

Louise rests on a bridge along Wisconsin 14 ("Old 14") on one of her long walks. This was the first east-west state highway in Rusk County, but other highways replaced it during the 1930s.

sweep the school-room herself. Libraries were so small, by the time a student reached the fourth or fifth grade he had read every book in the library. Reference books, almost without exception, were old and inadequate.

The supervising teacher was a link between the outside world and the small rural school of fifty years ago, and most of these schools were truly small. It was my duty to visit each school twice in a school year, and oftener if the teacher was in need of help. I was to give any suggestions that might help to make a better school.

I am sorry to say that a very small percentage resented a visit, but these were not so many. A young teacher in a small isolated school felt alone and almost helpless—there was so little contact with the rest of the school world. Perhaps just as important was the contact with the people of the community, and the great good-will and neighborliness that I found everywhere. It was a rewarding job and made me feel, even then, that the best crop this country raises is the fine boys and girls who are in our schools.

As one chapter of Louise's life ended, another began. When Louise became pregnant with their first child, she and Archie decided to move to the LaBerge family farm east of Ladysmith and make a go of farming. When they first started they raised sheep and dairy cows, but they would eventually concentrate on dairy farming. The commitment to the farm was a commitment to hard work. The plowing, cultivating, and harvesting were all done with a team of horses, and of course all the milking was done by hand. Like most farms of that era, there was no running water or electricity; all the cooking and baking were done on a wood stove, and tasks such as washing clothes—or people— required pumping the water from the well, heating it on the wood stove, then washing with a harsh homemade soap. Food preservation consisted mainly of canning large quantities of all manner of fruits and vegetables, various types of jams and jellies, and even meat.

In addition to the immense amount of work in running the household, Louise had twelve children in the first seventeen years of her marriage. Both she and Archie had come from large families; Louise had six siblings and Archie had eight, so it was not surprising that they too had a large family. She already had seven children in 1929, when the Great Depression hit. Like many farm families during the Depression, theirs was a no-frills life of subsistence. After 1929, there simply was no money to buy machinery or appliances to make life easier. However, the dairy farm and the large family garden always provided enough food to eat. The

Louise feeding sheep on the LaBerge farm, 1920.

family continued to grow during the Depression years, with the birth of five more children.

Along with this large family came the inevitable childhood accidents and illnesses; the house was quarantined a number of times with one disease or another. In the summer of 1933 a real tragedy struck when Bob, the oldest child, was stricken with polio. The family was quarantined for six weeks, during which time a neighbor had to do their grocery shopping from a list left in the LaBerge mail box. While the children suffered through their illnesses, Louise taught them how to knit, embroider, crochet, and quilt to help pass the long days of inactivity.

It seemed that no matter what the hardship or tragedy, Louise was the force that kept the family together. Her fortitude was especially evident in the late 1940s when Archie was stricken with cancer. Life dealt this cruel blow just as the farm had begun to overcome the financial hardships of the Depression and most of the children were grown. After a long and painful struggle with the disease, Archie, still only fifty-nine years old, died in December 1950. Louise remained on the LaBerge farm for about five more years. By then, all of her children had finished high school and were on their way to their respective careers. She then moved back to the Wegner farm at Sheldon to care for her aging parents. After they passed away, she stayed on to care for her bachelor brother, Bob.

The following are memories of Louise by a few of her surviving children, for her children were her "career" for the last fifty years of her life. Written accounts of Louise's later years are almost nonexistent; she would never return to her journals again after abruptly ending her second "Little Book." One can, however, perceive her warmth, her grace, and her lively sense of humor in the memories her children have of her. In a very real sense, they continue the story of Louise's life.

Bob recalls that she always encouraged the children to read, and to work on their penmanship. While penmanship may not have had a major influence on his career as an electrical engineer, reading certainly did. "I don't remember too much about the winter when I first had polio," he says, "but I recall being bedridden all winter. I guess the doctor didn't have any experience with polio, because all he could prescribe was hot packs on my spine. We used five-pound bags of salt. Mother would warm them in the oven and then lay them against my back. I suspect that they did some good. I remember Mother doing all she could to get me comfortable, and then doing all the kitchen chores, and getting things laid out for the school kids for the next day. There was a lot of extra work that winter."

Betty writes: "When I was a junior in high school (1940–41) Mother had emergency thyroid surgery, and as soon as she recovered from that she had a hysterectomy. Both these operations were done in Madison, and Aunt Gertrude went with her. After Mother was released from the hospital, she spent several weeks recuperating with Aunt Margaret in Baraboo. Lorraine and I took turns staying home from school each day. We had ten lunches to pack every day, we baked ten loaves of bread every other day, and washed clothes on the alternate days. This stands out in my mind because we had first-hand experience of the amount of work and responsibility Mother had with her large family. Fortunately for us, no one became ill, and everyone was glad when Mother returned.

"In 1946, when I taught at the Kinnamon Indian School near Hayward, I usually took the 5:00 A.M. train to Stone Lake on Monday morning. On Sunday night I would go roller skating and then go to the late show. When I came home from the movie, I awakened Mother and she would get up and read until about 4:00 A.M. when she would call me. (Evidently we didn't have an alarm clock.) Then one of the boys would take me to the train. To me, that shows the dedication Mother had for her children.

"Mother had so many talents—sewing quilts, making clothing, doing beautiful embroidery, knitting, crocheting, and making perfect darning on the heavy woolen socks and neat patches on the overalls. She was also very good at painting and drawing, and we all remember her playing the violin and singing. Unfortunately, the thyroid surgery ended her singing voice."

Catherine says, "My memories are of our mother working so hard, and also the two bad ulcers she had on her leg. I remember when I was about three or four years old—just before going to bed—I would wait around for a time when she wasn't too busy and say, 'Gute Nacht, mein Mutter.' This seemed to please her, because she was teaching German to Betty.

"I also remember that during the nights when she nursed one of the younger children—and it was cold in the house on some of those nights—I would find something to put over her shoulders to keep her warmer. I think she had quite a difficult, challenging life, but she was always pleasant, interested, helpful, and upbeat. Yes, she was quite amazing."

Phyllis says, "She was mentally, physically, and emotionally a very strong person. My memories of Mother are of kindness, strength, love, and patience. A hot snack when we got home after our long walk from school—milk toast, potato soup, pudding. Even when she must have been very tired herself she sat up with us (the five smallest children) and waited for New Year's to come in. She was always busy cooking, canning, mending, etc., but if we came to stand by her she never pushed us away, but rather she leaned toward us, and we felt her love even though she couldn't quit whatever chore she was doing. Her body language was unmistakable. There certainly were times when she was angry at what we had done, but she never withheld her love. She was the quintessential mother!!"

Gene remembers a time around 1955 when he was driving his mother on a road along the Flambeau River. A woman in a car ran a stop sign and nearly forced them into the river. "Mother would never swear, but she blurted out, 'Swear at her, swear at her!!' So it was evidently all right for me to swear. Perhaps my most enduring memory of Mother is the way she nurtured her children. I don't recall her ever brow-beating us or cajoling us to do our homework, or to do well in school. She simply maintained an environment in which we *wanted* to learn and to do well. I recall asking her after I got married in 1962 how she created the atmosphere that was so encouraging. She replied, 'Just live your life the way you would like them to live, and everything will work out.' I am also grateful for the love of music that she instilled in us. Music has always been an important part of my life, and continues to be a means of enjoyment and relaxation. Music, especially singing, is an integral part of every family get-together, and I know that this comes from her."

Bonnie says, "Maybe it was because I was the youngest of the family that I had lots of individual time with Mother. She still was very much the teacher because I remember many of the lessons she taught even now. One story she liked to tell was about herself as a child. She had the notion that if she poured a liquid really fast, she could get more into the glass. Needless to say, she went through many spills before she figured out the answer—no difference, only more mess. Many times when I stubbornly insisted on doing things the hard way, she would repeat this story to me. Never scolding me but making herself the one who made a silly error. Another story she told me was about taking care of a young boy whose mother had told him just before she left, 'Now, whatever you do, don't put any beans up your nose.' Of course, that became the most desirable action for the youngster to take. When I went off to college, Mother said to me 'I don't mind any career you choose for yourself. But don't choose teaching. It's too hard.' Yes, I picked teaching and have been at it for thirty-six years, with no sign of stopping. I think Mother never really quit teaching. She just transferred her location from the school room to our home."

In 1968, a family reunion to celebrate Louise's seventy-fifth birthday was attended by all twelve of her children, sons- and daughters-in-law, and all of her grandchildren. A total of forty-five people were on hand to honor her. Little more than a year later, on December 1, 1969, Louise died of heart failure when a massive loss of blood following a severe nose bleed weakened her heart beyond recovery. December 1, 1969, was also the date that astronauts returned from the moon; Louise was alert and gave her full attention to the television coverage of the event to the very end of her life.

Louise's influence on education continued for many years because four of her children (Betty, Donald, Gene, and Mary) chose careers in education at the elementary, middle school, high school, and college levels. We feel confident that she would be pleased with this legacy.

The LaBerge family reunion for Louise's seventy-fifth birthday in 1968. Back row: Philip, James, Gene; middle row: John, Donald, Francis, Phyllis, and Robert; front row: Catherine, Betty, Louise, Mary and Lorraine.

REFERENCES

T. L. Mueller, *Mueller*, a history of the Mueller family, self-published in 1987, 165 pp.

History of Rural Schools of Rusk County, Wisconsin, edited by Jean Sanford Replinger, self-published in 1985, 212 pp.

History of Rusk County Wisconsin, written by the people of Rusk County. Ladysmith: Rusk County Historical Society, 1983, 372 pp.

"County School News" (a regular column by the county superintendent of schools), *Ladysmith News Budget*, 1910-1921.

"County School News," *Rusk County Journal*, 1910-1921.

"Local and Personal," *Rusk County Journal*, 1910-1921.

Louise Wegner's ledger provided much information on dates, places, and people for the time interval covered in her diary.

Louise Wegner's photo album provided dates and places for the photo captions.

The Editors

Gene LaBerge

Gene Ludger LaBerge was the eighth child born to Archie and Louise LaBerge. Born in 1932, he was named after his uncle Eugene (who died as a teenager) and his paternal grandfather Ludger. Like the rest of his siblings, Gene grew up on the home farm east of Ladysmith and attended a one-room country school (Maple Hill School) for the first eight grades. He walked more than a mile to grade school and more than two miles to high school in Ladysmith. For the first six years he was the only student in his grade, and graduated from eighth grade in a class of four. Therefore his experience included events similar to many of those described in Louise's journals.

His father died of cancer the year he graduated from high school, and a year later, in 1951, he was drafted into the Marines during the Korean War. Upon his release from active duty he enrolled at Superior State College in January, 1954, undertaking a major in geology. He transferred to the University of Wisconsin-Madison in 1956 and received his B.S. degree in geology in 1958, his M.S. in 1959, and his Ph.D. in 1963.

Throughout his education he received unqualified encouragement from Louise. Following his formal education, Gene accepted a post-doctoral fellowship in Adelaide, Australia, where his new bride, Sally, had received a Fulbright Scholarship. Their year in Australia was followed by a post-doctoral fellowship at the Geological Survey of Canada in Ottawa. In 1965 Gene and Sally accepted faculty positions at Wisconsin State University in Oshkosh (later UW-Oshkosh). Sally taught for one year and then stayed home to raise their three children (Michelle, Rene, and Laura), but Gene taught for thirty-three years, retiring in 1998. In addition to his teaching, Gene initiated a geological mapping program in northern Wisconsin for the Wisconsin Geological Survey in 1968. This project continued each summer until 1983, when he accepted a position with the U.S. Geological Survey to continue the project.

Although he spent more than summers doing geological mapping, his teaching was always the major interest in his professional life. During the course of his career, Gene received every faculty award for teaching and research for which he was eligible at UW-Oshkosh, as well as an international award given in 1995 for outstanding contributions to the geology of the Lake Superior region.

He is co-author and co-editor of two books: *Precambrian Iron-formations* (1987) and *The John Barlow Mineral Collection* (1997), a study of a major mineral collection, and is the author of *Geology of the Lake Superior Region* (1994).

Louise's philosophy of lifelong learning has provided the encouragement to undertake new challenges. Gene kept journals of major trips taken as part of his professional life, such as his year in Australia, several months in South Africa in 1964, a trip to northern Canada in 1965, to China in 1982 and 1987, to Greenland in 1985, and to Russia during the coup in 1991. Thus he was fascinated by Louise's journal when it surfaced nearly twenty years after her death. It brought to light a woman he had never known, one who was a very accomplished person, and so much more than just

"Mother." He showed it to his daughter Michelle in the hopes that they could make a publishable book from it. And when the photo albums also surfaced, the project seemed more feasible. The rest, as they say, is history. This book will honor her memory.

Michelle Maurer

Michelle Maurer, the oldest daughter of Gene and Sally LaBerge, was born Michelle Louise LaBerge, named for Louise Wegner. She grew up with her two younger sisters in the little town of Omro, Wisconsin, where she graduated from high school in 1984. She attended Augustana College in Rock Island, Illinois, graduating with a major in English literature in 1988. She then went on to one half-hearted year of graduate school at Washington University in St. Louis, studying the lives of medieval saints.

Michelle spent most of the next decade traveling throughout the U.S., working at various odd jobs—as a bartender, in an orchid greenhouse, as a stage hand for a small theater, cooking in a vegetarian restaurant, and machining valves for snowblower engines. In 1997 she married Gary Maurer, a young man from Kiel, Wisconsin, and in May of 1999 they became the parents of a baby boy, Jacob August Maurer.

Gene and Michelle had first discussed publishing Louise's journals in the mid-1980s. Gene had more or less recruited Michelle as an English major and young aspiring writer. However, Michelle couldn't find an approach to the text that would have set it apart as a historical document. It wasn't until the appearance of Louise's photo albums in the early 1990s that Michelle saw the "hook" they had been seeking. The pictures of Louise and her family brought to life the events in the journals and portrayed the people in her life as both very real and unique characters.